Blind Sacrifice
Portraits of Murderers

Blind Sacrifice

Susan Gabori

Cover design by Terry Gallagher/Doowah Design Inc.
Cover and author photo by D. Hausmann
Printed and bound in Canada

We acknowledge the financial assistance of the Manitoba Arts Council and The Canada Council for the Arts for our publishing program.

Canadian Cataloguing in Publication Data

Gabori, Susan, 1947-
        Blind sacrifice: portraits of murderers

ISBN 1-896239-61-7

        1. Murderers—Canada—Interviews. I. Title.
HV6805.G32 2000   364.15'23'092271   C00-900172-7

And if one does not know the shadow, one knows nothing.

Ka: Stories of the Mind and Gods of India
—by Roberto Calasso

Contents

Introduction

To kill another is only human.

In eight devastating portraits, that frightening conclusion emerges from Susan Gabori's fascinating study of murderers who've confronted their acts and themselves. With startling consistency, *Blind Sacrifice* demonstrates that only those who accept this lesson—the sheer inevitability that their crime is part of their humanity—can move on to the semblance of equilibrium we call normal life. And in the very diversity of her subjects—male, female, old, young, gay, straight, ethnic, native—Gabori demonstrates that the truths emerging from her portraits are universal.

Killing is also human because it's so frequently a matter of imitation. None of the individuals portrayed in *Blind Sacrifice* lack models for violence. In all cases, Gabori's killers outdo their models. None of the abusers who plant the killing anger in their young charges are murderers themselves. But they are deadly breeding grounds for their victims, who eventually outperform them. Unable to see beyond the barriers of anger without lashing out at the bars, victims can comprehend the futility of violence only when they become the ultimate abusers themselves.

Blind Sacrifice's landscape certainly won't appeal to the politics of the day, which holds that the vast majority of people with emotionally devastated lives do not respond by becoming killers. The politics of the day, however, misses the point, which is that it's not about numbers. The hard truth is that some people will always kill others, not because they want to, but because they cannot escape the need or impulse to do so. Rory's heart-rending response to the author's touch, even as he falls back into the abyss, is *Blind Sacrifice*'s unforgettable contribution to that proposition. And the fact that society does not and should not excuse the violent taking of life in no way detracts from that reality.

The politics of the day would also have us write off *Blind Sacrifice*'s subjects, with the death penalty, with harsher sentences, with harsher prisons and with the abolition of parole. In some ways, Gabori's work is grist for the mill. It was only in prison, hard-liners will point out, that *Blind Sacrifice*'s protagonists seized on the opportunity for change.

True enough. But apart from the fact that, on this aspect of the argument, the hard-liners conveniently ignore the numbers game when it suits them, they point to high recidivism rates as evidence that society doesn't treat offenders harshly enough: their response is again inappropriate. The question isn't whether we need harsh prisons to rehabilitate people, but rather: What is it about the prison experience that prompted self-restoration in Gabori's killers?

The answer, I suggest, is that prison does indeed present opportunities. The high walls can shield people from the pressures that contributed to their dilemmas, distance them from haunting memories, free them from the burden of providing or the guilt of not providing—for themselves or others—and let them escape the stress of daily decision-making, even living, that has proven too much for them. A world in which all is mandated, all is routine, and much is predictable can be the highway to insanity or the guidepost to rest, and peace.

But temptation is more alluring than opportunity, and conformity of habit an easier choice than inner change. And that's the problem with prisons. They present far more temptation than opportunity. Violence for the violent, drugs for the dependent, a recognizable subculture for those who cannot tolerate the mainstream. And for the white-collar criminal, prison provides distance from shame, from the scrutiny of peers, from the probing of the media. For all who have broken the law, the temptation of prison is in its hidden comforts; not the TVs or the canteen or the conjugal visits, but the warm familiarity of one's own kind.

What *Blind Sacrifice* demonstrates, then, is that even murderers can take advantage of the opportunity for change. Surely the lesson is that, in our society's treatment of offenders, we must focus on opportunity and disrupt familiarity. For those who've spent most of their lives being punished, punishing themselves, and frequently as a last resort, punishing others, ever-harsher punishment is familiar. They're dulled to it. It comes with the territory, a territory they've always known, and a territory where there's no opportunity for change.

Some, like Gabori's subjects, resist the temptation, resist the familiarity. They are the few strong ones among the many who are weak, who need our help, not our wrath.

Julius Melnitzer

After almost two decades as a criminal and civil trial lawyer in London and Toronto, Ontario, Julius Melnitzer spent two-and-a-half years in prison, where he authored *Maximum Medium Minimum* (Key Porter). He's now working as a freelance journalist specializing in legal, justice and prison issues.

Preface

The murder was a blind sacrifice to their anger, fear, pain. These were not appeased. The shock of such an extreme deed cracked the thick outer crust of their defense: their armour against the outer world. Prison forced them to stop and be alone in their cell. It gave them time to open their eyes, think, see what they had done and why.

I set out to interview murderers who had faced their actions and themselves. As I discovered, these were not easy people to find. They were a very small percentage of the prison population.

I had a personal reason for writing this book. I wanted to know where people escaped to, found solace, when squeezed into a tight corner with no obvious means of exit. Everyone, at some point in their lives, experiences such a trauma. At such times it helps to look at extreme situations to better see and understand your own position and discover your own limit of malleability, your own capacity to stretch. For me the act of murder and prisonment definitely fit the bill: you cannot get much more extreme than that. I presumed that in such circumstances one's only doorway to solace was within, toward oneself. How does one find that route?

My previous book, *A Good Enough Life,* asked the same question— where do you escape to when your desperation reaches an extreme high? That book looked at people who were terminally ill. They showed me that before you can face your death, you have to face your life. By that act, you face yourself. Then you are free to die in peace. The subjects in that book were as difficult to find as in this one. People are not fond of facing their life. Anger, self-pity, blame seem an easier route. The few that I found showed me that they had retreated within, into solitude, to that inner centre, to find balance and peace. But they had died. Can the knowledge the dying had gleaned be carried back out into the arena of action, into daily life? How? For answers I had to find a new set of people who fitted similar criteria, had experienced a similar level of desperation—people who were so shocked by the reality they found themselves in that they were forced to redefine themselves. This book contains them. The murderers found identical answers to the dying, but they had a chance to take their discoveries further, into actually becoming what they had found within.

The murderers I chose to interview also ended up finding and facing their centre. Not an obvious route to freedom. Before they arrived there they had to face their fears, their anger, their background. Then, stripped naked, without the conditioning of the past, they could create a new life.

The exception to my stated criteria was Rory. He was 60 years old at the time of the interview. He had looked at himself, faced his pain and his crimes and was out of prison for 30 years. Then he had a relapse to his old ways. His emotional disintegration began around the time of the interview. Sharon is another example of someone who had slipped back into old patterns. It took her another 13 years to regain her footing.

Books have been written about crime, prisons and the law that puts people away. I have tried to explore the human side of crime; look at the reasons why people commit murder. As Sister Helen Prejean, who works with prisoners on death row in the U.S. and author of *Dead Man Walking*, said, "There is more to people than the worst thing they have done in their lives."

Who are these murderers? Where do they come from? I asked about their background: parents, siblings, friends. They revealed startlingly tortuous childhoods that quickly led to brutal, highly charged and dramatic lives.

What reason do criminals have for becoming criminals? At a very young age these people disconnect from the self. The chaos of their lives and the need to survive in such brutal conditions demand all their attention. Over time, one negative experience piles on top of the other. There comes a point where all the repeated hurt, pain and anger become so tightly packed into one's being that it explodes. That is when murder takes place.

The distance needed to travel from violent crime to self-knowledge is enormous, filled with numerous pitfalls and often strong peer pressure to stay within the criminal fold. Facing oneself is painful and difficult. The journey within is a solitary path requiring courage and inner strength. How does one move from terrible darkness to self-understanding?

Often prisoners feel detached from their crime or will not remember their actions, which is why remorse is so hard to achieve. But detachment from an extreme deed, such as murder, can only mean inner fragmentation, such as people who suffer from a split or multiple personality, where they are totally out of touch with their centre; often one part of them doesn't fully know what the other is doing. This inner fragmentation needs to be healed before a person can become whole. On the way to wholeness deeds and emotions must be faced.

We follow them as they discover the essence of who they are, the meaning in their lives. We witness the tremendous effort it takes to let old patterns go. These portraits show the journey from crime to peace, from fragmentation to wholeness. This is not a book about crime but about individuals struggling to be.

Finding these people, with the help of the parole board, took two-and-a-half years. All interviews have been taped, transcribed, then edited and structured. The chapters are based on the person's own words, remaining true to his/her natural rhythm of speech. I have also tried to remain true to the confusion of tenses that were sometimes used.

For some it was impossible to follow a chronological line of questioning. I would be asking about a time when they were 10 years old and they would skip to when they were 25. I would bring them back. Again they veered off. They would jump around in time. I wanted to allow them the freedom of association while keeping a firm grip on the rudder, with a clear eye on destination.

People related their stories over several weeks and often months. Each session took between two to four hours. Those who embarked upon the interviews did so because they wanted to give a sense of totality to their lives, a sense of its movement from past to present. They also hoped that in some way others might benefit from their experience.

I wrote this book in the hope that everyone would find something of value. Reading about such extreme lives, such bleak existences, hopefully can help us all to face our own darkness and give us clues to find the clearing. Then we can move toward self-understanding and summon the courage to be free.

LOUIS

Before doing the actual interview Louis wanted to meet me, to talk casually, ask questions. The initial meeting lasted nearly two hours. It was relaxed. I had the impression he wanted to get a sense of who I was. He asked what else I had written and why I had embarked on this project. The conversation also touched on philosophical questions which clearly interested him. At the end of the meeting he readily agreed to be interviewed. He was the only one who actually asked to meet me before the interview.

Tall, slim, with a mustache, French Canadian, Louis (46) was sparse with his words, contained in body language and facial expression. At the first interview he clearly stated that he decided to participate because it would give him an opportunity to see his life till now, to get an overview. He rarely offered more than asked, though he willingly answered my questions and I never had the feeling that he was trying to hold anything back. He spoke easily but his answer to one question seldom brought forth other memories. I continually had to feed him more questions. His answers were to the point and nothing more. This was a difficult interview. I had to think hard; his replies did not always readily lead to the next question. As we covered his childhood, he cried openly, without embarrassment, and said, laughing between tears, "I didn't expect this."

I think I'm one of those people who needed a shock to wake up. Had I not done what I did, not gone to prison, I would not be the person I am today. Prison gave me the opportunity to think. And what I've learned cannot be taught. You have to discover it yourself. But it takes a trigger. The murder was an accident. Unplanned. It was a terrible act, I don't wish it on anyone. But it did happen and I have to take responsibility for it.

Raymond was a regular client when I was doing prostitution. He was 12 years older than me and I used to go to his house on weekends. I didn't really like him. But then I was kicked out of the house at 19 and needed a place to live. At the time my life was going nowhere. I didn't have money. All I had was a couple of pairs of jeans. I told him about the problems with my father and that I needed a place to live. He said, "Don't worry. I have a country house. I will take possession of it in a month and need someone to take care of it. It's perfect timing."

In the meantime he offered me his apartment. He was a teacher and had only one month left of school. He said, "I know you just left your family. Take the time to relax. Read or listen to music during the day. There's no need to look for a job. There will be plenty of work on the country house. And I'm going to provide everything."

In return I gave him sex. It was convenient for me. I didn't continue the prostitution. Before I had been doing it for money to buy drugs. Now he was giving me drugs.

Three years earlier he had bought a country house and rented it out to be able to pay back the bank. He thought he was renting to an individual guy who turned out to be part of a motorcycle gang. He was actually renting to a motorcycle gang from Three Rivers. They rented the house because it was big; the land was 445 feet wide and the house had three floors. Also, it was on a lake and easy to grow pot in the backyard.

One day, when we went to collect the rent, the house was full of garbage bags filled with pot. And we saw machine guns on the table. We also saw them drying plants in the basement. So we knew what was going on. At first the relationship between the motorcycle gang and Raymond was good because Raymond was also smoking. Their lease on the house was almost up and they were supposed to move out so Raymond could repossess it. Raymond said, "I don't want to renew my lease on the apartment when I have a house. You have to move out by the time the lease expires in July." But they didn't want to leave because they had to harvest the marijuana plants.

Raymond threatened to take legal action. They got nervous thinking someone could discover the pot. So to stop Raymond from taking legal action they kidnapped me and put me in a room on the third floor. They were using me as hostage so Raymond could continue to teach at the school but wouldn't call the police. They guarded me with a gun and didn't know if they would have to kill me or not.

These guys can use brute force, but *think*, that's something else. One was totally feeble-minded, moronic. He was always moving around the house with a long knife, pretending to shave with it. He was unstable and the others knew he had to be controlled. I was scared of him. If one of them would have said, "Kill him," he would have executed me without a second thought, just to prove he was part of the gang, to look good.

Raymond regularly called from the city and they would pass me the phone. He also came from time to time. He parked at a distance and I could see his car lights flashing. On the phone he would say, "I'm going to be there at 10 o'clock." I knew that Saturday and Sunday, at 10 o'clock, I just had to look out the window. I could see his car lights flashing near the church. He said, "Try to escape. You know I'll be there at 10 every Saturday and Sunday." Tension was building. The date for the expiry of the lease was getting closer and closer.

In one of the phone conversations, Raymond said, "OK, Louis, I finally bought two guns. Try to escape." They kept me locked up on the third floor. I had a foot-square space to escape. I had to put my leg through first and hold on with my hands. I couldn't make any sound. I was scared because I had to jump from the third floor. When I finally hit the ground I ran toward the flashing lights of the car. It took me a half-hour to reach it. What you see in the country can be far.

Only the moron was home, so we immediately went back to the house armed with the guns. We chased him out and stayed in the house. That night we didn't sleep. The next few nights one of us slept while the other was on guard. We stayed in the house to prevent them from coming back. One guy came to get us. Apparently he was dangerous and armed. He was driving too fast. He missed a curve just as he was coming to the bridge near Three Rivers and crashed, killing himself. Otherwise, I would probably be dead today. The motorcycle gang never came back and we ended up with the pot which Raymond sold to someone.

We bought two guard dogs for security and we lived with the guns. When we went out in the fields we took them with us. When I was cooking in the kitchen I had the gun and the dog beside me. We hid the guns when Raymond brought his students to the country.

Raymond taught French to 12- and 13-year-olds in an all-boys' high school. He brought some of his students to the country house for the weekend. I didn't like that, not because I was jealous but I saw myself in those kids. When I told him, he said, "I don't do anything." But I sensed that something was going on.

A couple of months after I was sentenced my sister came to visit me in jail. At the time she was living close to where Raymond had been teaching. She said one of her co-workers had asked her to thank me for killing that guy. He had abused her son.

After we moved into the country house he took a room with a friend of his during the time he was teaching. That friend was also gay and teaching 14- and 15-year-olds at the same school. During the week I was alone in the country, free, smiling, taking care of the dogs. On the weekend, when he came up, I had a long face.

The original two dogs we bought had puppies and then the puppies had puppies. I raised and trained the dogs. Some we sold. They were Alsatians and German shepherds. The Alsatians were beautiful. I loved the dogs. Outside we had enclosures and cages for them. When I went cross-country skiing I always took all the dogs. They ran beside me. There could be 20 at a time. Never less than 10.

Because the house was old he wanted to renovate everything. I put down wooden floors. The ceiling of the dining room had big wooden beams that had been painted over. I stripped off the paint and finished the wood. We found a 12-foot-long Victorian table at an auction and put it under the wooden ceiling. It looked gorgeous.

He invited his friends, who were other teachers from the school, to the country. I cooked supper for them because I'm a pretty good cook. I like to cook. That was the easy part.

Raymond wasn't giving me money. He provided for my needs but that was all. I stayed because I didn't have any money to leave. The only thing I knew how to do was prostitution. All I had to look forward to was going out to find customers, day after day. I asked Raymond for money many times. He said, "If we want to sell the house we're going to have to renovate it. Put in a wine cellar, a swimming pool, tennis courts. Then it'll be worth a fortune. We'll sell it, travel and you can have money."

He said we were a couple. But I didn't feel like part of a couple. I was alone in the country during the week, working. He only came up on weekends. It felt more like the owner of the house and his slave.

Every time I asked him for money we got into arguments. He said, "But you don't pay rent here. I give you food."

I said, "Yeah, but I work for that. At least give me something to spend." He would buy me a carton of cigarettes but never gave me the money.

Every summer he took part in a Spiritualist Fair. He trained his friends and me how to do palm reading, how to react to a little sentence. The basics. It's a hoax. I would read a palm and say, "You're nervous." Everyone is nervous sometimes. You have to have key words to make people talk.

I said to one woman, "There is alcohol around you."

She turned around and told her friends, "He's very good. He just mentioned I live on top of the liquor store."

Which is not what I said. People who come to these things are very gullible. You just say a couple of words and they do the talking. Basically, you develop the ability to make people talk.

We started at nine and finished at 10 at night. The fair was in an arena for ten days. It was $20 for 10 minutes and people were lining up. He easily made $10,000 at one fair and we did this every summer. I always built the kiosk we worked out of and he never paid me. The kiosk was portable, planks of wood that can be assembled and moved around. In the kiosk we all sat side by side with only a little partition between us. A big table with small partitions and 15 people doing readings! Twenty dollars for 10 minutes. It was like a factory.

We did different towns. We were like a circus. He always had his friends who were making money on the side, no tax. At night we packed all the $20 bills into brown bags. And the worse part was that he paid the others but he never gave me a penny. All the money we made at the Spiritualist Fairs was going toward renovations and buying stuff for the house.

Two-and-a-half years into the relationship we had a big party. People were smoking pot, taking acid. I had some punch and got completely zapped. As I was drinking the punch I could feel myself getting very high, too high. I went to the bathroom cabinet knowing Raymond always had some Valium. I took some to bring me down and lost consciousness. I woke up in a nuthouse, behind bars so I couldn't escape. I didn't know what had happened to me.

I lost some days there. I know there was a party. I know I had a blackout. Some people took me to the hospital. At the hospital they pumped my stomach. I think I took too much Valium. The doctors thought I was suicidal so they transferred me to the psychiatric unit. I was totally out, like in a coma. I had a little room. Then there was a big area where all the nuts were jumping around and talking to themselves. I had to wait in line to get my pill. Exactly like in *One Flew Over the Cuckoo's Nest*. Slowly I came to and said, "What am I doing here?" I wanted to talk to the doctor, the nurse. No one said anything.

One day Raymond visited me. I said, "What happened?"

He said, "You tell me. Why did you kill Napoleon?"

All the dogs had grand, important names. I said, "What?"

"You killed Napoleon.

"You're sure?"

"You were stoned and you killed Napoleon. You should know better."

We got into an argument. Finally the doctor came and brought me back to the cell. A couple of days later he opened my cell and said, "You're released."

I said, "Yeah, but that doesn't tell me what happened."

"I can't comment. You'll have to ask the people you're living with."

Raymond picked me up. He was angry at me but he also blamed himself. He said some people had put acid and other things in the punch.

By then he probably would have liked to kick me out of the house and get someone else. We hadn't had sex in the past six months. He always criticized me. I could do nothing right. But he still needed me to work on the house.

I built a big terrace in the back, all alone. When he came up on weekends he never lifted a hammer. One summer I rebuilt the barn. When I finished it he surprised me with a canoe. I was really happy. He drove me twice to the river with the canoe, then said, "Do you think I'm always going to drive you? Forget it." The river was far and there was only one car, his. So I got to use the canoe twice.

Should I leave? Should I stay? Was I digging myself in too deep? Can he help me? I was stuck. I couldn't see the end. He was talking about a wine cellar, a swimming pool, a tennis court. It could have gone on and on. Sometimes I would get up in the middle of the night and work on the house, anything. I couldn't sleep.

The last two years I was with him I tried to commit suicide twice.

Both times with a plastic bag. That was my favourite trick. We had guns. I could have used a gun but I didn't think of it. I always tied a plastic bag with a rope around my neck. And I was always the one to untie it. Once I tried when he was in the house. He was downstairs and I was in the bedroom upstairs. The second time I was alone. I said to myself, this time I'm going to succeed. I turned the rope a few times around my neck and it was very hard to undo. I pulled and pulled. I got lucky. Air came into the bag from the back. I came very close.

I never said anything to Raymond. I never told anyone. Those last two years were just arguments. Toward the end we were hardly talking to each other. I could have gone any time but I didn't. I was weak. And I had stayed with him for five years!

During those years I had no contact with the family. I went with Raymond to escape my father. Then I discovered I was in the same situation as my mother was with my father. The psychologist in prison explained that to me later. That's why I really understood my mother. The psychologist said I probably didn't leave because I had no place to go and I was kept on the hook by the promise of various things. And I was getting no money. Raymond made me think, yes, we'll do things together. But it was getting me nowhere.

We had a big basement and he wanted to build a sub-basement for a wine cellar. I was left alone, digging this cellar with a shovel. Raymond never helped. He was the intellectual one. I was digging dirt all week long. The first thing he did when he came up for the weekend was to see how far I got with the cellar. He always said, "That's all you did? You should have done much more." And he got mad.

We had lots of fights. I said, "Hey, I'm digging with a shovel. At least rent a drill to help me break the stones." He never did. Sometimes there were big stones and I had to take them upstairs and outside. I had to create pulleys or I took them out by hand. I was doing work for which you needed at least two men and machinery. For him everything was possible and he couldn't understand why I was having trouble.

I sometimes worked 12 hours a day. He came down on weekends and said, "It's not finished yet?" I was like a slave. And I saw no way out. He never helped me. He provided me with a roof, a place to sleep, but I don't have to be a slave. I told him that one day when he came down to the basement to inspect my work. We began to argue. Every weekend we had the same argument. I tried to explain what I had to do and how much work it took. He didn't care. I kept a rifle in the basement while I worked, in case the motorcycle gang showed up. It was overhead, on hooks fastened in the ceiling. We were yelling. I got angrier and angrier. Instead of giving him a slap on the face, I took the rifle and shot.

I put him in the wheelbarrow and, like one of the stones, with a system of pulleys, took him out to the yard. He was taller than me and weighed over 200 pounds. I managed, by sheer willpower, to take him out. I felt, that's it, he won't disturb me again. I felt total relief.

I took some money from him, money I thought he owed me. I drove his car to the village and then hitchhiked to Montreal. In Montreal I took a room in a hotel. I wanted to do something but I didn't know what. It was a Catch-22. I was free but free to do what? I was lost. How could I live? I wanted to kill myself. One night I put a plastic bag over my head, tied it with a string around my neck and tried to go to sleep. But it wasn't that easy. When I started to gasp for air, I thought I better find another way. I wanted to kill myself but not to hurt myself. When you start gasping for air and it's burning, it's painful.

I stayed at the hotel for a week, going around in circles. I didn't know what to do. I thought, let someone else kill me. Let someone else do the dirty work. I went to a nearby shopping centre and called the police. I waited. They didn't come. I called again saying, "Hey, when are you coming to pick me up?" They still didn't come. I had no more quarters. I went to the bank and said, "I want the phone to call the police." A girl gave me the phone. I called and got really mad, "Hey, do you want me or not? I'm going to go away."

It was around Christmas. There was a Santa Claus with kids all around. Finally the police came. They arrested me in the shopping centre, near Santa Claus. As they took me out, one holding each arm, I was not even touching the ground. Outside they threw me on the snow and took off my coat to see if I had a gun. They pulled up my shirt. I was naked right on the snow. It was cold. Then they put me in handcuffs. I kept saying to the police, "Just kill me, please." I was sure they would kill me.

I was taken to Parthenais, the detention centre. The next day they asked me to show them where the body was. When I saw him I felt nothing, I was numb inside. I was crying from the time I arrived in jail. I stayed in Parthenais a year, a year-and-a-half, and cried all the time.

I never called my mother because I didn't want to tell her I had killed a man. I called my sister. She said, "Your mother already knows, it was on the news."

My lawyer said, "I fixed it all. Plead guilty." I didn't care how many years I got, I didn't care about the sentence. I just wanted to kill myself. I pled guilty to second-degree murder and tried to kill myself during the hearings. I was totally depressed. After each time I tried to kill myself I felt completely empty for a couple of days. You feel you don't care about anything. You're only thinking of trying again.

There were three hearings to collect information. There was nothing about my background and nothing on the killing either. Some of my family came to the hearings because they were open to the public. My brothers came just to give me support. My mother came once but she was so sick. She was crying. She probably had a nervous breakdown.

I got a life sentence, a minimum of 10 years inside, up to the rest of my life. Some people who were sentenced the same year, for the same crime, got 18 years, some got 12. I got 10. It all depends on the judge's mood. Even if you plead guilty, the judge can say 25 years minimum.

I was sentenced in 1977, when I was 26. They moved me to the old pen, St. Vincent de Paul, and I stopped crying. A few months later, they transferred me to Archambault where there was a lot of tension. The day before I arrived there had been a murder. The bars were full of blood. The first month I was there I tried to kill myself. Suicide seemed the only answer. I couldn't see the light at the end of the tunnel.

That last attempt woke me up. I realized I was the cause of my predicament. I had put myself into this situation. It was for me to change it. I thought that when I tried to commit suicide with Raymond, I didn't think deeply enough. I thought things would change. Once the weekend was over, Raymond was gone and I was happy. I was alone. Now I said to myself, if I don't have the guts to kill myself, I'll fight to survive. After I decided to fight, believe it or not, I started to be happier.

At the time Archambault was maximum security. Maybe 20 percent of the population made use of the yard. People either stay in their cell or they meet friends in the pavilion. After a week I said to myself, if I'm here for life I have to see what the yard looks like. I knew things could happen in the yard. I said to myself, go ahead, go into the yard. If something happens you're going to have to defend yourself. But nothing happened.

When you're alone in your cell for hours on end, you think. You look at your life. You try to analyze what the past was about, where you want to go, how you feel about everything. And for the first time you begin to get a sense of yourself.

I was born in St. Henri. I had two older and two younger siblings. The oldest is a girl, Clair, then Philip, me, Robert and Paul. One girl and four boys. I'm the middle one.

We were poor. There were four rooms in the house. My parents had a room. My sister had her own room and the boys shared a room with two bunk beds and a window in the middle. There was just enough room to go in and out between the two bunk beds. One night, when I was 12, I woke up to find my father under the blanket, sucking me. You feel something and you think you're dreaming. Then you see it's your father and you're scared. I saw the others were sleeping so I pretended to sleep. I didn't know what to do. I was frozen. Then there was a noise in the room and he left.

After that happened we barely looked at each other. A couple of months passed. Then it happened again. The second time I woke up when I was ejaculating. Again I thought I was dreaming. He was really meticulous. Only his mouth touched me. When I realized it was him again I was really angry. But he didn't give me time to respond. As soon as I came he left the room.

The third time I woke up while he was under the blanket and kicked him. I said, "Hey, go away." He walked out of the room, drunk. But even after he got kicked out, he came back to try again but I always kicked him out.

During the day he avoided my eyes. You can look at someone but not really see them. I felt very uncomfortable. And I was scared to talk to him. I was also scared to talk to my mother. She was sick at the time with a nervous breakdown. She was on pills.

With all of us sleeping in the same room, I knew when he came in. When he wasn't trying to touch me, I knew he was doing it to one of my other brothers. We never talked about it but I could hear noises. I know he did it to all my brothers.

St. Henri was very much a village. The neighbourhood knew he was gay, he didn't hide it. Some guys said, "Hey, your father's a fag." I heard that when I was 12. I knew it was true because he was trying it on us.

My father didn't have a pattern of when he would come into our room. One month he would come in every night or even two or three times during the night. He'd come to see if we were sleeping, then come back later on. We didn't sleep very well those nights. When he abused us the tension in the house was high. Then there were periods of peace and we were a real family. Then the tension died down and he would charge again.

Whenever my father came home drunk, which was most of the time, we knew he was going to try something. Every time he was drunk I was going out the back door or by the window. We lived on the first floor. The window between the bunk beds faced the backyard. I pretended I was going into my room and went out by the window. All my brothers did the same. When I was older I sometimes stayed out the whole night.

My father never acted like a real father. He never threw a baseball at us, never took us to see a show, never came to the park with us. We never did anything. My mother never took us to a park either because we didn't have money. I know it costs nothing to go to the park, but when you have nothing decent to wear you don't want to go into public. You're ashamed.

My father was always a stranger in the house. He was either at work or in the tavern. He worked in a lumberyard for a while. Then he got fired. Probably because of his drinking. Then he did different factory jobs. He would bring home a man and introduce him as a co-worker. Everyone was a friend from work. Sometimes they were tavern friends and he'd bring some beer and drink at home. He had brought one guy home a few times. Then we found out that he was one of my father's boyfriends. When he was drunk there were no secrets.

One day he brought a man home. He was really drunk. He kicked my mother out of bed and said, "I'm sleeping with this guy tonight." She waited outside the room, crying. Later I discovered he was really rude to my mother after all the kids were born. Then she got a nervous breakdown, maybe because she found out he was gay. My father said she was nuts. When you're a kid you don't know what's going on. You believe your father, you think your mother is nuts. When my mother was in hospital, he would bring his boyfriends home and kiss them in front of us kids.

After my mother had a nervous breakdown, she also had trouble with her heart, she became diabetic. She was not eating well because the little money she had was for the kids. She became sicker and sicker. Also, she didn't talk to anyone, she kept all her problems inside.

I think he stayed with my mother as a cover-up. The rest of the family, like my aunts and uncles, knew he was gay but he thought he had camouflaged it. He was always going to parties with my mother and he had five kids. We seemed like a normal family. But everyone knew.

When he got drunk he boasted about his sexual activities, both with my mother and with men. How often, what positions. Your mother likes that too. He boasted about having both sexes. I remember when I was 14 he said to my aunt one Christmas, "You should see the way I take your sister." Normally he was a man but after a couple of drinks he was starting to look feminine. When he was completely drunk he was disgusting, a queen. That's when people started to leave. It was always the same pattern. He welcomed people into the house, but as the evening wore on he drank more and more, and he became freer and freer. He insulted my mother. He talked about his boyfriends. He was wide open.

My first sexual experience was with my sister. I was 12 at the time. I was watching TV and she came to join me. She was 18 and she was taking care of us when my mother was in the hospital and my father was out. At the beginning I felt uncomfortable, but when someone starts rubbing you and it's your sister, nature takes over. My father was really a bad experience. With my sister it was natural. I didn't feel bad about it after. We did it a few times. It was something to do when we were bored.

My sister was never close to my father except when she drank. She started drinking very young. When she saw my father drink, she went over and asked, "Can I have a sip, can I have a sip?" My mother was mad, saying, "Don't give her any!"

But he always gave booze to my sister. When she started to go out dancing, that's when she started really drinking.

I come from a sexually active family. When I was about 14 I slept with my brothers. I slept with everyone except my mother and father. All my brothers have had homosexual experiences. I had a friend who was my age and he was really gay. My father got him as well as my brothers. I also did it with him.

By then I was into drugs. Grass, acid. One day this gay friend and I went out together and he said, "Try prostitution. It's easy money." At that time I thought it was natural. It was 1967, Woodstock, everyone was naked and stoned. That was the context.

I did prostitution for the money and sometimes for pleasure. Some guys knew how to have sex and it was good. I learned things. The money I made from prostitution I used for alcohol and drugs. I never showed that money to my mother or the rest of the family.

When I was about 16 I did it with a man and didn't know he was a friend of my father's. One day my father brought him home. The guy recognized me and told my father. My father tried to attack me after that because, he said, "Now I know you're gay." And he wagged his finger.

I said, "Not with you, you're my father."

When I was 16 he slapped me. I stopped his hand and slapped him back. Since the age of 13 I've done judo, karate and kung fu. So when he hit me, I hit him back. He spun around and went right out of the house. Everyone talked about that for a long time.

I'm the only kid in the family he didn't hit. He beat all my brothers and sister. One time he beat up my older brother so badly he had to go to emergency. My brother said, "I should have done exactly what you did the first time he tried to hit you."

Whenever my father beat up my brothers or sister my mother tried to stop him but she was only 4-11. My father was 6-2. He could lift her with one hand. How could she have stopped my father? She was crying and screaming at him, but there was nothing she could do.

She cried all the time. I asked her, "What's wrong?"

She said, "One day, you'll understand."

She was always saying one day you'll understand. I can't say anything. She was a very good mother. She didn't want to hurt anybody, she was even protecting the wolf inside. She took a lot of shit from everyone, her husband, her kids. She absorbed all the shocks. She cried a lot and was very religious. She went to church every Sunday, asking God to help her.

She was afraid. My mother had gone to Grade 3 at the most. She didn't know how to read or write. What was she going to do with five kids on the street? She was also worried about her reputation. What were the neighbours going to say?

Around this time a new family moved to the neighbourhood and they had a son my age. We became close friends. For three years we were together all the time, sexually as well as otherwise. No one knew that we had a relationship. No one would guess that there was anything sexual. He was masculine and I was also masculine. He didn't like my father and my father didn't like him. My father used to say, "You're spending more time with your friend than your family."

We did things together. We went to the movies. In those days you had three movies for 75 cents. We used to play in the yard, go swimming. I liked swimming. I started swimming when I was a kid. In those days there were public baths, small indoor swimming pools where they had a few programs for kids. I got my bronze medal, so I was a lifeguard and a swimming instructor. At that time I was working for Flipper Pool Service as a lifeguard in private buildings. I did that after being a TV repairman didn't work out. I got it because the owner was gay and one of my customers. After I began to work the guy was my boss and we didn't have sexual contact.

Three years later my friend's family moved out of town. That's when I lost him. He was my first love. It was a nice relationship. He was a good friend.

By 18 I was always stoned and went heavy on drugs. My father and I had conflicts all the time. We disagreed on everything. He said, "All you think about is getting out of here as soon as possible to get stoned." We had arguments over everything. Sex was one major point. He wanted to try again. I said no. Him wanting to have sex was a big aggravation. Because I refused we talked less and less to each other.

My father tried to hit me a second time. I stopped his hand and said, "Don't even try. I'm going to kill you." And I meant it. I was going to kill him. My look must have told him I was serious. I hated him. That's probably why I killed Raymond. I wanted to kill my father. I thought about that many, many times. I think I killed my father when I killed Raymond.

Time in jail made me understand what I went through. Prison gave me the time to understand myself and my family. In jail I was more free than when I was out. Jail saved me, changed me. I never thought of myself before and I began to think.

Inside, my attitude, my mind, began to shift. When you ask people, "Hey, I just arrived, what's the best advice?"

"Just observe. Watch."

You watch but you have to be careful because the people in front of you don't like to be watched. You have to watch without watching. It's a game.

I already had practise observing in the country. When you take a walk you observe nature. You sit down and listen in silence. You see life around you. That's why I learned fast in jail. I already knew how to observe nature. In jail it's a different game but the principle is still the same. You observe others and you observe yourself. By discovering other people, you discover yourself. Sometimes you don't have a choice but to react in a certain way even if you don't like it. It's a question of survival. Tension is high. You have to fight fire with fire. You can't say, he's very aggressive, I'm going to try to calm him down. You try to calm him down, you're labelled a weak guy and weak guys get beaten up. You always have to be strong and show that you're stronger. To survive I became tough.

You're in a jungle. If you can't catch little signs left and right, you won't survive. For instance a ball can be in the field. If you don't know where that ball came from, don't just start playing with it. Leave it there. You have to observe to whom it belongs. I know someone who got stabbed for taking an empty cup from the picnic table to have a glass of water. A guy said, "Hey, he took my cup!" The next day he was killed. People are so tense they have to prove themselves. For little things.

Archambault had the most stabbings in 1977 and 1978. One week there was no stabbing and I thought, hey, what happened? That's how bad the tension was. In 1984 there was a mass murder in which three guards were killed. Tension had been building from day to day. You take a squirrel, put it in a cage and start teasing and hitting the poor animal, sooner or later he's going to react.

The first year I was at Archambault I met a group of very interesting people. They were the elite of the jail, which I didn't know at the time. I met this group through tennis. In the beginning I was just trying to help maintain the tennis courts to help out. They were clay courts and we hosed them down, then passed the roller over them. Some people played really well.

One day I said to one of them, "If you don't have a guy to play with I can play with you."

He said, "No problem."

We played from time to time and they discovered I could return a ball.

I had played tennis outside jail with Raymond. Originally I had learned on the street. But Raymond was a really good tennis player. He was considered a pro. Also, in the country, I used to bike into town where they had clay courts and played there.

Probably they accepted me into the group because I wasn't one of the tattoo guys doing weights. These guys didn't lift weights. Some were very, very skinny and they had more respect than the ones lifting weights. When the committee of inmates had a serious decision to make, they asked these guys what to do. Like sometimes Parliament doesn't make its own decision—they'll consult the businessmen. Besides playing tennis with the group, we had good conversations. We gave each other energy, strength. One of them, let's call him Apple, was really bright, a lot of class, culture. Even if he was wearing jail clothes, he wore them with style. He influenced me in that. He said, "You have to keep your self-respect all the time." He and his circle of friends—and he was very selective—all had a lot of class. I was lucky to have been included in the group. We never talked about crime. They didn't want to do cross-links. When a new inmate tried to join us and he was bragging about what he had done, he left the group by himself just because we didn't respond to that sort of talk. Some people in the group had done really big jobs. All had big-sentence crimes. But they never talked about what or how they did what they did. I knew they had done big jobs because there were rumours inside. When there are big names, there are write-ups about them in the newspapers. You know who they are. Inside everybody knows who you are.

Apple had done Brink's robberies. This guy was a brain. He and his brother robbed banks all across Canada and in the States. They imported hash, cocaine, heavy stuff. Another person in the circle was Paul Rose, who was convicted of killing Pierre Laporte. But he didn't do the killing. At the time they all agreed the person who gets caught takes the blame. This was a bright guy, a professor.

In jail you have to do a job. The people I played tennis with said to the sports facility, "Hire that guy, he's good." The sports facility paid attention to what the tennis players said. They had weight. I guess they recommended me because of the way I took care of the tennis courts. I had just arrived and they took me right away. I became secretary of sports on the inmate committee. When you're on the sports team you have the best salary and you don't do anything. It's a good job. There were two sports trustees and one secretary. The two guys who are trustees represent all the inmates and they fight for sports equipment with the administration. Then you have about eight inmates who take care of all the equipment. The sports department was also in charge of different activities that went on. Sometimes they rented electronic equipment and needed a guy to connect it. I always volunteered.

I played tennis with Apple for five years. In the summer you're on the tennis courts five hours a day. It's always the same people who play tennis. Who's going to play on the tennis court? It's like snobbism in society. People who have money. Or people who are healthier than Joe Blow. In jail it's the same thing.

At night we were able to build a camp fire till 11 o'clock and played chess. Apple was also a fantastic chess player. I finally beat him a couple of times. I learned to play chess at school. I always oriented myself toward mathematics, electronics, chess. They all go together. Everyone in the yard has their spot, their territory. We played chess and talked a lot, like philosophy.

They made me think about other things than just wake up in the morning, eat, go back to sleep. They helped me to expand my mind. They had a whole other area of knowledge than me. They had met different kinds of people, seen other cultures. They made me more aware. When you realize how much choice and variety is out there, you ask yourself, hey, where is my place in all this? You try to define your own taste. Hey, you went to Paris? How was it? But today, I went to Paris. I went to Africa, Columbia. I've taken a few trips.

Before, when I was young, I used to read everything. I liked history, geography. In jail I went through different periods. One of my periods was philosophy, then psychology. We exchanged books in the group and discussed them. These people gave me the opportunity to examine and debate ideas that changed my thinking, that brought me alive. I was lucky to find this group and fit into their circle.

But jail presents certain difficulties. They're always moving inmates around. Our group may start out as five but the jail can move two to another jail. But two years later they'll be back. You have to deal with that. The group is always different because you get moved around.

I spent five years at Archambault and the people I met helped to awaken my mind, excite my curiosity. Jail brought me alive. For a while I was the president of the lifers' group. At Archambault I was having a good time. Archambault had a swimming pool that didn't work. The inmates had dug that pool by hand. They paid for the lining of the pool, everything. Not the administration. The administration said, "You can't use the swimming pool this year. It's broken." But all the equipment was there for me to get it started. I made it work. I gave the inmates a swimming pool. Suddenly the administration discovered the pool was operating for already a week and people were using it. The inmates were grateful, they thanked me. So inside I didn't have a problem. I'm good with my hands. I like to work. But from Raymond I never got any thanks. In jail I got the thanks and I became more aware of what I could do. I discovered I was capable. That gave me a lot of satisfaction.

I was secretary of sports till they moved me to medium security in Cowansville. Some of our group from Archambault also went to Cowansville. At Archambault I thought I was feeling good but I realized I was just surviving. In Cowansville I started to relax more. There is less tension in medium. In maximum you can relax maybe 80 percent, never completely. But while you're there you think, I'm not tense. Same thing when you go out. Inmates talked about that.

My mother came to visit me every week. Sometimes she had lifts and sometimes she took the bus, a two-and-a-half-hour bus ride, even when she was sick.

I often said, "Stay home, I'll call you."

"No, I want to see you."

She never missed a visit. When I was in jail we got closer and closer. She was seeing me more than the rest of her children outside. From time to time we talked about my father, what it was like when I was young. I told her the whole story in jail. She sort of implied that she knew but she had no education and she didn't know what to do. I don't blame her. Don't forget her husband was providing the money to feed the kids. In those days you didn't have houses where people could go for help. She was in a Catch-22 situation.

In the beginning some of my brothers and sister also visited me in jail. For a while I was very close to my sister. Then it deteriorated. She was always defending my father.

Whenever I talked about him, she always said, "But he's your father. You should have more respect for him."

I said, "You can't understand because you're a girl. Those things didn't happen to you.

"Yes, I understand but he's still your father. If he did that it's because he loved you."

"Yeah, a little too much!"

My sister was always taking my father's side. When she was young she didn't get any attention or affection. She was close to our father when they got drunk together. Still today she regularly goes drinking with him. They go to parties together. She really likes him.

My father never came to see me in jail. I wouldn't have really wanted him to come but as a father he should have been there. I probably wouldn't have liked it but I would have understood. Deep inside I would have known I'm still his son. But he didn't show up. Never phoned. Whenever I called home I talked to all the family, never him. Not even on Christmas.

In medium security you can plan. In maximum you cannot. You cannot really study in maximum when you don't know if tomorrow there will be a murder or a riot or a lockout. In jail either you have a job or you go to school. At Cowansville I went to school. They forced me to do the last two years of high school again. Then they sent me to CEGEP. I did half my CEGEP and then joined the electronics department. I was good in school. In the family I was the only one who finished high school. In Grade 12 I studied electronics. I liked electronics. After high school I was a TV repairman for two months. The guy I worked for was a crook. That's why I left. When someone called to say their TV was broken, he'd say, "Change that lamp as well. We know that the lamp we put in is weak and the guy is going to come back in two months." He was teaching me how to be a crook, to make sure customers came back.

In jail there were only eight people in the electronics class. We had an outside teacher come in and it was almost like private classes. Once a physics guy came and we did some laser experiments. That was the good part about jail. If you know what you want, it's there. You have to be opportunistic.

I also did some correspondence courses in robotics. So I got a few diplomas which helped to get me into The Computer Institute of Quebec when I got to minimum. I could show I had a background in computers.

In Cowansville I managed to get a computer in my cell. I was one of the first inmates in Canada to have a computer in the cell. I discovered I could do things. At Archambault I discovered I could repair the swimming pool. In Cowansville I discovered I could do programming.

I began to see a psychologist at Cowansville because if you want to go to minimum, you have to pass an evaluation. I saw one at Archambault but he just asked straight questions. In Cowansville I visited a psychologist once a month for three years. We were just talking, relaxing. He talked about golf. Of course, that's another way of getting me to relax and get to my feelings. He didn't say he was going to analyze me. He said, "This is your period of the month to relax."

He was surprised that I didn't have a lover. He said, "You should find a man for yourself here. It'll help you pass the time."

I said, "No."

He said, "It's up to you."

Actually in medium security I had two lovers. I made love after six years in prison. One encounter was just in passing. A one-shot deal, just to relax. It was probably the first time, except with the friend I had as a teenager, that I had sex as an equal. Of course, there you have to be cautious, not only about the timing but also to find a place where you won't get caught. The second one took maybe two or three months from the first time I saw him till it actually happened. We both knew we wanted to do it. We finally did it in the shower. The timing for the shower was perfect and we did it without talking. We were both watching for the right time. We took a very long shower together and I'm surprised no one discovered us. When it was over I realized we must have stayed an hour or more in the shower. It was really something. We never did it again, though I did see him again. He was on my wing. We played sports together.

I gained confidence at Archambault and more in Cowansville. In Archambault I got confidence from the inmates I was friends with and I discovered myself. In Cowansville I did some theatre. Every time I mastered something I thought, what else can I do? In Cowansville my teachers had confidence in me. Like my electronics teacher who signed for me on my first day out. He believed in me. He also signed for me to go out and run in the marathon. I ran about three or four marathons when I was in medium. On weekends I trained in the yard.

After almost eight years I got into minimum. By then I had a good sense of myself. I saw that I wouldn't have to be in jail forever. I was ready to go on the street.

My mother continued to come and visit me regularly. In the last two years I encouraged her to go to an old-age home. You'll meet new people, maybe you'll find a new boyfriend. You need to change, to stretch yourself. She said, "Yes, yes." But she was a "yes" mother and she never did anything. She said, "It's too late now. I'm too sick and too old."

From prison I told my mother to go out. She did a few things but she got so little money from my father. I told her to go play bingo. Ask your sisters to take you for a drive. She used to be friends with some of her sisters. But she was often sick. Many times she lost consciousness in the shopping centre and needed an ambulance. She could lose consciousness any time. She would go out with her sisters and they never knew when she was going to need an ambulance. Her sisters and brothers didn't want to go shopping with her any more because they were scared. They invited her out less and less. That upset her. She said, "I should die now so I won't be a problem to anyone."

She came to visit me and I would try to cheer her up. I said, "Wait for me. I'm getting out soon and I'm going to need you." That brought her alive. It gave her hope.

When my sister came to visit me she said, "Mom and Dad are OK, everything is fine." But when you start to go out on three-day leaves you discover the situation between Mom and Dad is not fine. It's not the way you described it. I saw what was happening between my mother and father in a clearer way. I started to discuss their relationship with my sister. I talked to her about my father's attitude to my mother. She said, "You never understand," etc., etc. My sister is always on my father's side. So the relationship with my sister deteriorated as I got closer to going out.

In minimum I went outside to study robotics. The course was sponsored by The Computer Institute of Quebec. I studied robotics, programming, computers. It started at 7:30 a.m. I had to take the bus at five a.m., sometimes in the snowstorm, from the corner of the jail in Laval to St. Thérèse. It usually took me a good hour-and-a-half to get to school. In the morning and at night. Some of my courses were from five to seven, two nights a week and I arrived back in jail at nine in the evening. Then I had to do my homework. To do that kind of homework in jail is not easy. Then I woke up at four the next morning to go to school again.

In minimum I didn't really have friends partly because I was only going there to sleep. In summer, on weekends, I was on the tennis court. In winter I played badminton. I was talking to everyone but not talking to anyone.

I began to see that I could do something with my life. I never thought like that before. Before I didn't have a picture of what I could be, what life could be. I didn't have any dreams before I went to jail. No one showed me I could have a dream. I discovered it myself *(crying)*. When I remember those times…there are so many things I should have done but didn't. I didn't even feel happy before I went to jail. I had a father who was an alcoholic, a homosexual, a mother who saw nothing and tried to act like a mother hen. You grow up in a very poor neighbourhood. You just exist. What's going to happen tomorrow? What's going to happen the day after tomorrow? What are you going to do with your life? You don't know. You have no idea. When you meet other people you see there are different ways to be and you discover there are such things as goals. You meet people with different tastes and you ask yourself, what's my taste?

I was lucky to have met the people I did in prison. The group I was a part of talked about life, culture, not crime. Other inmates boast of what they've done. These people talked about the trips they took, the different cultures they visited. They talked about wines. Apple adored wine and he'd say, when you're out you have to taste this wine or that wine. He'd talk about the difference between wines. He described them so well that we could almost taste them. He gave us a taste by his description. He used to say about the other inmates, "They're stupid assholes. Look what they're talking about. They have no culture. They're talking about beating up a guy on the street or they're laughing about a break and entry they did. They're going to go out and come right back." I agreed with him.

The element that started it for me was talking to people like Apple, listening to them. They talked differently from the people I knew in my past. They inspired me to grow, expand. They gave me an education. I'm not the same person today as I was at age 20.

In minimum I could see the light at the end of the tunnel. I could see the day I will go out alone and achieve something. Finally, after 10 years, I got out of jail. You get a small bag and they say, "Go have fun." You're starting a new life. And you have maybe about $30 in your pocket. An uncle came to pick me up. I arrived at a halfway house on the 31st of December.

I was so alone and sad when I got out. I didn't go to my family right away. I needed air. I needed to see faces, to see trees, buildings. I walked a lot. The first two months I was out I needed to go to places where there were lots of people. I heard there was a meeting somewhere and I went just to talk to people.

Before leaving jail I enrolled in a program where they tell you how to find a job, how to pass an interview. So the first week I was out I looked up electronic firms and asked for the name of the person in charge of the personnel department. I then called back and asked directly for that person. If they ask who is calling, you just say your first name. They think you're a personal friend. You say, "Hi, I'm so and so, sorry to bother you but I'm looking for a job."

It took me a week to find a job as a computer technician. When I went for the interview I immediately told them I had just gotten out of jail. I said, "The rehabilitation program is going to pay half my salary for six months. I'm going to cost you half the price of a technician. Probably you don't need another technician but for half the price you can use an extra technician." He said, "OK, that sounds like a good deal." I sold myself.

I worked at Canadian Data repairing computers. After six months they hired me permanently. They didn't have a choice. I was good. Just give me one week to show what I can do. Jail and all the programs gave me confidence.

One time I was at NARCO, a petroleum company, and I met someone from our group who had a good position there. He just happened to come into the office when I was with one of the comptrollers of the company.

We said hello to each other, talked about his family. He asked me what I was doing there. When I told him he said, "You always liked electronics. I'm happy for you."

The guy was just listening to our conversation. When my acquaintance left, the comptroller asked where we met and I said, "In jail." He laughed. We both laughed. He thought I was joking.

My mother's place was a 20-minute walk from the halfway house. I used to pick her up and take her for walks. I was very available to her. After a year-and-a-half at the halfway house I went to live with her for six months. I didn't have a choice. She was really sick. While I was living there it was draining but it wasn't tense. I was pleased to be able to do it for her. I considered my mother a friend. I didn't see it as a responsibility. In those six months I saw my father maybe two or three times. After I came out of jail I only talked to my father superficially. We were very cold with each other.

I saw my mother was still living with my father and she was not happy, very depressive. They were sharing the same bed and he still slept with her. She told me. He was mostly gay but also bisexual. The last year before she died she said, "He still does it." That's why I tried to persuade her to go to an old-age home.

She said, "I want to die with my things around me."

I said, "But you don't have to share the same bed with him."

"It only happens when he's drunk."

So I took her under my wing. I became the mother hen because I thought she deserved to have at least a couple of good years. I gave her what I could.

For 10 years she regularly visited me in jail. She deserved it. It was a small sacrifice to take her for a walk, buy her something at the Dairy Queen, take her to lunch. It was nothing for me. I'm the only one who did that. The others had their own families.

After six months I got an apartment. When you start over again from jail you don't even have a fork or a knife. You start from scratch. Normally people at 38 have everything they need. When you don't even have a spoon you have to cut corners and share. My mother offered to give me dishes, cutlery, but I said no. All that comes from my father. I prefer to start from scratch. Now I have everything. A washing machine, a dryer, everything.

She was very happy when I got my own apartment. She was always saying, "Do what you want and try to be happy. You deserve to be happy." She understood but after a while she got depressed again. I realized she needed more than just a little boost. Now that I had my own apartment she could call when she needed to talk. That would help her but it drained me. I didn't realize how much energy she took. I didn't have time to live my life. I didn't have time to build things for myself. Her need was choking me. I needed to be freer. I explained that to her. But I saw right away that my mother needed help like I once needed help. She would phone saying, "Louis, please come, get me out of here." She asked for help. She took the first step. Some people never take that step. When she came to jail I talked a lot to her about what was going on with me. So she herself had opened a little, she was trying to expand.

In time she got more confidence. Still, she was very demanding in terms of energy. But after you gave her some attention, take her for a walk, she was fine. Once I took her out to lunch and brought a gay friend with me. She was very pleased, "Oh, this is your lover."

I said, "No, this is not my lover. This is just a friend."

"I'm sure he's a lover but you don't want to tell me."

She was upset that he wasn't my lover. When it came time to say goodbye, she said to him, "Big guy, come down and give me a kiss."

My mother is 4-11 and he was over six feet. She was funny. My friend really liked her.

She called me every day and we talked as friends. I took her out for lunch. We went to museums. We did things we should have done when I was a kid. She liked to eat at Dairy Queen in the summer. So at night I took her out for ice creams. Simple things, just to take her out of the house. She was a very good friend. We exchanged recipes. When I was trying to cook something, sometimes she would guide me on the phone. Or vice versa, because I'm a pretty good cook myself.

Canadian Data got a project to install a computer network in Africa. They needed a technician and told me to go. But they didn't know my status. They knew I had been in jail but not for what. And the client certainly didn't know. When you leave jail you're limited to 25 miles of your residence. All of a sudden I have to go across the ocean. I submitted the project to my parole officer who put in a formal demand. Thankfully, in a short period of time, I got a special permit to leave the country.

I was in Africa for two weeks. While there, I ate at the Canadian Ambassador's house twice. They provided me with a driver and a car. From regular Joe Blow I went to a pretty high level. A bonus attached to Africa was Paris. I stayed one week in Paris, all paid.

I got home. A few months later, on the 12th of November, my mother died. Two days before she died we had a long, long conversation. We talked on the phone for about two hours. She told me she was going to die. I said, "I love you so much but I understand you have to go."

She had heart problems, asthma, was a diabetic. She went into a

41

diabetic coma sometimes. She said, "If that happens again I'm going to let myself go. I don't have any more strength to fight."

We started crying. We just talked about things in general. From time to time we said, "Yes, I love you." I'm going to remember that conversation all my life. That was on a Thursday night. On Friday we briefly talked in the morning. On Saturday, when I arrived home, there was a message from my father saying your mother is dead. She died Friday night at the age of 67.

She never understood her body, she didn't recognize the symptoms between asthma, diabetes or her heart. Sometimes she took the wrong pill. If you take your asthma medication when you're having a heart attack, that makes it even worse. That's why from time to time she got really sick and we had to take her to emergency.

In a short conversation I had with my father after she died he said, "I gave her everything she wanted. If she asked me for a certain pill, I gave it to her right away."

But neither my father nor my mother knew her symptoms. I tried to teach her, "Listen to your body. Heart problems are different from asthma, don't ask for the pump. The pump is going to kill you." Obviously, she had asked my father for the wrong medication.

My aunt said, "Believe me, now it's going to be better for her. You did your best and she died in peace. She died when she wanted to die." Not only did I lose a mother, I lost a friend. But I was also released of a responsibility. Sometimes she was very demanding. My aunt said, "Now you're free. I saw what you were doing with your mother. Now you must take time for yourself." In that sense her death was a liberation.

I saw my father at the funeral. He was sad. But there was also a feeling of relief because four months after my mother died he married this guy. He must have had an affair with him while she was still alive.

The following Christmas, after my mother's death, my father invited the whole family, including aunts and uncles, and cooked a Christmas meal. My father was a good cook, even if I didn't like him. That was the last family reunion. When I arrived at seven my sister was already drunk. Everyone talked about my mother. After dinner, my sister said to me, "You're just a bloody queer."

My brother's children, who were seven and 12, were there and they didn't know about me. She really put me on the spot when she said that. Tension was high. I said, "I'm leaving. I don't have time to waste here."

That was the night I broke off contact with my sister. I didn't expect her to spit in my face like that.

In a three-month period, after my mother's death, nine other people died in my family. My uncle. My youngest brother was killed in a car accident. His wife committed suicide after his death. My oldest brother hanged himself. He was just coming out of jail and he couldn't face life. He was living alone a few blocks from my mother. His wife didn't want to take him back because he was violent. He was in jail the last time because he beat her. He had been in and out of jail all his life. He drank a lot, did drugs. To survive he stole. Most of the time he was on welfare. He was very violent. He got arrested more than once because he beat up guys with a baseball bat. His son, who was 14 at the time, discovered him in his room and cut the rope after he had been hanging for three days. The body was starting to decompose. Apparently he was very ugly and imagine a kid of 14 cutting the rope. He tried to save him. Apparently he even tried to give mouth-to-mouth.

On the 15th of March, four months after my mother died, my father had a big wedding that cost $50,000. He took out a large life insurance for my mother and when she died he collected. I didn't go to the wedding but the rest of the family went. My aunt told me about it. There were 80 people with a limo. There was a four-course meal, wine at every table, an open bar. A video was taken of the wedding. My father is 70 and he married a 35-year-old man. I had met him at my mother's funeral and again at the Christmas meal. He introduced us. Oddly enough, he is also called Louis, has my build and looks like me. That's scary.

After my mother died I was quite depressed. The owner of the company said, "Louis, you need a vacation."

I said, "I have no money and you know my status."

"It'll be a gift."

One morning he arrived and handed me an envelope with an airline ticket to Columbia and some money. Everything was paid for. He said, "Come back when you're rested."

The owner of the company was doing very well. Two years after my mother's death he sold the company to two brothers and in six months they went bankrupt.

I was with Canadian Data for 10 years, till they went bankrupt this past January, six months ago. When I lost my job I lost everything. They had provided me with a car, benefits. The bank returned a cheque of

$12,000. The severance pay from my ex-employer bounced. No job, no car, no money. What do I do? I'm an ex-inmate, I'm gay, I'm 46 years old. Try to find a job.

I didn't let myself get depressed, not after everything I've been through. So many bad things have happened to me in the past. I've been put to the test so often, today I feel I could face anything. Today I can see the positive in whatever happens. It's just another test. I'm no longer afraid of what could happen. I could lose everything tomorrow, my house could burn down, and it wouldn't bother me. I don't even have a house insurance. It's what's inside that counts. You're alive, you're healthy. The rest is all decoration, artifice.

I decided to go out on my own. It took me a week to find something. I joined a business that was run like a co-op. Everyone is independent but we share the same office, same conference room, same infrastructure. Everyone there works with computers. But they didn't have anyone to do their networking or their hardware. They were always subcontracting. Now they have me. I also went through the computer list of all my old clients, chose the best ones and they followed me. The other people in the office bring me business as well. Now I have a car, a cellular, everything I need.

It's great for me in the business I'm doing. Thanks to the experiences I've had in jail I can read people. I can size them up and know if they're trustworthy. Some people are like a wide open book. I'm not always right but I have a better idea than people who didn't have the jail experience.

Now, outside, I have the luxury to observe myself and make changes. Some customers don't pay. I have to get on the phone and I learn to observe their reaction. Before I was aggressive. Now I'm smoother. And I collect money faster. In a couple of months I learned a lot in the business because I took the time to examine what kind of mistakes I made.

I do the same thing in my private life. Sometimes I'm rough with friends and I try to correct it. I try to be more flexible, more diplomatic. Whether it's work or friends I try to be more aware of others' needs and make them more aware of my needs too. It goes both ways.

I may be poor but I'm happy. Before I wanted to make an impression. Today I don't care about image. Take it or leave it. When I work I have to dress. I try to look respectable. I meet presidents of companies so I'm not going to show up wearing jeans and loose sweaters.

Now I have more friends. I go out for supper more often. I have more of a social life. It's never too late. Today, because of AIDS, people prefer to exchange affection instead of sex. Before, gay people had sex to get affection.

I think circumstances made me gay. It wasn't a choice. I still have a conflict with that. I look at the human being. I don't have any barriers. I can probably make love to a woman. Maybe one day I will. It's been a long time since I have but they still have an attraction for me. I don't go with anyone. I don't like the regular Joe Blow. The person has to be pleasing both mentally and physically.

I can sacrifice a lot but not the food. I eat well. I like to cook good food, then finish the meal with a baguette, the rest of the wine and cheese. I treat myself well. I never did that before. I'm spoiling myself now. The small pleasures of life are very important. More important than a vacation. You can relax and treat yourself well every night at home or on the weekend. You don't accumulate stress.

Today I look at my life and I'm happier than I ever was before. Of course, there are days when you're not happy, your mood changes, but the ups and downs are less. You have less extremes the more stable you become. I discovered that. I think people who experience extremes of highs and lows are not very happy. Before I also had extremes. But now, when I have a problem, it's insignificant. A lot of friends come to me with their problems and I see them as minor because they haven't been through what I've been through. A little problem gets them upset. When someone dies or is very sick, that's a problem. But the rest...your TV isn't working? For me an average problem is not a problem. Everything already happened to me, so not much can surprise me.

It's been 12 years since I've been out. I still have a life sentence on my shoulder, even if I'm out. I came from far but now I'm happy. Maybe I'll never become very rich but at least I'm my own boss, I like what I'm doing. I feel more comfortable than before. Prison gave me life. It gave me the opportunity to find myself. Strange to say, prison freed me.

NICK

I read an article in the paper about a man who had been a member of the Mafia but after drugs, several murders, time in prison, did a turnabout, came to see "the evil of his ways" and finally, the light. I did not consider newspaper articles a reliable source for names but this was early in my interviewing process and I could tell the parole officers were not going to have an easy time finding the type of people I had requested. I felt I should do some independent research and pursue whatever clues presented themselves. I called him up, telling him about my project and requesting an interview. He said he was in the process of selling his story to Hollywood but he had another name for me, also an ex-Mafia man like himself. He gave me his phone number. I was not convinced but, unwilling to leave a stone unturned, made the call.

The voice at the other end was open, enthusiastic and seemed to understand and totally appreciate what I was trying to do. He was willing to participate and tell his story to help others. I felt hopeful. We set up a time for the first interview.

One sunny, summer morning he arrived at my house, an open smile and clearly eager to relate his story. I was immediately struck by his strong presence. His energy and enthusiasm were magnetic. He was of medium height and solidly built, evidence of having worked out. He seemed to have both feet firmly rooted in the ground. He exuded warmth though you knew he could stand up to any man. His voice was a resonant tenor that spoke with strength and conviction. The way he related even to the sad parts of his story had elements of wit, hopefulness and understanding.

Every interview I had with Nick (51) was like a jolt of high-voltage energy. He was always up, optimistic, full of good humour and totally confident. Yet he was open to accept another perspective and willing to consider other possibilities, to see things in a different light. He was ready to concede that he did not have all the answers.

Nick was clearly a survivor, ready for any challenge. He had always been a survivor, even while growing up with a physically abusive, alcoholic father and later while he was doing heavy drugs and working for the Mafia. The intensity with which he lived his criminal life is the same intensity with which he lives his present beliefs.

As he was telling me the early part of his story, including the period he was a drug addict, his sense of chronology was quite askew, the memories coming from a disjointed drug haze in which he lived at the time. I had to ask questions to keep him on track and do some fancy mental acrobatics to retain a clear storyline in my head and go back to parts that needed clarification. Listening to his tale was equivalent to a fast roller-coaster ride.

Now I love myself because God is in me. In the past I took all those drugs because of self-hatred, not knowing who I was, where to go, what to be. I didn't know what was right, what was wrong. Everything I did was bad. I used to provoke people in different ways so they would kill me.

When I came out of prison, I thought, I'm really a bad dude now. Then I started thinking I was worthless and began using even more drugs. My father abused me physically but he didn't demean me mentally. He taught me about work. But then he'd get drunk and beat me up. But I had never thought I was no good because of that. As a young kid I just did boy stuff.

I was born in southern Italy, in the Basilicata region. It was a town way up in the mountains, tough, hard, close to the earth. The first recollection I have in my life is hanging upside down on a chain in a fireplace. I was three years old. This was a walk-in fireplace with a chain to hang the kettle. They took the kettle off and tied me feet up and head down, to the chain. Then my mother lit the fire. I lost faith in these people. They're cooking me here. I'm barbecue. They're getting rid of me. Then they put me down. They wanted me to stop wetting the bed. I was so afraid after that I never wet the bed again. They figured they did the right thing because it worked. But I was angry for a long time.

My second memory was when my sister, Rosanne, and I were selling lupinis. She was five or six. Rosanne is a year-and-a-half older than me. She's first, I'm second. We're back home counting the money. She had the bad habit of counting money with her tongue out. I was watching her. The next thing I know my father comes in screaming and yelling. I look at what he is screaming at and Francesca, who was only 18 months old, was right in the fireplace. She must have crawled in there. Her legs were getting burned by the wood. He ran over, grabbed her and bam, kicked Rosanne in the chin. My sister's tongue split in half. The blood went squirting everywhere. She is screaming and crying. My mother wrapped her tongue up in gauze. Francesca wasn't burnt bad but the following year she died of dysentery. She just wasted away. I used to always look around for her to see where she was. I missed her.

The very next year Rosanne and I were walking on the mountain picking snails off the wall to bring home to my mother for spaghetti sauce. There was a blind kid on top of the mountain with his sister. He pushed a rock off and it hit me on the head. The rock crushed my skull. I went into a coma for three days. They thought I was going to die so they built a coffin for me.

Soon after my father left for the States, New York City. His father, my grandfather, was working as a janitor on Wall Street throughout his life. I was named after him. My father had a photograph of him. Then he moved to Bridgeport, Connecticut, because he didn't get along with my grandfather. Two years later Rosanne and I followed him. I was on a ship for 13 days coming across the ocean. What storms! They gave us life jackets. Put the steel covers over the portholes. Rosanne and I were throwing up. Thirteen days in this mess. Still I had my little daydream that money would grow on trees and the streets were paved with gold in America. All our relatives told us that. I got to New York City December 17, 1953. I didn't see no gold.

We were excited to see my father. Then he started beating us up. At night he would drink. I went down to the basement to get him a gallon of wine and saw all these empty bottles. In the two years he was alone here he must have accumulated about 600 of them. The very next year he and I started making wine. We made it for the next 18 years till he got sick. He'd consumed a gallon of wine every night for 35 years.

He was working in a foundry smelting steel. A hard, hot place. That was one of the things that troubled him. He was an artist. While we were in Italy he made money as a musician. He played the accordion at weddings. He worked on the land. He could draw. He had his friends. Many things kept him occupied there.

He was fun to be with, until the bottom half of the gallon. It was

Dr. Jekyll and Mr. Hyde. The first half he was sing-songing. He'd get the accordion out, start playing, draw, tell us stories, jokes. You'd enjoy being around him. Then all of a sudden, how come you've got those socks on? What's your hair doing like that? Every day someone got it. Me and my mother got it the most. He was a tyrant, a dictator. What he said was it. Rosanne and I prayed together to God that He would take him. We wanted out of this situation. Some of our friends had nice homes. We had a basement filled with barrels of wine. Those years were tough. There was no peace. We were terrified. You couldn't argue or have a discussion. If I voiced a different view from his, wham! You got it. A knuckle in the head. Kicks.

From the time I was 12 to 16, at two in the morning I went to deliver milk, came home, went to school, came out of school, went to deliver newspapers, came back home, had supper, and from seven to nine I worked in a bakery.

Second-year high school I got kicked out for throwing fireworks at this girl because she broke a date with me. I threw it up her dress and it burnt her thigh. The principal was hanging out the library window and saw it. He called the crossing guard to arrest me. I was rough, wild. I never did homework and always passed. I quit school when I was 16. But I studied in the joint. Now I have such a value for education. I understand its worth.

One day seven of us went to the recruiting office to join the marine corps but I was under 16. I went home and asked my mom and dad if they would sign for me.

They said, "No, because you have to work." They needed the money.

I said, "I'll send you money from there. They pay you in the service."

No, no. My father had bad experiences in the service. They killed a lot of people when they were in North Africa. One day, when I was about 15, I knocked on the bedroom door and the door swung open. On the bureau there was a bust of Jesus with the thorns and he was on his knees in front of that. Next to it was a picture of Mom and Dad. I had never seen him pray. When he turned his head I saw he was crying. I had never seen him cry. I closed the door. I felt I had gone in and caught him naked.

The next day we were getting ready to eat and he said, "Do you want to know why I was crying last night?" I wouldn't have asked him because we didn't have that kind of relationship.

I said, "Yeah."

He said, "I was thinking about all the men we killed in North Africa when we were over there in World War II."

My uncle got blown up beside him. He was standing on a land mine and he was in pieces all over the place. Years later, reflecting on that moment, I came to forgive him. He had a lot of hurt within him *(crying)*.

I didn't know what love was. I knew anger. There was never peace in our home. If I saw a fight I wouldn't run to patch it up, I'd run to get in it. So I met this girl. We started going out and not even eight months later she gets pregnant. I told my dad I'm going to marry her. I was 17. "Do you love her?" I don't know what this love thing is because I've never seen much love between my mom and dad. I've seen them fight non-stop day and night.

Then one of my buddies came home from boot camp and he had some pot. That was the first time I remember getting high on any kind of drug beside alcohol. Come on, light up another one. At that time in my life a joint and a glass of homemade wine was going to be my high forever. Let's go punch that guy, let's go break that window and steal that fur, anything.

I get married. Now I'm popping pills, smoking pot, drinking, selling heroin. My wife could tell me nothing. I was crazy. I made sure she had the communication with me that I had with my dad. What? What's your problem? I was dominant.

At the time I was working at General Electric. There was this manager and he would boast about all the money he's got. I don't have nothing. He lived in this old house on the hill and the mountain was his, handed down from family to family. He'd always brag about what he had, what he just bought. I bought a new car for my daughter, a pearl necklace. I was on the night shift. I hated it. The work was boring so we got high. It was a nasty time. I didn't know where I fit. I wanted to fight. I was so angry. One day my first crime partner who I'm dealing drugs with says, "Let's go rob a house and get some money today."

I said, "I know where to go." I knew where the manager lived. I wanted to rob his house to get even with him for bragging all the time. We broke into his house, stole some pearls, a few silver coins and some other stuff. That was the very first time I stole anything.

He knew I did it. One day he came over and said, "Nick, all I want is my daughter's pearls."

"Why are you asking me?"

"I know you took it."

"I didn't take anything from you but I know you're a braggart."

I walked away from him. He couldn't report me. He's got no proof. He just knew. He must have gotten some readings off me. After I robbed him I was cocky. Before, I was more obedient, doing my work. Then I used to go alone to steal. Ringing the doorbell. Nobody was home, BAM, I just kicked the door in.

Stealing went along with getting high. It was part of the package. I didn't need to steal for money. When I started stealing I was married, living in my mother-in-law's house. I was working, laying floors, carpet, linoleum, tile, that was my trade, and selling drugs too, so there was no reason to steal.

My friend gave me a .45 automatic. When I got that gun, you couldn't tell me nothing. At night I would go into places and steal. The next morning my mother-in-law and wife would go looking for rings, earrings, necklaces, jewellery. I never robbed anyone who didn't have nothing. I'd only go to the rich areas. We also did stores. One night this guy and I stole $9,000 worth of TVs. Back then it was a lot of money. I released my anger with stealing.

Then my daughter, Gina, was born. I promised myself I was never going to be a father like my father was. I got four kids and I never hit any of them. Dino, my son, was on drugs for many years. He shot a kid. He went to jail. I used to take him into the woods and teach him how to shoot every weapon, how to treat people, look them in the eye, shake their hands, not mushy but firm. I taught him what I thought was a man at that time. My value system was macho. When I came out of prison I realized that everything I had taught him wasn't right. Then I had to unlearn him, like I had to unlearn. Now he has a son, married, has a beautiful job.

My mother-in-law and her husband knew I was selling drugs. When someone was coming over and I wasn't home, they'd give it to them. They made money, too. One day I was in the shower and the cops are banging on the door. When I heard that, I wrapped myself in a towel and tried sneaking out the window. There was a cop out there. "Get inside, man!" He had a billy club. This was 1966. They took all the marijuana plants. I grew 60 pounds out on the front lawn. I got arrested and charged for growth and possession. One to five. I did nine months.

I was in jail, sitting down. How did I get into this mess? I tried to figure out who got me busted. I asked a friend of mine, also an inmate, who worked in the records office to see if there's a complaint. The records say what your charges are, who the plaintiff is, and what you're accused of. He said, "The plaintiff is your mother-in-law." I couldn't believe it.

I was 18 years old in Connecticut State Prison, 22,000 men. I was the youngest guy and everybody was checking out my ass. I was scared. As soon as someone came around me and said something I didn't like, I punched him right in the face. I learned that people respected you if they feared you. The baddest and the toughest ones were respected the most, so I learned to be badder. Prison life is a different world. The killers are the most respected because you know he's capable of killing you. Then bank robbery and armed robbery men are second in line. There's a hierarchy of crimes. I didn't have any status. Drugs are pretty low.

That first sentence I learned to read, to enjoy it, love it. I had never read before. There were no books in my house. My father only read the Italian newspaper. Reading took me out of doing time. Then one day I saw this big blue book called *Best Loved American Poems*. Rudyard Kipling. I found peace in poetry. Poetry seemed to speak to me more than anything else at that time. Then I had to write a few poems.

I remembered my mother showing me a letter my father had written her when he was in the Second World War, when he was a prisoner of war in Greece. There were little red carnations drawn on top and he wrote her a little poem. That was the first poem I read. It touched me. But my father is a bad guy. Yet he did stuff like this. Wow, that was nice.

In prison I found peace because my father, that tormentor, wasn't there. I was free. The worse and hardest thing about doing time is the people you do it with because they're maniacs. Everybody is a bad guy. There are no good guys in prison. Still, when you're in your cell, reading, there's peace. I became free while I read.

Toward the end of my prison term I'm in solitary confinement for 30 days. Two in the morning I hear a little piece of paper come flying in. "Congratulations, it's a boy." The nine months I was in prison, my wife was pregnant again.

I went home and there was Gina and Dino. But I didn't go back to my wife when I came out of prison because she was living with her mother who had set me up, got me busted. I went to live with my dad and mom for two weeks. One night I heard my father yelling in the kitchen. I was just going to sleep but I got up and came out. I saw him beating my mother.

I said, "You don't put your hands on her anymore."

He yelled, "Who do you think you are? You go to prison, now you're a big shot. This is my house. You don't tell me…"

"I'm telling you."

I walked over to him and wrapped my arms around him. I was strong then. I was lifting weights. I learned how to box. He was heavy but I picked him up, carried him into my bedroom and threw him on the bed. I said, "You don't put your hands on her no more."

"Get out! You're not telling me what to do!"

"OK. I'm going. But I'm coming back. Don't put your hands on her anymore." He didn't punch me or nothing. He was shocked like I was shocked. My mother didn't say anything. She was frozen. That was the last time he ever put his hands on her. I'm proud that I did it and didn't hit him.

I got a job, floor covering. I saved my money, got an apartment, fixed it up. My wife and kids moved in. Then I saw this go-go dancer. I was never faithful to anybody. That's all my father talked about, women. When they were kids how they used to do this or that to women. I grew up thinking you smoke, you drink and you screw. You screw as many as you can. Now I'm faithful.

So I'm messing around with this go-go dancer. My wife gets wind of it. The next thing you know she took all the stuff and went back to her mother's house with the kids. Two weeks later I got busted. I'm back in prison. I did 11 months. In that time the immigration department came to see me because I wasn't a citizen of the U.S. They told me if I signed this waiver I would go scot-free to Italy. If you're on parole or in prison, you can't become a citizen. My mother became a citizen not too long ago. My father, never. He had this thought in his head, I'm an Italian, I'm going to die an Italian. They wanted to deport me. I didn't sign it. A few months later I learned that I was divorced. This was the best thing that could have happened to me.

Meanwhile, in prison, some of the guys I became friends with would go to the library on Wednesdays and I would also go. They would be on the law side and I'd be on the novel side. That's how I got into W. Somerset Maugham. Later on I read Irving Wallace's biography of Sigmund Freud. Then I got into reading books by Freud. All prisons have exquisite libraries. All the classics. Literature is a beautiful world. Words are powerful. I was locked up altogether 13 years. During that time I read a lot. And from that I learned to write. In books I learned how people communicated with each other and how you expressed feelings using adverbs and verbs. I learned how to describe in a letter what was going on around me, where I'm at. I would look at the dictionary. Sometimes I would write a letter seven, eight times until I got it right. By the time I finished it would be a work of art. My sisters and ex-wife have many letters I wrote. Sometimes I read the letter I wrote to other prisoners. "Hey, listen to this." The bad thing is that right away, if they like it, they want you to write their letters. Write to my mom, my girlfriend.

I read *The Razor's Edge*. That really touched me. You learn truths of human nature. After that I was really interested in learning about mysticism. There was a character in there who was a mystic. Another character became enlightened. I wanted to know about this power. Then I became a mystic, in my own sense, through drugs and acid, wanting to tap into this power. First I wanted to manipulate others, get them to do what I wanted them to do without me even having to speak with them, manipulate their thoughts simply by willing it. For instance, when I was on acid and coke, this one guy owed me $3,000 and I'd will him to pay. Man, pay before I come over and shoot you, put a gun in your face or knock you over. While I'm willing him, the phone would ring. I'm coming to bring you that money. The higher I got, the more I could do. The more drugs I could shoot, the more power I would have.

I came out. The day I was coming home, Laura, the go-go dancer, came to pick me up. Went home, told my parents I was divorced. Laura and I lived together for about six months. We were getting high, doing acid, smoking pot. One day I went to this hangout and this chick was walking by. She called me a name. I said, "Yeah, that's me."

She said, "I'm sorry, I thought you were…"

I said, "It's me anyway. I'll be whoever you want me to be. Come on, let's go."

I conned her. I sweet-talked her. Then I went to her place and stayed the night.

When I came home Laura goes, "Where did you go last night?"

I said, "Don't start with me."

I caused a fight with her. Then we got high, did some pills together. All of a sudden I see her so evil. When she was talking her face was contorted. She looked ugly and bitchy. She kept nagging and I punched her right in the jaw. I cut her lip and she went down. Then I realized what I had done. I grabbed her and forced her to have sex with me. I went to sleep. I woke up and she was gone. I went to her house and her mother came out with a gun. "Who do you think you are?" A week later Laura came back but in that week I ended up going with another girl.

The worst thing is that I never had a vision of building something with another woman. My focus was tonight, in bed, that's it. I just wanted action. At this point I was robbing liquor stores with guns. Cathy, my younger sister, heard about it. She had just gotten married to my brother-in-law and he's mob, professional gamblers. He had big-time money connections. They figured I was going to kill somebody. They wanted to open up something anyway because they had so much money. They said, "Let's open up a nightclub in Atlantic City on the Boardwalk." We went there, ended up buying a little place. Called it the Climax Lounge. I was excited. We fixed the whole place up, the walls, the bars. I'm good at construction. He goes to Las Vegas. I'm left there but I don't even know how many shots there are in a bottle of whiskey. I don't know anything about running this place. I get a manager, have four barmaids, two bartenders.

This barmaid who worked for me wanted to introduce me to this chick, Dolores, because I had some speed at the time. She wanted to buy. One thing led to another. Dolores stayed with me, fell in love with me, I fell in love with her. But she was a speed freak. She's making deals, selling the stuff for me because she knows a lot of people in the area. Her two brothers-in-law rob a pharmaceutical company for two 55-gallon drums of speed. Now they come to her and ask if I want it. We start selling speed in Connecticut, New Jersey, around Pennsylvania. We're making so much money. I don't even care about the nightclub anymore.

Then these three guys she knew in Philadelphia wanted to buy some speed. I went there. Ethyl, who was carrying the speed for me from Atlantic City, and I met these three other guys over at this fourth guy's house. There is speed, coke, White Lightening, which is also a hallucinogenic, a Sunshine barrel of acid. I had been up at that point three days straight. I was high. Many times I would be up three or four days in a row. I took the acid, crushed it, put some water in it and drew the syringe. One of the guys said, "Yo, man, not here." I wrapped it up in a paper napkin and we left. The three guys, myself and Ethyl get in the car. I told the guy who was driving to slow down. I took out the syringe and POW. Then I could see through walls. I could see water going through a pipe. I could see past the pipes into the next room, a little baby laying down in a crib. I could see the mobile. I could see a couple in another part of the house watching TV. Man, I couldn't focus in or out. Vince, the driver, was going to ask me something and before he does I answer him. I say, "Two more streets and you take a right." We were going to get my bag of clothes that I had over at this girl's house.

When we get to the house he rings the doorbell but no one comes to the door.

He says, "Let's go."

I say, "No, there she is, she's opening the door."

I see her on the other side reaching for the handle but I see no door, no matter in between.

He goes, "What are you talking about?"

The door opened. I said, "I came to get my bag of clothes and my coat."

I took them. We get in the car and are driving away. We all go to South Philadelphia where I have my apartment. I had four apartments. Bridgeport, Atlantic City and two in Philadelphia, North and South Philadelphia.

As we get there and we're getting out of the car, I say to Vince, "Leave my jacket there."

He says, "This isn't a bad jacket."

He puts it on.

I got angry but I couldn't express my anger because I was so high and I was so without my own strength or willpower. I just followed all three guys and Ethyl up the stairs. I put the key in the door but I was too weak to turn it. Vince took the key out of my hand and opened the door. We walked in.

He said, "You got it?"

"Yeah."

I put it on the table. Everyone took the syringe out and we all shot it. Vince says, "We'll take an ounce each, this is good stuff."

I went in and got the scale, came back and the stuff was gone. I said, "Where's my stuff?"

"You took it."

I say, "You guys are playing with me." But I was talking really slowly. I was positive that I had put it on the table. I went to get the scale. When I came back it was gone.

He said, "You took it, Nick."

"No. Look man, I'm not playing with you guys." I went to the room, got my gun, loaded it and as I was putting the shells in, they were like big, huge, long mortar shells. Five of them. I came back out. This guy, one of the three, had a straw hat on and I pointed at him and said, "Take your hat off." As he was taking his hat off something came to my left side and just moved me over. I was trying to resist. My whole being was moving to the left. I don't remember pulling the trigger. What for? I wanted to see what's under this guy's hat. Bang! The gun went off. The bullet went through his brain. He fell and landed on my foot. I see the blood coming out of his head and going on my shoe, on the floor. Right next to his chest area, as you walk in the winter time when there's steam coming out of your mouth, I saw the shape of a person with no features, like a mist going through the ceiling. The mist came right out of his chest area and it went straight up.

As soon as I shot him I left. It felt like I never touched any of the steps as I was going down. There was the door of the person living on the second floor and I could see right through the door. I could see a lady sitting there looking up at me as I was coming down the stairs. As I get downstairs and touch the sidewalk, all of a sudden...

"Man, what happened up there? He's dead."

I turn around and Ethyl is right behind me. She says, "Nick, do you know what happened?"

I point the gun at her.

"No! Don't."

I said, "You made me do it."

"It wasn't me, it was the drugs."

I put the gun down. "Let's get out of here."

We went to a restaurant. I called a couple of guys in Connecticut and said, "Come and pick me up, it's an emergency." I had a flute with me because I play the flute every now and then, and a gun. We waited three hours in the restaurant. They showed up. We got in the car and went over Ben Franklin Bridge. As we're going over the bridge, the driver looks in the rear view mirror and says, "There's a cop car."

I said, "Pull over, quick."

I roll the window down and throw the gun in the water. Two cop cars come over. One pulls in front of us, one pulls to the side of us. I said, "Whatever you do listen to the flute and go with me. Go with the sound, don't stay here."

I started playing. I played ourselves out of there. That's what I did with my mind. Ethyl and I are sitting in the back seat. He's sitting in the front with another kid. I forced them, "You just listen to the sound and go with me, go out with me." All of a sudden the driver gets in the car and says, "OK, we can go."

We go back to Connecticut. I called up my sister and she called my brother-in-law. I told them what happened. I went home to talk to my father. I was still high. I told him I killed a guy. My father didn't know what to say. He just looked at me. Then he thought for a long time. He was thinking and thinking and then said, "Better him than you." My brother-in-law came to pick me up. Stayed in a motel for three days. He sent a driver who drove me to Montreal. I ran out of money. I go back to the States to do a drug deal so I could make enough money to go to Italy. I'm supposed to be going to Italy. My plan was to come to Montreal, get in touch with a couple of my relatives and they're going to give me some phoney papers. It was all set up.

I arrange a drug deal in the States. I call three guys and they have to put up so much money. Then I go to this guy's house in Atlantic City to get the speed. For five minutes I'm sitting there. The front and back door break in. I'm surrounded by state troopers.

"You're under arrest. You know what we want you for?"

"Yeah, I know."

I was high. I stayed high for three solid months on the acid I killed the guy with that night.

Busted for first-degree murder. Then they broke it down to second-degree murder. They said, "Do you want to take a lie detector test?"

"Sure." But you can't take the test till you get an attorney.

I got a real hotshot attorney from Philadelphia. He comes and says, "Better than a lie detector test why don't you give them a sodium pentothal, a truth serum, test? That will hold up. They can contest the lie detector because there are variables. If you submit to a sodium pentothal, there are no variables, the prosecutor can't contest."

I said, "OK, I'll do that."

They transport me to the hospital from prison. The doctor is trying to inject the needle. He's not getting the vein. I said, "Give it to me, man, I'll show you how to do it." Bam, I got it. I injected the truth serum and what a high that was. Float. I sat down and I'm on video.

He asks, "What's your name, where do you live, where do you come from, how did you get to Philadelphia and what happened?" I told them exactly what happened and then he says, "When you left, who picked you up?"

I said, "These two guys."

He says, "What's their name?" I wouldn't tell him. It hurt. He asked me another question and then it didn't hurt. I thought, this thing really works. I'm going to test this now. But I'm high on that stuff, you're really floating. Still, I'm aware of what's happening. I didn't want to tell them the names of these two guys because I didn't want to implicate them, but it hurt to hold back.

He goes, "When you got to the bridge, what did you do with the gun?" I already told them in the written statement. I decide I'm going to lie.

I said, "I had a…" and I couldn't even talk. It hurt inside. I said, "I threw it over the bridge." Then I felt much better. This thing is real. Honest, I thought it was a bunch of junk you see on TV.

Three months after the sodium pentothal test, I'm in the county jail, waiting to go to court. I'm sitting there in a big cell by myself and then I remembered what happened to the speed. I had put it in the bag, zipped it up, took it to the room with me. Then I hid it. I came out with a scale to weigh it and it was gone. I couldn't find it. Oh, no. At least before there was some kind of a reason for me killing this guy. I thought they had stolen my stuff. That week my attorney came and I told him exactly what happened. He saw the hurt I had. He said, "Would you like me to recommend a counsellor you can talk to?"

The counsellor gave me a blotter test to see if there's any brain damage. No brain damage, no nothing. He said, "You're impulsive, that's your nature. You have to learn to forgive yourself."

They presented the results of the sodium pentothal test to the judge. I pled guilty to involuntary manslaughter. The judge said, "I'm sorry, we do not have adequate facilities to give you proper counselling. You have a drug problem." His wife, mother and his kid were there in the court-room. When the judge said that, they put the cuffs on and, walking me out, I went over to his mom and wife. I didn't know them. I said, "I'm sorry." That's all I could say.

I went back to the county jail and met a couple of guys that knew him. Turned out he was my girlfriend's sister's fiancée. He had gotten divorced and was going to get married to this other girl. When I went to this guy's house to buy the speed, my girl, Dolores, had called the cops on me.

After the county jail I went to state prison. I did three years at Graterford, Pennsylvania, out of the five to 15 for murder. There wasn't a month someone didn't get stabbed there. The deputy warden got killed. The Black Muslims wanted their own prayer time and they wouldn't give it to them. They only had Catholic and Jewish services. There were 27,000 men in this prison and about 18,000 were Black Muslims.

When you first get to jail you're despondent, confused, grasping at anything to give you some strength. They lock you up and tell you when to eat, when to drink. You don't have no rights. When anything of value comes into your heart, a touch of love, a touch of care from anybody, through a letter, you absorb it, you read it over and over and over. The whole five years I was locked up, my main sustenance was correspondence. I lived for that. If I didn't get no mail, I'd write. I didn't care. I'd write to Gina, Dino, my sisters. I'd write to my girlfriends. I had a whole bunch of them. None of them were mine, I'd just make it up in my mind that they were mine—oh, darling, when I come home... I'd get all perverted and I'd express it. I'd mail it to them. One girl in Atlantic City, another in Philadelphia, in Bridgeport, Connecticut. They'd respond.

There are guys who watch TV and masturbate all day long. One day this tough guy comes running out of his cell yelling, "She's dead, she's dead." Who's dead? He's talking about some chick on *General Hospital*, a soap opera. He used to masturbate over her. There he was crying. That's it. He lost all respect. This chick died on TV and his life collapsed.

I'm working in the butcher shop. That's the best job because no one can mess with you because you've got the meat cleavers, knives. Everyone stays away from you. But I had become a vegetarian. To try to make amends for the killing…I never had a relationship with God, I never read the Bible…I said I'm not going to eat no more meat. For five years I never touched a piece of meat because I felt bad for having killed this guy.

I did a lot of thinking then. I thought and thought. I never thought as much before or after. I was so self-conscious about everything because I killed this guy. I wanted to understand everything. I read all the classics. I even tried to read the *Iliad* but there were no periods, commas, nothing. I was getting screwed up in my head. Where do I stop? I read Gurdjieff. Ayn Rand. *Thunderbolt. The Valley of Horses. Clan of the Cave Bear.* What a powerful book. Reading got me closer to the self I was looking for within me. The true person that's in each of us. God has created us to be strong, healthy, caring, gentle, compassionate, understanding. That's the guy I was searching for inside. I started seeking. I felt bad for having killed a guy for no reason, for being overdosed. I was trying to make some sense out of the life I was living.

Books gave me hope. Hermann Hesse's books touched me the most during this period. *Narcissus and Goldmund. Siddhartha.* It made me think about the hurt I had caused my parents. It revealed so much to me about who I was and where I failed in life. I began to look at my emotions. My faults. I did drugs because I didn't want to deal with reality. I didn't like where I was at, my social status—to hide it I became tough. That's what mobsters do. They hide their ignorance and social level by putting fear into people's hearts. You fear me, I've got respect. I also did drugs to blot out the pain my father had caused me. From Hesse I learned that the things that cause us pain end up later to be such great wealth and beauty. Then I read Edgar Cayce.

The five years I was in prison I came in contact with why my father was such a maniac, a tough guy, an alcoholic. He grew up without his father. Must have been rough for him. He was in the war. I looked at what I had done and he hadn't done. He didn't lead a crooked life. He didn't do no drugs. He didn't go around beating up guys to collect money for the mob. He didn't even have a guide. At least I had someone, even though he was bad. He taught me how to be a man. No matter what comes, you can survive. The moral values. Be honest, true, sincere. Say what's on your mind. Keep your word. So I accepted him and forgave him. He used to complain that no one named any of their boys Pasquale, after him. That's a real dishonour for an Italian. When he got drunk he'd say, "No one named a Pasquale." I knew it hurt him. I was determined that I would have a son called Pasquale.

Dolores had bought me a flute but when I got busted they took it away. In prison, I mentioned it to this kid, Bernardo. You know, I had a flute before I got busted. I'd like to have one again, especially now that I have a lot of time. It cost $150 and I didn't have the money. One day he goes, "Nick, this is for you. My aunt died last month, left me an inheritance and I bought you a flute." Wow, that was great. I ordered a few music books. Before I didn't know what I was doing. Now I wanted to know where the notes were. I spent the next five or six months studying. I wanted to know more but I didn't know how. Some people are musically inclined. Me, I have the desire but I don't have the ear.

All of a sudden a new guy comes down the block. Percy. A short, black kid. He hears me and goes, "Man, you play that thing?"

I was going through my scales. I said, "I'm learning but I don't know how to learn much more."

He said, "Let me see it."

He starts to play. At the time Roberta Flack was on the charts and he played her—*Killing Me Softly with Your Song*. He played it so well.

I said, "You've got to show me that."

I can't play by ear. He taught me the whole song, one note at a time. A month later he gives me a music book. Then he's teaching me riffs. Then I wanted this Van Morrison song—*Moon Dance*—so bad. "It's a fabulous night for a romance and the stars they light up your eyes..." I learned that with him.

I played one summer night in a band in prison. I was so nervous. These guys throw chairs at you if you stink. The first song I played was *Summertime* by Ray Charles. Then I played the Van Morrison song. I got such a nice applause. It made me feel so good. I had a band backing me up. Nine other guys. Percy was there. He could play any instrument.

I only did five years for the murder because I had taken a sodium pentothal test and because of good behaviour. I had gone along with all the programs. I thought I had gotten my act together. I knew how to play the flute. I was a handball champion. I was a vegetarian for five years.

When I left prison I had to go to the immigration department in Philadelphia. They were deporting me to Italy. They allowed me to make a phone call. My brother-in-law came with $4,000, gave it to the immigration department and I got out on an immigration bond.

A few days later I went over to a friend of mine and saw this babysitter. She was so pretty, 17 years old. I'm 31. I thought, no one has touched her. I walked over to her and said, "What's your name?"

"My name is Karen."

"Do you want to have my baby?"

"Are you crazy? I don't even know you."

I said, "Well, you'll get to know me and then you'll have my baby."

The very next day I got her phone number and went to her house. Remembering all the Spanish novels I read about how they would serenade with the guitar, that's what I did. I serenaded her. Her parents came out and I told them, "My purpose for being here is that I'm going to marry your daughter." I asked them for her hand. She fell in love. It was beautiful. We married.

Karen knew I had come out of prison. I didn't tell her what for. I was so fast and slick. You couldn't catch me. I'd twist everything you say to make you think you said something else. You wouldn't even know what you asked me. I answered you and you'd think that's what you asked me. I was so manipulative. I didn't even know I was doing it. I was doing it just out of con. I'm sharp, man. You need me. I'll teach you this. I'll show you that. When Karen finally got the whole story, she had been adapted to it so it wasn't such a shock.

I got a job as a butcher. I know how to cut meat. One day I smoked a joint, drank a little wine at lunch, went back to cut meat. I sliced the tip of the nail off and a little piece of my finger. I got so mad, I took the knife and threw it into the wall. I walked over to the owner and said, "That's it, I quit."

I went to see a friend and said, "I need a gun."

"Come on, man, didn't you do enough time already?"

I said, "I've got this chick, I really dig her, man. I need money."

He said, "You're not going to get it with a gun. Get a job."

"If you don't get me a gun I'll get it somewhere else."

"OK, OK."

When I got the gun I was going to do bad. Then Frank, my brother, wanted to open up this diner. I went and asked my mother for some money and she said, "Nick, I don't trust you." Frank went and asked her. She loaned him $3,000. I got mad. You give him the money and he's 10 years younger than me. I felt bad. But we opened up and called it Frank's Old Time Diner.

The diner was Budd's Diner before. It was an old trolley car that had been moved from one town to the other on tracks. I buffed the railing, all brass where you hang your hat and coat when you come in. Marble counter, brass seats that swirl. It was a beautiful place. It shined. When the old customers saw that I buffed it all and made it so clean, they all came in and Budd himself used to come in. He used to teach us little tricks. That place was exciting.

My brother had worked in the kitchen of Bridgeport Hospital. My mother knew somebody and got him a job. He was a short-order cook and taught me how to work on the grill. The grill I enjoyed. I didn't want to cut celery, onions. Eggs over light, scrambled. I enjoyed that. Flip hamburgers and hot dogs. I was front-row action and I was built. I was pumping up. I was boxing. I had a nice white shirt every morning. People came in, "Hey, Nick, you're looking good." "You, too." I enjoyed it.

Everything is going well but Frank won't give me no money. He'd give me $20 now and then. I've got Karen and an apartment across the street. We're all living together. He'd go to the discos. He's a professional dancer. Even today, he, my son and my son's half-brother rent halls and have disco contests. The modern dancing. So he's giving me no money and I'm getting upset. At the end of the week I've got to pressure him. He handles the money, goes to the accountant. That's not my thing. I never did that. My money is to spend, not to account to somebody.

Karen is pregnant. Pasquale is about to be born. She's really big. She would come in in the morning. She was really suspicious because in the past I wasn't faithful to anybody. But I didn't mess around. I wasn't doing no drugs for two years and I was faithful to her at the time. She would always come in and sit there. Then she'd come in behind and help me clean.

Then friends of mine, mob guys, they have these ships of marijuana down in Florida to unload. You have to have speedboats to go to the big boats and bring in 200, 300 pounds at a time. They said, "Nick, do you want to go down and work with some of these guys. You can run a crew for us."

This guy just wanted to help me make some money and he knew I could run a crew. Guys would listen. I said, "I can't. I'm on parole." Every two weeks I had to report to my parole officer. This job was going to take at least three months. But I wanted to get rid of my brother.

I asked Frank if he wanted to go to Florida. He said, "How much money do I make?"

I said, "Forty dollars a bale. And there are thousands of bales."

He said, "Sure."

I got rid of him. That made me feel better. Now I can run the place and get me some money. The only problem with me was that I'm no good at managing money. I spent it as fast as I got it. My sister would come in to work and she was robbing the till. My sister and my wife's sister were stealing every day. My sister taught her how to steal. I didn't care. I said to a friend of mine, "I want to sell some pot." He brought me 100 pounds the next day. I put it in the back. I said to my sister and sister-in-law, "Whenever someone comes and gives you a code, cornbread, you take them in the back, give them whatever they ask for and then write it down." They wrote everything down and I went to collect the money. You want to steal my money? You have to work for me. They knew what they were selling and they wouldn't steal that. It's just a code of ethics. If they sold 10 pounds I'd give my sister another $300. Everyone had money then. You don't know how fast you can make money with drugs. I take a package from here to there, I get $10,000. One hour's work. But whenever I sold drugs I always used.

Frank came back from Florida with a brand new Cadillac and $80,000 cash. They were doing so much cocaine you can't sleep at night. In the 1970s cocaine was the elite high for people making money in the drug world. At night they'd have big cocaine parties in Miami. Those people had orgies. To sleep they do heroin. Frank had made a few trips back. The only problem is that down there he started doing a lot of cocaine. Before he was straight, now he is on drugs.

Pasquale is almost born in the diner. I went home from the hospital the day he was born and my father goes, "So what did you name him?"

I said, "Papa, I named him Pasquale." He had a large belly and I never seen a belly shake so much in my life. He was proud. The only goal I had was to have Pasquale with Karen. Once I had him I had no more goals. My focus, my vision, was only to get Pasquale for my father.

I didn't see beyond that.

Then I met this Colombian kid. I said, "You're Colombian, you got cocaine."

He said, "No, for cocaine you go to jail."

I said, "An Italian has wine and a Colombian has cocaine."

I kept bugging him and bugging him. Finally he brought me a little bit. I went to these guys I knew and they tested it. It was 90 percent pure. They handed me $10,000. I went back and we started. I'm making money selling pot besides. I'm getting high. I would still get up at 4 a.m. and open the diner.

My brothers-in-law are bookmakers, guys who take bets illegally, the mob. I went to collect money for them and got 10 percent. If someone didn't want to pay, they would send me. They knew I had balls. I went to collect with a newspaper, the *Bridgeport Post*, because I lived in Bridgeport, Connecticut, wrapped around a pipe. All you see is a newspaper rolled up. You don't see the pipe inside. "You got that money?" He started giving me a story. "Look, you don't understand, my kid's sick."

"Man, that's your problem. You gonna pay the money or I've got to give you the news." BAM! I hit you over the head with the newspaper. You got the news.

If I don't get the money with the news, I get a big bottle of Coca Cola. Empty it out and fill it with gasoline three-quarters of the way. Put detergent on top. Then put a rag in it. Light it and throw it through a window of their betting office. The glass breaks, the flame ignites and explodes, but the detergent acts as an adherent agent. It sticks to the wall. The soap sticks so it burns good. The following day we call them up.

"Next is your house. You gonna pay the bet?"

"OK, man."

And they pay. You gotta put fear into them. With illegal activities you can't go to a policeman.

I did have a little scruples. If it was next door to a house where people lived, or upstairs where people lived, I wouldn't do it. Even though I was crazy, I didn't want to hurt nobody. But if a guy would not pay I would crack his knee caps with a piece of steel or a baseball bat. A guy owed $20,000. Me and a couple of my guys put him in a van and just kept cracking him. Busted his kneecaps and then just rolled him out on the street. Called the ambulance, they picked him up, and took him away to the hospital. The next day he called his father and asked him to come and pay the $20,000. They had the money. He just didn't want to pay. You had to hurt him.

I felt it was my job. This guy isn't going to walk too good for the rest of his life. When you break joints they never get repaired. I knew this. I go to them and say, "I'm going to bust your knee caps. Are you going to pay that money? Don't give me a story, man, you're not going to walk right after this. I give you the option."

Another thing is when a bookmaker opened within two blocks of another bookmaker, the mob asked me to torch the joint. I used to like lighting fires until the last one. A bookmaker, a friend of mine, had opened up close. But these mob guys were my family, plus I worked with them. So they told me, this guy opened up over here. We warned him. Take care of him. I went to see him. I took a look at his place. He had a dropped ceiling. The next morning, at 4 a.m., I went there first, before the diner. Climbed on top. Put a hole in the ceiling. Poured in 10 gallons of gas. Lit my lighter and it went so fast. The dropped ceiling to the roof had created a pocket. I hadn't thought of that. As I turned to jump off, it blew up beneath me. I thought I was finished. I went up and down and saw flames coming out of the hole. I jumped. Got down, got in my car and split. I go to my diner. Right away I put on my apron, my hat and get the coffee going, the home fries. At 4:30 a.m. or 5 a.m. I had more business than ever. All the firemen were coming in for coffee: My diner was three blocks away. The only diner open at that time. And in the back I had 40 to 80 pounds of pot every day that I was selling to dealers. The diner was my front. Everyone knew it. The cops knew I was a dealer there.

As I'm selling and doing a lot of cocaine, I sold the diner to my ex-wife. I was making too much money illegally. I went to this guy's house to bring him a package of coke one day and I see a syringe. I took it with me and started shooting coke again. Before I was sniffing, but when I saw that syringe something came over me.

I start doing coke all over again. I also start carrying my gun. I got two Colombian partners that are getting it right from the source. I made a lot of money. Had a drawer filled with money. My wife could have whatever she wanted. She'd share the money with her mother. I didn't care. She was like my little baby doll. But I mistreated her. I was so paranoid on coke. "Who did you let in the house?" I put a gun to her mouth. "I know you let someone in the house." I was shooting coke all night long. Stabbing, sticking needles in my arm. I used to be up three, four, five straight days. You never, never have enough of that thing. It's a demon.

This kid was going out with my sister and my mother didn't want him going out with her because he was a bum. She asked my other sister, Chris, if he could live with her because he had nowhere to live. She asked him to leave after two months because he never helped to pay the rent. He wouldn't leave.

She called me. "Nick, come and get him out."

I came and said, "Get your stuff and let's go."

I drove him downtown. The next day he went around to my sister's house and robbed it. But I wasn't in town. She calls the cops. They come, she gives them his name. One of the cops was his uncle and they didn't charge him.

Four days later I came back. In those years I never left my house without a gun. I had two guns, a .25 automatic in my pocket and a .357 in an upside down holster over my chest. I used to call it my American Express card, never left home without them. I drank a bottle of wine and went to look for him in the liquor store where he was working. I told him to come out. He cursed at me and pow. He went down. He got up and ran. I go to my car and hear, "You don't come down here to beat up on my people." His uncle. The two of them are standing together. But the uncle has his arm in a cast with a support holding it up.

I took one step and he said, "Shoot him." Pow! The kid shot me. The first bullet went in my arm. I ran toward him. I wanted to throw him a punch. I threw a left but nothing happened, my arm didn't move. I freaked out. He put four more bullet holes in me. They ran away. I feel my legs getting wet. The blood is going down. I'm getting weak and I start walking. I thought if I got in the road someone has to pick me up. I walk to the middle of the street. I knew if I went down I was dead. I said, I'm not going down, and I stood in the middle of the street. All of a sudden I left my body and it was all dark but somewhere there was a little light and I was heading for it. As I was going for the light I started thinking about Pasquale, Dino and Gina. Oh, no! I fought again. I have to stay here for them. For the first time in my life I called on God. I looked up at the heavens and screech, just like that, this car stopped in front of me and two women were in it. Then I heard, "I think he's drunk," and they took off.

Just as I'm getting ready to fall backwards I hear this dude in front of me. "Brother, do you want me to take you to the hospital?" A Spanish kid. When I got to the hospital they wanted to give me anaesthesia but I said no because I knew I was going to die. There was no strength in me.

The cop said, "Who shot you?"

"I don't know." I'm thinking I'm going to get these guys.

I woke up and have a respirator at my throat. Tubes in my nose. My brother, sister and my wife were standing there. They had been there for three days, taking turns. Then the doctor came and explained he took out my left kidney, my pancreas was severed, and they cut a chunk of my liver out that was all damaged.

I'm recovering. Nine, 10 days in the hospital and I'm thinking how I'm going to get him. I got both of these guys tied to a chair. But the one that shot me, I got a knife in my hand and I'm digging his eye out. I'm seeing this in my mind. The uncle is sitting there watching me dig his nephew's eye out.

As I'm thinking about this, a Jamaican lady who mops around the beds calls to me. "Nick!" How did she know my name? I never spoke to this woman. "Nick, let it go. Evil will follow the wicked all the days of their lives. You've got to let it go."

How does she know what I'm thinking? Days later I'm thinking about them again. Again I heard, "Let it go. Evil will follow the wicked all the days of their lives." Every time I thought about revenge that phrase would come into my mind. It was like an associated part of my memory band and I couldn't split them. I couldn't just enjoy my thoughts.

I stayed in the hospital for 40 days. While I was in there, my father was dying of cirrhosis of the liver in another hospital. Before I got shot I was visiting him every day with Pasquale and Dino. He asked my Mom, "Where's Nick?" They didn't want to tell him. He went into a coma once. He went into a coma twice. He has no more liver left. He was yellow like a banana. When I came out I went straight to his hospital. My arm was all wrapped up. My hand didn't work for 11 months. As I'm going down the corridor with my mother his head is sticking out of the room. My mother is shocked to see him up. He hadn't been up for months. He was crying when he saw me and I hugged him.

"Nick, it's good to see you. It's not good when the son dies before the father."

Two days later, as me and Dino left the hospital, this big black crow squawked at us. I looked up and said, "It looks like he's crowing at us. Dad's going to die. They're messengers of death." I read about ravens in Edgar Allan Poe. Three o'clock that night he died.

I went to go collect some money from this guy and he said, "Your brother was here last night. He told me it's your birthday today. I've got a gift for you upstairs. Go get it." I went upstairs. I open the door and there was this chick lying in bed with a bottle of wine. Now I never cheated on Karen. Everything was saying, go. My feet were going backwards but everything else was going forwards. I ended up jumping her. I had a good time but when I left I felt empty, guilty. Why did I do this?

I got home and she never used to wait for me. It's 3 a.m. and she's up. I run off to the shower to get the smell off of me. Then I went to bed and to overpower any doubts she may have, forced me to make love to her so she wouldn't think anything. When I woke up in the morning my wedding band, which said Love Forever, was snagged on some of her hair. I pulled off my ring and looked. Love, split, Forever. I went to see my best friend who owned a jewellery store. "Can you fix this?"

Six-and-a-half months later, at another party where I went to bring a package of cocaine, there she was. The same girl. She moved on me. I did it again. I went home and Karen was sleeping. When I woke up the next morning I went to wash my face and I felt a little scratch. My ring had split in the same place again.

After that I got really nasty. The next chick I saw, bam. I screwed up already, what's the sense? Let me just keep on. Because of the guilt inside of me, I'm doing a lot of drugs now, drinking like a maniac. While Karen was in the delivery room with our second son, Kenny, I was shooting up in the bathroom of the hospital. I kept going into the delivery room to see that she was all right. I was doing drugs wherever I went. My licence was under suspension. I went to court to try to get it back and while I'm waiting for the judge, I went to the bathroom and shot some cocaine. It didn't matter where I was. I was a drug addict. Thinking faster than you, knowing more than you. Nobody knew nothing. I knew everything.

I buy a quarter-of-a-million dollar house, nine rooms, in a nice residential area. One solid acre of land. It's about 100 yards off the street.

I had put $90,000 down. She's all excited. One night, before we move from our old place, I'm shooting coke at someone's house and it's about 4:30 a.m. I get this overwhelming feeling, I've got to go home. It's just getting daylight. I go home. Open up the door and see my wife, her sister, my son and her brother huddled in the corner of the couch. They're terrified.

"What's with you guys?"

"Listen!"

We had oak floors and everything was squeaking. I pull out my .38. I go running down to the basement. There's nothing. But the floorboards above my head are making noise. I go upstairs and they're scared.

"Nick, do something!"

I grab the phone book and look up a church. I call St. Patrick, not far from our house. It's 5:30 a.m. now. This lady answers. The priests are all sleeping. She asks me what's wrong. I say, "Listen, the house is going crazy."

The clanking and the banging. She could hear it. "What do I do?"

"Light a candle and pray."

I said, "Karen, get a candle!"

She went into the kitchen, got a candle, lit it up.

"Everyone come here, we've got to pray. You know how to pray?"

No one knew how to pray. But I knew how to say Our Father and Hail Mary, stuff they taught us in school. The floorboards are going crazy. "Our Father who art in heaven, hallow be Thy name, our Kingdom come…"

The floorboards grew quiet. I called back the church. I want to know what's going on. She answered the phone again.

"Thanks, it worked."

"Do you live near a cemetery?"

"Yeah, behind the woods is the cemetery."

"I don't know how you did it, but somehow you brought evil spirits into your home."

"Thanks." I hung up.

I went downstairs and got my syringe. Everybody is upstairs making breakfast. I want to do a shot of coke. As I was about to do it I heard tapping. I'm thinking, I'm bringing them in with all these drugs and crime. I say, "That's it, huh, I'm bringing you guys in? Are you guys spirits?" Another tap. I shot the coke. I could feel them. I went upstairs and had something to eat. I was rushing.

After breakfast I was making up packages of coke. One-ounce bags, two ounces, doing my work, rocking it because a lot of people liked it compressed at that time. In the late 1970s rock cocaine was the fad. It's three o'clock in the afternoon and I'm thinking, I want to see you punks. I get a sawed-off shotgun, a .357 Magnum, and put them on the table where I'm working. I get a crossbow with an arrow in it, a machete my partner brought from Columbia, and put them down. I filled three syringes with cocaine. I put one in one arm but don't shoot it, the needle is just hanging there. I put one in the other arm, another in my leg. I'm thinking, if I get that high I'll see these punks and we'll have a shootout. I shot the first needle. I get the rush. I shot the second one. Now I get this bright light, like I'm looking at a fluorescent light. I can see nothing but bright, bright light and I hear, "No, no, no!" Loud. "No, no, no!" I shot the third one. Pitch black. I'm not here. I don't see me. I don't see no walls. No floors. No nothing but three demons. One in mid-air, the ugliest, the most fearful thing I've ever seen in my life. They're dark grey linear creatures. If you could put a face on a thing that face would be hate, fear. They had so much fear and hate deep in their eyes. The one in control commanded the other two by will. Me, I had no will. One seemed to be down and was pulling me but I didn't have a body. I had to go. I had no choice. The other one had me by the shoulder. The two of them were pulling me. I had never been so scared in all my life because I was going where I didn't want to go. I thought of my father, and then I thought of God as Father. Suddenly I remembered our Father who art in heaven, hallow be thy name. Now I was going the other way and they had to come with me. As soon as I said amen, I could see the walls again. I could see me. That day I didn't get high again. The next day I started shooting once more.

My partner and I were going to see this guy who was buying a kilo of coke. He said to me, "Take only half, I'll keep the other half here to make sure everything is all right." I took the half and went to the Dunkin' Donuts.

This guy I knew pulls up and says, "You've got it?"

"Yeah. You got the money?"

"My guy has it over there."

I go to my car to get the coke and, as I open the door, a long double-barrelled shotgun comes to my head.

"Drop it! You're under arrest."

Five state troopers from the vice squad come out from behind a wall. They had my hands cuffed. Threw me down on the asphalt. When they had said, "Drop your gun," I dropped it on the asphalt next to the car. Now I saw the cop, instead of using a pencil or anything, pick it up with his hand. He put his fingerprints all over it. They take me to the state barracks.

I get there and the cop says, "OK, if you want things to go easy on you, tell us where the other guy is."

I said, "What other guy?"

"We know we only have half the package."

"Can I ask you a question? Where's your next raid going to be?"

"That's none of your business."

"That's right. This is a football game. You're on one team and I'm on the other." I walk away.

He yells after me, "You're not so tough. You're going to be up in the penitentiary rotting."

"No, I'm not because you got shit on me. While I'm playing my flute, you're going to be down here teaching your agents to keep their fingerprints off the gun."

"What?"

"He got prints on my gun. That's his gun."

He starts yelling and screaming and I'm laughing.

My partner stayed away for about a month and then called me. We started dealing again. Now I'm really doing hard drugs. I was going crazy. I used to have calluses on my hands from gripping a gun all night long. Paranoid. Looking for people in the house. No one's there. My kids are sleeping. She's sleeping. I'm walking through our nine rooms with a flashlight in one hand and a gun in the other. As the high would wear off, I'd look at myself and say, what are you doing? I'd get a syringe. Shoot some more and it would start all over again.

My partner owed me $18,000 and he didn't want to pay. I called him up and said, "I need the money."

"I don't have it."

"I'm coming to your house whether you have it or not."

I get to his house and he's not coming out. His girlfriend had two little kids inside. I start yelling. The only reason I'm not blowing down that door is because of those kids. I look around and he had a van. All souped up with a fridge, a TV. I blow the doors apart with my shotgun. "You're next, man." I leave.

On my way home his girlfriend called the state troopers. They had a roadblock out and busted me. I had my sawed-off shotgun in my socks and they found another gun under the seat of the car. Plus they found two syringes in my pocket, one of them loaded with coke. They took me to the state barracks, then to the county jail.

In the county jail I'm sitting in the dayroom waiting for the phone. I would get on the phone at this time and talk dirty to my wife. "Put your head down your pants, honey, tell me what it smells like. You got your nipple.

"Yeah, I'm rubbing my nipple." This is the garbage I'd make her say. So it's my turn to get on the phone. I've got 15 minutes. Everyone gets 15 minutes. This kid is on the phone. I say, "Get off the phone, man! You're on my time." I've got to find a way to get out of this joint, of not doing the 20 years. They've got me for the coke, the gun, the sawed-off shotgun. I'm in the dayroom with all these guys waiting to use the phone. I'm getting madder by the minute. I'm going to punch him in the face when he walks out so the other guys understand they don't take my time. All of a sudden I'm looking down between my legs and see all these little pieces of paper on the floor. I pick one up and it says, "The Lord is your strength and your refuge." When I read that, something came over me. I didn't care about punching him anymore.

When the guy gets off the phone I grab this piece of paper and go talk on the phone. But I'm not talking dirty. I get off the phone and my mind's ticking. Somehow I've got to find a way to get out of here. I look at the piece of paper which is still in my hand, "The Lord is my strength and my refuge." A peace came over me again.

I ask someone near me, "Where do these pieces of paper come from?"

"Some guy yesterday ripped up a Bible."

Then a guy came in and said, "I've got some coke." Snorted a few lines. I'm getting nervous and paranoid. I go in my cell and try to read. I can't concentrate.

The next day a guy offers me some pot. I knew so many of them. I was a big shot in there. Everyone is trying to give me this or that. I smoke a joint. I get paranoid again. I go into my cell. I'm thinking, I'm getting high no more.

On a visit, my son, Dino, who is 12, smuggled in a carbide rod to cut the bars of my window. But I only managed to cut three bars before the carbide pieces wore out. Then the guards come to check and find the bars cut. I go to solitary confinement for 30 days for attempted escape. As I'm walking down the corridor with my pillowcase over my shoulder, with my toothpaste and toothbrush, a guy says, "Yo, Nick." And he threw me a little book. The New Testament. Like I said, I was a hotshot, a gangster-type guy, and I was older than most of the other guys so they gave me things. I was about 35 at the time. The others were young jitterbugs.

I had been in solitary four times before that. Never have I heard anyone doing less than 30 days. The first day I'm there I set up all my stuff and start reading the New Testament. The next day I'm reading again. In 28 days I finish it completely.

Ten minutes after I close the Bible a guard opens my cell and yells, "Pack your stuff and let's go."

"It's only 28 days."

"The warden says you're free to go."

As I'm leaving a guy gives me some pills and says, "These will make you feel good." Ten white pills. I take two. Nothing happens. I take another two. Nothing. I finally take eight and my tongue swells up so much I can only breathe through my nose. That night I didn't go to eat because I couldn't swallow. For three days my tongue is swollen. On the third day the swelling starts to go down. I see the guy who gave me the pills.

"You're a sick punk."

He says, "No, you're supposed to take the white with the blue."

"You didn't give me no blue." That was the last time I got high.

So I had read the New Testament. Now I have to go to court. My lawyer says, "For $50,000 you probably do two years, for $30,000 two to four years, for $20,000 five to 10 years."

I said, "Twenty-five thousand is all I've got."

I got five years from the state for the sawed-off shotgun, another five years from the feds for the sawed-off shotgun because it's a federal weapon. I go to Danbury, Connecticut, a white-collar prison. The president's men got busted there. I only stayed 40 days and then got shipped out. Had I stayed I would have learned some things, would have made some good contacts. But I was a level four, security level, because I had done time before. The highest security level is six. There, guys were all level ones.

My head clears now. I'm not doing any drugs. I'm missing my wife. I'm realizing all the stuff I did. Karen was a good young lady. I messed up her mind. I used to beat her and put a gun to her head. At night when I was high on coke I'd be walking around the house with a gun and she'd yell out, "Nick, what are you doing?"

I go in the bedroom, "Shut up." She's scared out of her mind. "Who did you let in the house? Where are they?"

Then I get transferred by plane to Atlanta, Georgia, a federal penitentiary. It's a monster of a place. Your cell has three walls of steel. You wake up in the morning and your hair stands straight up from the static electricity. I'd have hair all over the pillow. You've got to walk tall and be on guard every minute. Swearing is all you hear all day long. You punk. You piece of motherfucker. I stay in Atlanta, Georgia for a month-and-a-half. Then I get transferred to Texarkana, a town on the Texas and Arkansas border. There, a lot of guys wanted to tattoo me because I had no tattoos. My father taught me when I was a kid, you want to write, write on paper, leave your body alone. In Texarkana there were so many Mexicans with tattoos on their necks, on their eyelids, spiderwebs on their faces. Frogs. The Madonna. Leopards. Snakes crawling all over. They kept bugging me. "Man, you're virgin meat." "Let me do you. Back up! I'll punch your face."

After that I go to El Reno, Oklahoma, right outside of Oklahoma City. The Bible belt. When I'm there they tell me in 30 days you have to find a job or you go to solitary. I only have two days left. This guy I'm playing cards with, he's a bank robber, he didn't want to lose me as his partner, says, "Go upstairs and ask this guy, Gary Evans, if he's got a job for you."

"What does he do?"

"They fix TV's, radios, smoke alarms, telephones."

I went up there. I said, "I'm looking for a job."

He had an aura about him. He was clean. He says, "Do you know anything about communications?"

"No, I know construction and crime."

"Usually I like guys who know a little something but I like your eyes. You can start Monday morning."

At the time, every day I went back to my cell thinking, I don't want to sell no more drugs. I'm feeling bad about the life I had lived. I'm going to miss my kids again. I screwed up my life with my first two kids, Gina and Dino. Now I'm screwing up with Pasquale and Kenny. I hardly even know Kenny. Now Karen's phone is disconnected because she can't pay the bill.

Monday morning I went into Gary Evans's office. He says, "Nick, do you know anything about the Bible?"

I say, "No, but I read the New Testament when I was in solitary."

He says, "What do you know about it?"

"Nothing. I just read it."

"Well, guys that work for me have to read the Bible or you can't work here."

"No, I don't read no Bible."

"It's your choice. You want to work here, you read the Bible. You don't want to work here, you don't read the Bible."

I say, "I don't have a Bible."

"I have a Bible." He gives me the King James version. "In 30 days I'd like you to memorize a scripture."

I knew poems by this time. I had memorized poems by Rudyard Kipling. I knew poems on top of poems. I went to my cell and opened the Bible. My eyes went to Proverbs 3, Verse 5 and 6. "Trust in the Lord with all thine heart; and lean not unto thine own understanding. In all thy ways acknowledge Him, and He shall direct thy paths." After I said it once, I wrote it down and I think I've got it. Nothing surfaces. I look at it again. I can't get it. I'm getting mad. Why can't I get this? Three days later I finally got it. Now I memorize another one. Luke 12. I'm finding it a little easier. James 4. I like the King James version. It has thee and thou. Three months after I memorized Proverbs 3, Verse 5 and 6, I don't want to swear no more. Swearing was my conversation. That's all I knew. Now it hurt to swear. I'm thinking, maybe I won't do drugs when I get out. Maybe I can have a different life. I'm getting some hope. But at night I'd wake up with all those bad words. Every night. I put in a request to see the psychologist.

He called me in. I say, "I tried to stop swearing but at night I wake up with all these bad words."

He says, "Let me explain something to you. Your memory banks are recorded implants. In order for you to reimplant the implants you need to memorize something on top of that. Every time a swear word wants to come out, place something on top. As a tape recorder."

I said, "Thanks."

He says, "Praise the Lord." This is the Bible belt.

They had said instead of doing five years I can get out sooner if I do the drug program. The man in charge of the drug program is a born-again Christian. But he can't preach the word of God to us as a form of therapy. So what he did was make photocopies of the Psalms, enlarge them, and put them in front of us. Three times a week we'd go for a session. I'd read the photocopies. "The Lord is my strength and refuge." So this is where those pieces of paper I found are from when I wanted to punch that kid who was on the phone.

Now I'm hungry for the word of God. I get to Matthew 6, Verse 25. "Do not worry." I've got to memorize this. I went to see Gary Evans. "Gary, I memorized a scripture I want to share with you. Matthew 6:25." By the time I finished tears were coming down his eyes.

He says, "I've watched you and I've seen God work through you the last few months. Come here."

We looked outside and it was snowing.

He says, "How many snowflakes are out there?"

"I don't know."

"Millions. Every second there are millions upon millions. But every one of them is different. There are no two snowflakes alike. And in all the people out there, there is no one like you. That's why you got those special fingerprints. You're unique and, because you're special, God has a plan for your life."

Something happened to me.

"Do you want to be born again?"

I said, "You mean I could be like you?"

"No, you can be like you in God's Kingdom and He will take control of your life from here on. When you pray He'll tell you different things. Do you want that for your life?"

I said, "I want that."

"Ask God to forgive your sins."

"Please forgive me for all the sins I ever committed, Lord."

"Ask Him to come into your life and give Him your love."

"I ask You to come into my life and take control because I don't want to live that life no more." When I said that, I got such peace. In prison I became free. The power of the word of God set me free.

I read and prayed. I wrote everybody about what happened. I wrote a letter to Karen and told her we're going to make a new life. I wrote her a poem that was called, "Forgive and Forget." I drew flowers and bees.

One day the priest was sharing in church. He said, "If you've got an enemy on the block, and I know you've got enemies, when he comes walking down, before you look at him, before your anger rises, the minute you see him, say to yourself, I love you. Watch what will happen."

This is pretty crazy. I'm going to do it. This guy Brodis, a big, black guy, used to bother everybody. He wasn't abusive but he just got on your nerves. I had a lot of arguments with him. I never fought him physically but it was close many times. After this Sunday afternoon, as he's walking by, I say to myself, I love you. I didn't want to say it. I wanted to punch this guy out. But I'm going to try this. He just looked at me and walked past. I keep doing this. In time, for no apparent reason, we become friends all because in spirit I'm saying I love you. We're talking and he started changing. He wasn't bothering that many people. From then on, any time there was someone who was getting on my nerves I'd say, I love you. I learned to be more compassionate. Break through that fear, I've got to be like this.

I get transferred to Dallas, Pennsylvania, for the parole I owed for the murder. Ten years because I messed up. They gave me a hearing. They're going to evaluate you as the time goes on to see how much time you're going to do of the 10 years. The guys I had seen 10 years earlier thought, here I am again, a loser. But they respected me. I was a bad guy but I had a good heart. I would always defend the underdog.

The fourth day I'm there a guy comes up to me and gives me a piece of paper. It says "The Emmaus Bible Correspondence Study Course." Free of charge. I filled it out. Sent it in. They sent me two books. You do one. You fill out the answer sheets and mail it. While they're evaluating your scores, you're doing the other book. By the time you finish this, they send you two more.

I'm studying like crazy. I got good marks. When you finish a book, they send you a certificate. You are certified to be a minister of the Gospel of John. You are certified to be a minister of the Gospel of Luke. It's a legal college. I'd mail my certificates home to Karen. She wrote to me every month. She'd come to the visiting room, sit on my lap, hug me and kiss me. Then she lost the house. The first year my partner paid the mortgage. Gave her $400 a week, every week. He used to bring the money to her mother and her mother would give it to her. He didn't want to go to my house thinking they'd be watching for him. A lot of the time her mother would rob her. That's why we lost the house.

I'm studying and growing and really enjoying it. The TV's blasting, guys yelling and the minute I started studying, the Lord would shut my ears. My average score was 87. I finished and they asked if I wanted to do an extended course. I was thinking about it. Then my counsellor calls me down. "Nick, we've evaluated you." I wasn't supposed to get evaluated for four more months. "You can go home now." I know this is God talking to me.

Karen doesn't know the day I'm coming home. But she knows it's going to be this month. I call my son, Dino. He's now 17 years old. He's doing drugs. He's got a girlfriend. By now he had done six months of jail. I ask, "Do you know where Karen lives?"

He says, "Let's go first to her mother's house to find out."

When we went there, she was all cold. "Oh, it's so good to see you home."

I said, "Where is she?" She gave me the address. As we were leaving, something within me made me turn. I looked up at the window and saw my mother-in-law on the phone.

It only took a few minutes to get there. Karen was coming out with clothes under her arm as we were going in. I was so happy to see her. I grabbed her and hugged her. She was shaking, trembling. I misconstrued it to believe, in my own mind, she was excited. We went upstairs and I said, "Where are the boys?"

"They're coming." It's only a one-room apartment. There were mattresses on the floor. Stinky little beds for my kids and I left them with a $250,000 house. We talked but she just had no conversation. She was cold and afraid. I've got a letter in my pocket that she wrote last week saying, "Honey, I can't wait for us to start our new life together."

About five minutes later Pasquale and Kenny come in. They were six and eight years old. I said, "Where did they come from?"

"They came in a cab from my mother's."

"I just came from your mother's and they weren't there."

"They had taken a walk."

She's lying but I don't want to cause no problems. It's my first day home and I'm horny. When we go to bed she is cold. She couldn't give herself. But I did what I had to do.

The next day she wants to leave. We walked the kids to school. I said, "Let's go back to the apartment."

She says, "Let's go shopping."

I said, "What shopping?" I want to do what I want to do.

Again she was really cold. While we were doing it I just felt like turkey dung. I picked up my kids from school. That night again she was cold. She's distant. The next night, when we go to bed, I just put my arm around her and she starts to scream.

The lady next door yells, "Don't be afraid, I'll call the cops!"

I yell, "No, don't call the cops!"

She calls the cops. I hear the sirens. I leave.

The next day I call her and say, "What's your problem?"

"I'm afraid that you're going to strangle me while we're sleeping."

"Why?"

"I'm not in love with you anymore. I'm in love with someone else. I have been for a long time."

"Why didn't you tell me that when I was in prison? I would have just taken you off my back. We would have gotten a divorce. I could have come home to start a brand new life. Why didn't you tell me?"

"Because I was afraid that you were going to kill me."

"If you were afraid I was going to kill you, then why did you go out with the guy?"

At this time my mother had a boyfriend with an apartment in the same building as her. He moved in with my mom and gave me his apartment. I'm staying away from Karen because she put a restraining order on me. If I go by there I get arrested. But I'm going by anyway. She's living with this guy and I'd be out there calling him. He's a Spanish kid. "You spic!" I lost my Christianity. I wasn't reading the Bible. I want her, man. He's got my wife and kids. He ain't getting them. I'm obsessed. I'm walking around her apartment building. "Come out here!" They're scared to death. He's already afraid of me because of my reputation. They're still together now. They have two more kids.

I went to see my kids one night at her brother's house. That's where she said I could go see them. The street was a sheet of ice. It had rained and then frozen. Me and my brother are walking on tiptoes. As we turned the corner there they are. He had his arm around her. When I saw them walking like that I snapped. I lost it. I punched him. There is a garbage barrel with a rake in it. I pulled out the rake and started beating him. I kicked him in the head. She jumps up on top of me. I slipped and went down on the ice. He opens up a six-inch knife and sticks it in my back, in the only kidney I got. When I saw the knife I grabbed him and he slipped. He tried to stab me again and I went at him, punching him left and right. I broke his nose. His ear is bleeding. I'm kicking him in his head. As I'm going for his throat, my brother jumps on me. He was slow to stop me because he's been a heroin addict for 10 years, otherwise he would have stopped me earlier. "Nick, don't do it!" I get in the car and we drive away. They're screaming and yelling, especially her. "You'll see, you'll go back to prison, you animal!"

I said to my brother, "Let's go home."

He said, "Go home? Look at you." Blood was coming out of my side, just pouring down.

"I'm taking you to the hospital."

In the hospital the cop asked, "What happened?"

I said, "This guy asked me for a cigarette and I told him to get lost. As I turned and walked away, he stuck me in the back."

He wrote it down. Five minutes later he came back. He says to me, "You know the guy that asked you for a cigarette, he's beat up bad. You're under arrest."

He puts handcuffs on me and handcuffs me to the chair.

All of a sudden it hit me. Here I am under arrest. I have a hole in my back. He's still with my wife and kids. I'm going back to prison. I was lost. I had a little book that helps with Scriptures in my pocket. I'm reading it and crying. I beat up this guy so bad. What happened to me?

They take me upstairs. I'm under protective custody. There's a cop outside and I'm not allowed no visitors. I'm cuffed to the bed. The cop is with an organization called Cops for Christ. He says, "What are you reading there?"

"I'm trying to get some comfort. I messed up pretty bad."

"The Lord will never leave you. He'll watch over you."

I say, "Thanks." But I'm not listening. I'm feeling depressed.

The next morning another cop is out there. He says, "Your brother came to visit you. I'm just letting you know. You're not allowed no visitors."

"Thanks."

A half hour later. "You mother came to visit you."

"Thanks."

Not even 15 minutes later this little black guy comes walking in, Pastor Obi from the Hosanna ministry I used to go to. He's a pastor now but he was a drug addict, a card shark, a pimp, he had about 30 prostitutes. Then he became a pastor and opened the Hosanna ministry as a recovery centre, 97 percent recovery rate for drug addicts. The Bible is the only thing they use. I used to go in three times a weeks. Learn how to pray, understand spiritual warfare. Someone calls you a jerk. What do you do? You call him a jerk in return? That was my way. I learned through the Bible and Pastor Obi, someone calls you a jerk, you say, I'm not a jerk, neither are you. Now they have no comeback.

I said, "How did you get in?"

"I just walked in. That's God." He says, "Brother Nick, this morning I was praying for you. God put upon my heart that you're trying to get a slick lawyer. You're trying to get some fast cash and the right judge to straighten this matter out. That's what I was thinking about. But you know, Brother Nick, you're a Christian now. You've got a God in heaven. Your Father knows what you're going through and He'll take care of you. Put your trust in Him."

As he said that my spirit rose and I knew I was going home. I knew it was going to be OK. "Thanks."

From the hospital I go to the county jail. I go to court. It's unheard of for two people who have been in a fight to have the same lawyer. Johnny, my wife's boyfriend, and I, we had the same lawyer. I said to him, "You can't be his lawyer and mine. This is conflict of interest."

"Don't worry. This is no longer a criminal case."

When they first arrested me they were going to charge me as a habitual offender, a career criminal. Thirty years mandatory. I was scared out of my mind. That's why I was trying to think, I've got to get money and a lawyer. Instead of a criminal case the lawyer turned it into a domestic case, domestic violence. Three years' suspension. One year probation. I never got a suspended sentence in my life. I've had 13 1/2 years in prison, 14 arrests, 19 convictions. The judge says, "You're free to go." Instead of doing three years in prison, they're suspended so long as you walk right for one year. If within this one-year probation you get arrested, you have to do these three years.

Pastor Obi saw my problem that I couldn't let go of Karen and put me onto Sister Gemma, a counsellor. She was counselling me because I was going to kill the guy my wife was with. I couldn't get a handle on my anger. I had been seeing Sister Gemma about a month by then. I had two or three sessions with her before I ended up in jail for beating him up.

I didn't know how to let go. The anger was still there especially after he stabbed me. I'm doing my best not to sin with any woman. I didn't want to commit adultery, fornication with anyone. But if He doesn't send you one thing, He'll send you another. He knows your weaknesses and that's where I was weak. Sex. Here she is with another guy, he's not her husband, I'm her husband and she's screwing him. But I wanted to walk right with God. This chick walks up to me and says, "Hi, Nick." She stayed the night with me. I felt like real dirt. I went to church that Sunday and stayed strong for a while.

Then came another chick, Debbie, a millionaire. My friend's girl-friend. She had him locked up because he stole some art work from her house. I'm trying to get her not to prosecute him. We became friends and then she just jumped me. I said, "No, this is sin."

"No, it's not sin," Debbie says. "It's normal."

I thought Karen would come back to me if I was pure but I was weak. I didn't want to succumb to these women but just a little eye contact, a little talk and all of a sudden…I did not want to have sex. I wanted to live holy. That's why I was in torment all the time. But I also wanted to have sex for the pleasure, to feel like a man.

I'm at the Hosanna ministry. "Hi Nick, how are you?" She kisses me. We're sitting in the car and next thing I know I fall asleep. I woke up and she's on top of me doing it. We stayed together for five months. There was something sexual between us. The pain that I was carrying and whatever she was carrying made the sex so exhilarating, so crazy. The heat, the burning, the passion. One night we went out, had a few drinks then came back. "You," she said, "you murderer, you creep."

I said, "Shut up."

"You filthy no-good…" She was drunk. POW! I knocked her down. I went to sleep.

The next morning she was gone. I hear bum, bum on the door. The cops. "You're under arrest." I went to jail. I had $1,200 in my pocket and it was $1,000 bail.

Sister Gemma kept telling me, "Nick, you're not ready to have a relationship. Get all that garbage out of you. You know how many years of garbage you're carrying? You're loaded down. All that you're going to draw to you is what you carry. You're going to draw some of the same garbage."

But I didn't understand. I was thinking with my penis, not with my brain.

I used to try to share the word of God in our therapy session but Sister Gemma didn't want to hear that. "This is not a Bible study," she'd say. "This is a counselling session."

I was so used to evading the issue. I had these schemes. I didn't know they were a part of my makeup. A drug addict, a hustler, a street guy has learned so many ways to get away from the truth, to deal with manipulation. He manipulates his own self non-stop, day in and day out, that he doesn't know what the truth is anymore. How do you feel? I feel angry. What does that feel like? I feel like ripping someone's eyes out. How would that make you feel later on? I'd end up crying sometimes. Or I would yell at her. She knew how to get at my feelings. I got in touch with the hurts and anger when my father beat me up. I got in touch with how I felt when I killed the guy, how I felt when I watched his mom and dad in the courtroom. How did it make you feel? It made me feel like trash. What does trash feel like? What's it smell like? She used to get me into every bit of it. I do that now, having learned that from her over 29 months, every Friday or Thursday. Never missed one session. Always left there feeling freer, something else got released. She taught me that, if you don't get in touch with the pain, it'll always be there drawing like a magnet other things that destroy you.

Why did you read the Bible? Another thing that came out with Sister Gemma, slowly and gradually, is that in prison I got to know the word of God for Karen. I did a lot, not for my own personal growth but for her. When I came out she wasn't there anymore. She was with somebody else. I felt everything I did was for nothing and I was in a rage. That's what made it so hard for me to let go of her.

The immigration department was trying to deport me because of the sawed-off shotgun. It was 12 1/4 inches and fit into a terrorist category. That was a tool the judges and my lawyer used to keep me in their claws, to keep me paying for a new hearing, a new this or a new that. "There's a new clause I just found. I'm going to submit it to the court and it's going to cost you $3,000. We're going to have a new hearing into your case to see if you're staying or not." Always they kept me hanging on a string. They'd never kick me out but they'd never remove me from the undesirable aliens list either. The last time we went to a hearing I heard the judge say to the lawyer, "There is no remedy for him. But the eagle's eye is over the shoulder." I didn't understand what that meant. They continued talking. "We'll have another hearing in six months and we'll see what the progress of this dossier is."

At the conclusion of the hearing we're walking out. My immigration attorney is powerful, has seven offices all over the United States, in California, Miami, Boston, New York City, which is where I used to talk to him. He said, "Nick, we'll apply for another hearing next month and it'll cost you $3,000."

I said, "What's the sense when I heard the man clearly say that there was no remedy?"

He said, "You don't understand."

"What did he mean when he said the eagle's eye is over the shoulder?"

"That's courtroom jargon."

"I know, but I'm paying you and I want to know what he said."

"It doesn't concern you."

"Everything in there concerns me." I'm mad now.

I told Sister Gemma about what happened in court and she said, "You know what you have to do now? The man said there's no remedy and you don't feel good with the lawyer, so you have to dismiss him."

At the same time she gave me the name, address and phone number of another attorney. But when I fired him I didn't contact the other attorney. Five weeks later I get a letter from the immigration department to be deported.

I got deported to Italy the first week of January 1992. When I got to Basilica, I had gone back in time, 5,000 years it seemed. My cousin in the U.S. had a house in our hometown, so I stayed there all by myself. I was hurting when I first got there. I was in my little room and I cried. When am I going to see my kids, my family?

I've got to light up the fireplace in order to eat and keep warm. There's no hot water. Man, cold. This is primitive. How did I get here? People still went to work in the morning with donkeys. It's way up in the mountains, 3,600 feet above sea level. Women who have lost their husband or child dress in black. This is crazy.

It's a little hick town with 960 people, me, my Bible and my clothes. But because I was alone I came closer to Jesus than I could have ever come in my life. It was just me and him. I didn't know nobody there. I had a lot of problems with the language but in a year I learned. My cousin from Milan came and introduced me to the priest who took me under his wing. If he was going somewhere to inaugurate a church he'd take me. We got to be really close.

I went to Rome six times, to Naples five times, once to the Riviera because I have an aunt up there. I earned $850 in 11 months by painting houses. But I was never without even if I had nothing in my pocket. People would send me money. Every once in a while friends sent me $50. Every once in a while my sister sent me a couple of hundred dollars. I wouldn't ask. I just prayed. Lord, I only have $20. Next week I'm going to need some money. Bam, I'd have some money.

I was going to a Bible study there on Thursday nights. There was a policeman. He was more what an FBI man is in the U.S. My papers to acquire my passport had arrived at his office and he said at that office it takes time unless you're a big man and can pay big money. For someone like me it can take a year. He said, "But I've got an idea, since I'm a cop and you're an ex-criminal and only God could have put us together, I'm going to do you a favour. I'm going to tell the government what kind of a guy you were in the U.S., the crimes you committed, and you're going to do the same things here. It's to our advantage to make out a passport quickly and get you out of here." A month-and-a-half later I got a passport.

All of a sudden my mother came to visit me in Italy. She said, "Nick, I brought you $1,400. I want you to go to Canada."

A cousin of hers had died there and when she went to the funeral she saw how nice everyone lived. She thought if he was here at least he's close to us in the U.S. My cousin said, "Tell him to come. We'll receive him."

I flew from Italy to Canada. To Montreal. I came here on a tourist visa. I was going to come here for six months, go back to Italy, pray for more money and then come back for another six months. This way I can be close to my family, my children. But God had other plans for me.

I met Carol at a birthday party the first month I was there. Three months later we got married. Carol's father helped me out. We worked together. We were partners. He's a professional house painter and also an abstract painter.

We did some work for mob people. One day while I was painting the house of the key Mafia guy, the police come to arrest him because they had sunk a boat and later found 750 kg of coke in it, $50 million worth of coke. I'm on top of the roof, singing. Then one day I was in the garage talking to this other wise guy. He had everything, power and wealth, but I had freedom. I looked around in the house and there was no temptation. Nothing. I felt bad for them that they're in this game. A phrase jumped into my mind: a man's wealth is contained by the things he learns to do without. I thought, I'm wealthier than him. I've got me.

Everyone in my family got saved, thank God. They said, "Get out of here. I can't take it no more." But I found a jewel and they had to get it.

Dino had started going to the Hosanna ministry with me back in the States. Gradually he gave his heart to the Lord.

Pasquale is 17 now and he's got a baby boy called Nick. I've got two Nicks. Dino's son also. Pasquale isn't married yet because her father won't let her till she's 18. She's only 16. But he's taking responsibility for the baby. He sees the child every day, buys all the clothes. I told him, "Pasquale, whatever you do be faithful, don't cheat on her." I told all my boys that. And I was the biggest pig of all.

I want to bring people into God's church. I want people to come in from the dark. But you have to reach the bottom first. The bottom will be different for different people. I want to go into prison and tell the guys I know what it feels like when you're waiting and you don't get a letter. I know what it feels like when you're not there for your kids at Christmas. When you want to kiss them good night. Right now I can't get into the prisons because I don't have my residence. So I go to soup kitchens and give testimony, let people know the life I lived and what God has done to bring me into His kingdom. It's a privilege. I tell them that. It's a privilege that God uses a filthy criminal, a nasty guy like me. That's what I was.

Sometimes I don't know how to speak, I'm too gruff. That came from having to survive in the joint. What? What are you looking at? What are you talking about? You had to carry your shoulders high, be bold and be ready to fight at all times. It's so hard to tear down. But I'm working on it. God is blessing me. He's taking it away.

When I first became a Christian I was ashamed to do something good. What is she going to think? It took a long while to understand, if it's good, do it. Excuse me, let me do that for you. I was so unsure of my new growth, my new life. Is she going to think I want to take her to bed by offering this? Now I don't hesitate. The other day this man fell on the street. I immediately got out of the car to help him up. Now I don't give a chance for doubt to enter. I just go do it. Get bold about it.

BERT

I met Bert (43) at a talk I gave in a minimum security prison. During the discussion period the references he made about his mother attracted my attention. She refused to let him call her mother. "What are you going to do about something like that?" he asked rhetorically. There was no rancour in his voice, no bitterness. Afterwards I approached him to say I was looking for certain types of people to interview for a book I was writing. From the comments he had made, he sounded right. Would he be interested? He wanted to help out but said I had to be certain he was indeed right for my needs. We agreed to meet the following week and talk.

The interview had to be conducted in prison. I arranged a meeting with him through my contact there. It was set up in one of the lawyers' interview rooms.

He was boyish-looking with dark, curly hair. Said he is 5-7 3/4 but rounds it off to 5-8. He was solid, muscular. He worked out at the prison gym regularly but said he had always done weight training, even before prison. Beyond the powerful and bulging muscles of his arms and thighs, he was clearly of small build.

The first time we met, he was very open, friendly and pleased to talk. He was helpful as I searched for an electrical socket and when I had trouble with the tape recorder. At the end of the first interview he wanted to know if I still thought he would qualify for my book. His concern was more for my project than himself. Once I assured him that I was interested and wanted to continue, we set up the next interview.

Part of him was like a cuddly, affectionate teddy bear. I was struck by how his natural being seemed so at odds with his criminal activities and the place where he was. He was gentle in the way he talked, the way he acted. His desire and need for warmth was touching, heart-rending.

It's nice to be able to put it out, not to analyze it or figure it out. Just unroll the carpet. How did I get to where I am? When did I drift? Up on that tree in the backyard, I used to be above everything. I could see all over the yard, over the roofs, the neighbourhood. I was safe up there. No one could get me. The higher I climbed, the farther I went from anything. I had my favourite nook and used to whittle pieces of wood with a knife. I cut myself up on that tree. I still have the scar. Every time I look at it I remember. That's when I started to drift.

I was at my grandmother's at the time. That's where I saw my mother. She came twice for my birthday. She bought me my first two-wheel bicycle and told me that was the last one I would ever get. I treasured that bicycle. The next time I remember her coming with a card that had $20 in it. Money. A twenty on my birthday was a regular thing. But she never came again to see me.

When I was young I learned that in life money and things made you special. When my brother and sisters would come over, I was the littlest one but the best one. My grandparents gave me money so I was the best pal to be. Money creates respect.

All of us would only see our mother when we were young and she would get us on Christmas. We were all in the back of this Lincoln Continental. We drove around and got to look at all the decorated houses. Phil was driving and we would sing Christmas carols. We just drove around their neighbourhood. There was Don, Lorna, Christine and myself in the back. Then there was Paul and Elise in the front seat, her children from the second marriage.

My mother was ashamed of us, the first set of children. I couldn't call her Mother in front of anybody. I had to call her Ann or Mrs. Burke. We were friends of the family. Later in life I called her Mother. When one of her children answered the phone I would say, "Is Mom there?" Around my twenties I insisted that was my mother and I was going to call her Mother or Mom.

I wouldn't see her for three or four years. Then all of a sudden I would drop by. She used to give me hell. "Why do you always pop in on me?" I used to walk into her house and she said, "What if I have someone here?" I pop in on my grandmother. I don't knock. I just open the door. When I go to my father's place, I walk in. That's my home. As I got older I got very resentful but never said anything to her. When she wouldn't come to testify for me at court, I told her if I saw her again I was going to run her over. She left me in a lurch at a time when I needed help.

Philip, her second husband, the fellow she ended up running off with, was my father's friend. He owned a motel. She used to work there. I have a hard time trying to understand why she didn't take us. Somebody in my family once said, "You were a mistake."

My mother left when I was six or seven months old. My father often said, "You were still on the old lady's tit."

At my grandmother's I can remember seeing all these nipples for bottles on the counter. She used to bathe me in the sink and those nipples were right in front of me. I have a vivid memory of that.

I've never been able to figure out why she left my father. He still loves her today. I asked a few questions and my father of course blames it on her. But now Philip married the secretary with the body. My mother had gotten a little bit overweight for him.

Vicki was an early sweetheart of mine. I was going to see her on my tricycle over this steep hill. I waited at the top. The light turned green and I started to peddle. I took my feet off the peddles but by the time I got to the bottom the light had changed to red and I went smack into the side of a taxi. The taxi driver asked my name. When I told him, he knew my father because of the garage, so he phoned him.

I was sitting in the back of the police car. I had broken my wrist, bumped my head and had bruises. I was hurting. I remember my father coming. I was crying. He gave me a backhander and said, "You stupid little bastard, what were you doing on the hill?" Then my grandmother got there, pushed him away and took care of me.

When I was young I was down at the grandfather's garage all the time but he never paid any attention to me. I was left in the back playing with the trucks and cars. That's where I learned to start a vehicle without keys. I was tinkering or I was in the back shed where we had a bunch of old motorcycles. My grandfather had race bikes.

My grandmother used to leave me alone a lot when I was young. She worked at the garage with my grandfather. She was an accountant for his business. After a while I liked to be alone. In a way it served me well. Now I don't mind being alone at all. I've got an inner peace. I'm happy with myself.

She told me not to touch nothing and I was into everything. One day I was playing with lighter fluid and poured it on the varnished table.

I did a design on it, then lit it. The fire went all around. I panicked and put it out but it left a mark on the table. My grandmother asked where the mark came from and I said I spilled ginger ale on it.

Around that time I also fired a shotgun. I had seen it on TV and knew my grandfather had shotguns in the basement. I went downstairs, got the gun, brought it up, loaded it. Went out the back door and pulled the trigger. It put me through the door, on my butt, and scared the living daylights out of me.

I ratted on myself because I showed my grandfather all the little holes these pellets had put in the henhouse in the back, which had been turned into a garage. All the parts from the two motorcycle parts dealerships were there. We had just painted the front of it. My grandfather started kicking me in my ass. My grandmother came out and said, "There'll be none of that around here."

I used to sit up in a tree and daydream. I remember floating all around. I had a family all right but it was imaginary. I had a sled with dogs. I was up north and lived in a bush shack. I had a mother and father who used to trap for a living. We went to hunt and fish. I got it all from television.

This went on for several years. That's the only family I had. I used to use my brain to go away. I used to build in my head. I didn't have very much reality to my life. Everything was fantasy. I lived in your world, here, I participated in it, worked in it. But everyday life was not a reality. It was a part that I played. The eight-to-five work, the rough part, was my father.

I've never been me. I'm only me now, today. I've always been someone else, what someone wanted me to be. If you had hurt me, I had blocked it so actually you didn't hurt me, but you did hurt me and I just stored it. I put it on deep freeze but it melted. The wall came down after my grandmother died.

I was slow as a child. That's the only way I know how to put it. I had a very hard time tying my shoelaces when I was a kid. I just couldn't get it. I was excellent in anything mechanical. I could take anything apart and put it back together. Blindfolded. To search for something inquisitively, I could do it. Up at the cottage the burner on top of the stove didn't work. I was only a child but I knew enough that there was a fuse around. So I got underneath on my knees. The fuses were at the bottom and my grandmother was trying to look for the fuses on top.

I found it and said, "See, I'm not stupid, Nanny."

She said, "Who calls you stupid? You're not stupid" *(choking back tears)*.

I looked at her and said, "Dad calls me stupid but see, I'm not stupid." She told me that I wasn't stupid and don't let anybody tell you in your life that you are. My grandmother could tell me anything and I'd believe her. It was wonderful. My life with her was perfect. I was very, very close to her. I was her pet.

I knew where everything was up at the cottage because I was always by myself, always walking around. One day, while picking pine cones, I met the old woman who lived in the woods by herself. Everyone was scared of her. They used to call her the old witch. I was leery but also curious. When I saw her through the pine bush, she scared the shit out of me. She looked like what you see on pictures of old witches with the white long hair, thin with raggedly clothes. She was old, old, an old woman.

I befriended her. I was eight or nine. We became very, very close. Every day I used to row over there on the lake and walk up. I would get her water in pails because she couldn't carry them anymore. We used to collect pine cones which she burnt because she liked the smell. She had a wood stove. I used to chop some of the wood and bring it in for her. I brought her bread and butter. From a can she gave me round, hard, coloured candies with the icing sugar on them. That was my reward. Then she died.

This is when my aunt's boyfriend did something nasty to me. When she died he took me up there and wanted to see what was in the house. The door was locked. He shoved me in through the window so I could open the door to let him in. And he stole the stuff there. The old oil lamps with glass bottoms and the wick. I had nightmares for years and years and years after because I felt so damn guilty doing that.

Up at the cottage I spent all the time by myself with my grandmother except when the other families would come up on the weekends. It was supposed to be mine but it never turned out that way. The grandfather did a lot of funny things, like selling the cottage. The whole family built it together. I can remember carrying lumber around and whacking nails in. The boat was also supposed to be mine. The grandfather sold that too.

On Sundays my grandmother and I went to church and to Uncle

Elm's, her brother's, in the afternoon. We always took something. Uncle Elm had a farm. I went in to say hi and then I was out the door, gone. The haylofts and the cows, chickens, pigs, and what's this and how does that work and I'd wander in the fields, see the bull. We had Sunday night dinner up there, her and I.

I saw my grandmother braiding her mother's hair. She had a room that faced south in Uncle Elm's house. There was always sunlight in the room. She lay on the old brass bed, all handcrafted with a handmade quilt on top. I remember patches of different colours. Her hair was hanging down the side. I swear it was to her feet. I don't remember when she died. I remember going to the funeral.

In the first years when I used to go to my grandmother's, before I started school, my father used to dump me off there in the morning and he'd pick me up at night on his way home, which would be about seven o'clock.

At the time my sister, Christine, was two. She was the third youngest, I'm the fourth youngest. Don was the oldest and then came Lorna. From my oldest brother to me you're looking at six years. They lived with my father. They were just people I knew, before I knew who they were. I went there at nights and on weekends but I wasn't part of it.

This went on for two years. Then it gets to be a pain in the butt for them. My grandmother has to pack me up every night so it's better that I just stay there. Now only on the weekends does my father pick me up and take me home. This is when I run into the stepmother. She's the babysitter. He needed somebody to look after the other kids. The old man brings her out and drives her home. This is the way their relationship starts. Then she moves in.

I was a bedwetter. My grandmother used to make me wash my sheets. When I went to my father's on the weekends and he found out that I wet the bed, he grabbed my hand and rubbed my face in it. Then I got smart. If I wet the bed I would take the wet spot, turn the sheet around and put the wet spot at the bottom. I also remember sleeping with the dogs in the doghouse. I was more comfortable there than I was in the house.

Tiger wasn't supposed to be in the house and I always got shit because she also used to wet the bed. When Elsa came home the mattress would be wet and I'd take the blame because I wouldn't tell her that I had Tiger in the house.

Early on I remember seeing Don, Lorna and Christine throwing eggs at her and she was throwing eggs at them because they caught her with her false teeth out. They were laughing at her. But she was an old bitch. I slept in the basement and she locked the door on me. When you're young, you're up early and I couldn't get out. And I just shudder at the thought of eating one of her meals again. She would give us salmon with green pea sauce on toast. It was horrid. Baloney fried up with potatoes and mashed turnips. Hot dogs and hamburgers. There was one glass of milk at the table and a jar of peanut butter. I used to take a big scoop because I knew I wasn't getting any more. We'd get a backhander for taking too much. You couldn't eat when you were hungry. I used to eat the little coloured dog biscuits with Tiger. I'd give one to Tiger and I'd eat one. I had to open the cupboard to get the food for her. She couldn't have any either. We were supposed to stay out of the cupboards. You couldn't even go into the fridge to get a glass of milk. You had milk with your supper and that was it. Sometimes I'd be eating and my legs would shake up and down. Of course the table would shake and you got shit for it. She had a ring with a diamond and she would turn it around and whack you in the face. She backhanded you, "Wait till your father gets home." Or, "I'll teach you." She was always screaming in a shrill voice. Terrible. I can still remember it. This woman had already lost her children because she was very, very abusive. Social services had taken them away.

Also you had packed lunches that were sickening. White bread sandwich with pickles on it. It's made the night before and it's soggy, damn terrible. I just threw it away. With my grandmother I had meals. Not that there wasn't a meal on the table. But she would feed us some disgusting slop while she would be gobbling down a T-bone steak. She would eat all the steak that we were supposed to get. Then, of course, Dad would come home and she would serve him meat and potatoes.

Once Christine said, "Put these on."

I said, "Why?"

She said, "Because you're going to get the strap."

Then my father came into her room and she got the strap. I saw her get strapped a lot. I felt very sorry for her and very angry toward my father. Usually he slapped her on the pants but I guess he caught on to the idea that she was putting on five or six underwear so it didn't hurt as much. He pulled the underpants down and gave it to her straight on her bottom. Then it was me. I had never been spanked before. Where did this come from? That was the first time I started to see all kinds of violence around me.

Christine was sort of troubled too. She thinks I got the worst end of the stick because I was dumped all over the place. No one wanted me. She said this in court. The longest I've stayed in one place is since I've been locked up here.

After a strapping Christine and I used to laugh it off to take the pain away. Once I tried to stop him and I was told if I didn't sit down, I'd get the same. So I obeyed. She was the one to get the majority of the straps with the belt because she resembled my mother the most, other than myself. The strap was a piece of a mud flap. Thick rubber with strings through it to give it density. That's what makes it very strong and durable. I also saw Don and Lorna getting the strap. When we talked about the beatings we always used to laugh about it. Do you remember the time we did this? Ha, ha.

Sometimes the strap depended on Elsa because she was the one who caused all the problems. My stepmother would turn his anger toward us. No matter what he was mad at, she would blame it on us. We were always the brunt of everything, even if she had done something wrong. The lot of us never spoke because you always had to watch what you said, when you said it and how. Even if you were right, you were wrong. I never said nothing and always used to walk and talk with my head down because then I didn't have to have that direct eye contact. I never walked with my head up until 1988 or 1989. That was the time I went to see the psychologist at Archambault and put everything out on the table and started to feel better about myself.

My father was a very troubled man. Now I see that because he very much stayed to himself after the divorce from my mother. He deeply loved her. He was very, very hurt when she left. He never wants to talk about it. It's too painful to him.

When I was young and my father had the Hudson Service Station, we used to have Saturdays together. Then life was great. On Saturday we went across the street from the Hudson Garage to get bacon, eggs, beans and toast at Charlie's Diner. This was a Saturday ritual and then it stopped. All the caring in his life stopped sometime after that point. I remember working with him at the garage. Those were good times. He still had the hydroplane. My father and grandfather used to race boats, cars and motorcycles. After he got rid of the station is when life went for the shits. I remember my father chasing me around this big pot-bellied, round coal furnace with octopus arms. He was 6-2 or 6-3 and I was only small. I would run all around this furnace in the basement which was my room and he couldn't catch me.

Now I start school at my grandmother's. I flunked Grade 3. Stuart, Roy and I learned how to steal cartons of cigarettes from Dominion. Stuart walked in with a coat and put it on the cartons of cigarettes, which used to be at the end of the aisles before they opened up the smoke shops, and pretend he was looking for his mother. Then you come back and grab your coat. When you grab your coat, you grab two cartons underneath your coat and walk out. We only did it once. Stuart was selling them to get some hot dogs, candies and junk. I got three packs of cigarettes from the carton and just puffed. When the police asked him where he got them from, he took them to see his father who was very strict and said we all stole them.

We all went to juvenile court. We were given a one- or two-year probation and had a curfew at nine o'clock. That was my first experience with the courts, at age seven or eight. I wasn't really obeying my curfew and was in trouble all the time in school. My father takes me away from my grandmother's when she said she couldn't handle me anymore. My grandmother finally dumped me off too but I still loved her dearly.

I cherished the ground that woman walked on. I used to dig up her garden. Every spring I would take out every window of that house and clean them with vinegar and newspaper. I used to take her shopping on Mother's Day. She loved to go for walks. She used to say, "Look at the colours of those trees." As a kid I used to row her around the bay in the country. She sat at the back of the boat and I rowed. We'd chit chat.

When I moved to my father's is when I moved from heaven to hell. I called my grandmother crying on the phone, "I want to go home. I don't like it here."

She said, "I'm sorry, I can't. I can't. Your father has taken you now."

I think he took me because he figured he was going to beat it into me. That's when the kicks in the ass, the backhanders and the strap really started. I didn't get it very often because he and I were more physical, more hand-to-hand. Fist-to-fist. I hit him back. I gave him a couple of good shots there. He's a big man. He swung at me and I ducked, came up and gave him two shots. He didn't move. Just looked at me. We wrestled a few times when things got out of hand.

Everybody would sit around the Christmas tree. He'd hand out all the gifts but he wouldn't give me any. Butch doesn't get nothing. He would say, "Santa Claus didn't leave any gifts because he's been bad." If I didn't pass at school or when I acted up he'd shave my hair off. I'd have to go to school like that and I'm in Grade 4, 5 and 6. He even shaved my hair off when I was in seven and eight. He was constantly humiliating me. You were like a target. I'm in Grade 8 and he buys me a pair of oil-resistant, service station attendant work shoes which had a great big thick black sole with a little heel, a round toe and laced up. "Here, you won't wear these out." The day he bought them for me I went outside and kicked that football all day long till I ripped the sole off the boot. Then I got beat for it and got my head shaved. But he was my hero. I loved that man passionately and still do. I guess because he used to say, "This is my son." That's one thing he was never embarrassed to say, that I was his son. Anywhere, anytime, what I've done, it didn't matter. When my father presented me, "This is my son, Bert," I felt 10 feet tall. It made me feel great that he would identify me as his son. My father wasn't ashamed of me.

I've always tried to portray my father. This is where the conflict came in my life. I've always played that great, aggressive, stern person which I'm not. My father was rough, tough, gruff, no tenderness. But he was a man. He worked all his life and he worked every day. He always had food on the table but he gave you no money. You didn't get an allowance for taking out the garbage.

In 1963 or 1964 I move to my father's and in the same year, when I'm nine or 10, we moved houses. My grandfather owned the house my father had lived in. My father had renovated the whole house. He put up a two-bay garage outside so he could do some tinkering at home on his hot rods because he was still racing at the time. My grandfather sold it to the National Conservationists of Canada. We left our friends and moved into this cramped space. I was stuck in a room with Don. That's when I noticed a significant change in my father. I think there was a lot of anger between the two of them after that.

I was probably 12 when Larry was born. He had cookies, milk, juice, any time of the day, any food, anything he wanted. My father used to bounce him on his lap. When Larry cried I noticed him becoming very agitated and violent. He'd spank him. My father could never stand a baby crying. Tears were a lot of things that never came out. If you cried, "You want something to cry for? I'll give you something to cry for if you need your crying now." Like when I was young we went to an auto show. My father had a 1957 GMC half-ton. I put my hand on the door when it was open. He came around and swung the door closed while my hand was in there. It hurt. I was crying a bit. "What are you crying for, you stupid little bastard? You think that hurt, I'll give you something that hurts." And you get slapped on the head.

My sisters had to look after Larry. They changed his diapers, did his laundry, fed him his bottle, washed the bottles. Elsa was a lazy tyrant. Lorna left when she was 16. She walked out the door and went to live with my mother, went to nursing school and became a nurse. Don had gone to live with my grandmother to finish his mechanic licence. Christine left shortly after. I ran away. Larry must have been two or three by the time we all left. I think this was her goal to get us all out of the house so it would be just Larry, her and my Dad. My grandmother told my father, "That bitch of yours drove them all out of the house."

Then I was living on the streets and ran into Alphie, who was the president of Satan's Choice at the time. He said, "Go and live at the speed house." Methadone. It was a cracker joint with blood splattered all over the place. I spent three or four months there. I've seen a lot in that time. I've seen a few of them stiffed out. Then I went to Raymond's. He's living with his parents. But he's adopted. I move in there, downstairs in his basement. The two of us were stealing cars. We were just joyriding them. It was just transportation to drive around and be cool.

Around 1967 or 1968 both Raymond and I were 14 and we ended up in a training school for juveniles for a stolen car. Another fellow killed himself. Shot himself in the kitchen after he had killed three girls. It was a car accident. It was night. He was driving fast. They were walking on the road and he ran into them. He drove home and couldn't handle it. He was 17 at the time. Raymond and I were really close.

There were four of us in the stolen car, including Raymond and myself. Raymond is driving and we get chased by the police. We're coming up to the bridge and all of a sudden these lights hit us. They laid a track of lights across the road with a belt of these steel prongs to blow the tires in the car. Raymond hits the breaks. I jump out, took 30 or 40 tumbles, and ran. Raymond followed me. They get Raymond first, then me. They took us to juvenile hall. Raymond is in the next cell. We're talking and rolling cigarettes in thin Bible paper from butts we stole out of the ashtray.

I'm in juvenile court one day and the old man walks in. The judge says, blah, blah, blah, next week. The old man comes back next week. The judge says, "We don't have the full reports yet." My old man stands up and says, "Look, I don't have time for any of this fucking bullshit. Either send him up the river or send him home."

So I went up the river to training school. You were beaten there. I spent many a night scrubbing the floors with toothbrushes. I never had contact with my father the whole time I was there. Never wrote me. Never came to see me. I was in training school for eight months.

They gave me parole. My father picks me up at the bus station. I'm home. I go back to school for two years, Grade 7 and 8. I was too hard to handle. All the teachers gave me away. The last year my desk was in the vice-principal's office. That was my classroom. No one can control me. I'm too active, too high-strung. But none of these stupid sons of bitches asked if there was anything wrong at home. Not one. Obviously something was amiss because I wasn't retarded.

When school was over I was dumped for the summer at Clem's in Clarence Creek. My father packed things for me but I didn't know he was packing for me. The whole family goes up to Clem's.

Comes time to go home, I get in the car. "You're not going home, you're staying here."

"What?"

I'm there and I don't know these people. I know Clem because I've seen his dogs and watched him race. He's got 14 Siberian huskies. We had a bitch, Timberwolf, in a pen, which was bred with Nicky, a Samoyed. Clem went up north on sled teams for the government. He had his own sled team which he used to race.

He's at work all day and I've got this little brat running around. His son is a lot smaller than me. A terrible little kid. As I'm cleaning out the dog shit, he teases the dogs with sticks. I was very happy when the bitch bit him in the ass. I used to watch her for hours and she'd go back and forth in the cage. She was a gorgeous beast. I got her to eat out of my hand. I felt sorry for her because she was caged up. She was a wild wolf from up north.

I had just finished graduating from seven and eight and was due to start high school. I was happy to go there because I wanted to play football. I was quite aggressive and loved contact sports. This was the beginning of summer. During a fight with my father he was twisting my arm and said, "I'll kill you, you son of a bitch." I bolted and took off. I went to my mother's and my mother wouldn't take me. Then I went to my grandmother's and she took me in for the summer.

I started to look for a job. I caddied, carried golf clubs for people. I made $3 or $4 a day. Then I ran into Brian, an old friend from school. Maybe three years older than me.

He said, "What are you doing?"

"I'm working in Hull, at the golf course."

"How much money are you making? I know where you can make a lot more money than that."

He showed me what he did. We're down at the beach. People go to the beach, take their clothes off, put their clothes, wallets and purses in the car. He opens the car, takes out the wallets and away we go. It's big money that's coming out of these purses and wallets. I never did any of the stealing, I was the one to watch when people came. I'm working as backup.

Now I'm going out with Carol. I'm living at my grandmother's. She's living at home around the corner. We've been together for some time. Carol runs away from home because she's having problems with her mother. She came to me. I used to bring her in through the bottom window in the basement. I'm 16 at the time. She's 14. Carol's been there with me for a few weeks. We're both virgins, we're still exploring. One night we had intercourse. I never thought there would be blood. My grandmother came down and did the sheets. She knew what had happened because it was in the spot. It didn't come from me. Carol was tabooed. She was no good for me at all. I was my grandmother's treasure. Any woman involved with me was no good.

Carol wants to run away now. I stole my grandfather's car and money. Her and I head up to cottage land. We don't go to our cottage. We go two cottages down from ours. I know how to get in because I was a kid there. We're up there three or four weeks. Then all of a sudden the police are coming in one door. They charge me with break and enter and possession of a stolen car. I'm going to jail. In the courtroom I said she knew nothing about the car, the stolen money, the break and enter. It was supposed to be my grandparents' cottage which was down the lane. My grandfather charged me with theft. I go off to Guelph. I got 18 months. I do eight.

When I got out the first person I ran into was Steven. Steve was into crime here and there and he was a lot older than me. We started to hang together. Steve and I spent one winter in a 1964 Pontiac with a plug-in heater. We ate Kentucky Fried Chicken, drank beer and did crime. We weren't great big criminals. We had enough to put gas in the car and toot around, but not enough to pay rent.

Then me and a friend of mine rented an apartment. That's when I first started the safes. It was paying the rent. Carol and I ran into each other on the street. When we came back together, it was like sliding back in. It was nice. I started to drift away from my criminal activity, weaned myself off. They'd say this is what we're doing now and I'd say, "I'm not going, I'll pass on this one."

I was working at the garage when we got married. The marriage thing came up because she was pregnant. We paid for the wedding ourselves. I was 21 years old. We got married in 1977 and Gavin is born the same year.

I was in the delivery room for eight hours. Gavin is born. She's put in a room. That night I was feeling very insecure. I went home with a woman and slept with her but didn't have sex. I knew her. All I wanted to do was talk and nestle. I went back to see Carol the next day.

It was a very hard time for me. I didn't have any sense of responsibility. I guess having Gavin sort of scared me. I was now working for Ontario Hydro. We bought a home. There's a mortgage payment every month. She wants to go back to work. There are daycare payments. I had the hydro bill, the heating bill, car payments. The responsibility took hold. I was home most of the time building picnic tables with Gavin.

We had some excellent times. We'd go to her father's for Christmas, stop in at my father's, then to my aunt's. Her father and I used to golf all over. We golfed for a charity match.

Then I went to work for Hobbart Manufacturing, restaurant equipment. I was a service technician, doing inspections. I was the representative of the leased machines, the service manager. It was a good job.

My criminal friends, any of us at that time, probably would have done anything for the other, especially Steven and I. He'd call me at three in the morning because he wanted me to come down to make sure no one in the bar jumped in on him. And I'm working the next morning. But I go. Then, of course, I have to explain myself. "Where are you going?" "I have to go out." "Why?" I'm not good at that. I felt guilty for going to help him out, but if I don't go I feel guilty as well. Here is that honour bullshit. I felt like telling him to leave me alone. I'm not interested in your bar fight.

I was in a bar one night and got a severe beating by two guys for nothing. They wanted a dollar and I wouldn't give it to them. They busted my cheekbone and jaw. There were these two guys I knew who didn't do anything about it. I was in the hospital for a good month.

If I got into a fight Steve, stepped in and I was the same with him. I went back and started hanging out with Steven again. When I went back I had two metal wires sticking out to hold up the top jaw. I went back for the security that I had before. Then Frog came to see me and said, "It's been taken care of. Don't worry."

After that I was with Steven and he said we're doing these safes. But they could do only three safes and I have a mechanical intelligence.

I said, "You're pissing around with $5,000 in these safes when there's $80,000 in those other safes. Let's take one and find out if we can open it." I can go into a building and come out the other side and tell you what kind of alarm system they have and what kind of wires in it, how many steps it takes to cross the floor.

In the summer, at the same time I was doing safes, I would set up the community barbecue in the park. Drink machines from 7-Up were set up. For the Children's Hospital I used to go around to Zellers, K-Mart, Toy Mart, and speak to the managers. "Look, what toys do you have here that are broken or are not good? I want those toys."

I made quite a bit of money with the safes. Carol at first wasn't aware of it. I let the money trickle in very easily and in very small quantities. She was a straight, straight person except for her younger years with me. Then on the weekend I said I had to go away on a job. I would come home and there would be cash.

The police had us under surveillance. They're following us. There is an OC, organized crime, on the record. We've been working all this time and they haven't been able to follow us because I go here, turn there, take a left, get out of that car, go in this door, step out the back door, get into another car, and then I leave. I'm organized.

They have the surveillance out for six months before they actually pop us. We're charged. The hen is out of the bag at home with Carol. I'm in jail. I call her. Everyone hears about it on the radio.

A few of my friends living in the area came over to see her and asked, "Does he have anything here?"

She said, "Go in his tool shed and look."

I had some tools there, expensive and elaborate tools for opening safes. Gary took everything out of the place and hid it at his place because the police were obviously going to come and search.

We get out on bail. I go home. Carol is tripping. Gavin is probably three at the time. I get 89 days and three years' probation. Then I said, "That's it, no more." I had a little bit of money put away. Carol and I had moved to a new house. I wasn't going to get involved in crime. I had stopped. I hadn't associated with anybody for a while and things were fine. All of a sudden these guys come back into my life. They're broke. They had spent all their money. That's when I had this turmoil about me owing them because I had grown up with them and they had helped when I came out of jail and they had accepted me when I was younger. Steve was family. You don't turn your back on family. When they came, I hummed and said no. They came back and I said no. They came back a third time and I said yes.

They wanted me to go out west with them and do two jobs. It caused conflict at home. She said, "Don't, Bert, something is going to happen. Give it up. We're happy here."

I could never really sit down and say, "This is why I have to go." I was frustrated because I felt so guilty. I was leaving and didn't want to go, but on the other hand I had this honour bullshit. Honour among thieves. It's a heavy ethic to break.

We go to the airport. I bought all three plane tickets, paid for them cash, and gave false names. I had rented a Lincoln Continental that was waiting out there.

The girl at the rental agency asked, "What's the occasion?"

I said, "It's a funeral."

"My God, I have a white Lincoln for you."

"Don't worry about it. I'll stay in the back of the procession."

We drive from Calgary to Edmonton and we come back. I'm satisfied. We have $14,000 each. Now let's go. They said we could do one more before we go back. I'm totally against it so I really wasn't going in on the second one. I was sitting outside in the Lincoln searching a map. I was sort of playing six while the other two were going in. A policewoman pulls up beside me. "Do you have any identification?" I reach down because my wallet was under the front seat. When I reached down she drove away. When she drove away I started the Lincoln and went the other way. Then there was a chase. They got the dogs out after me and arrested me. I went to jail. I phone Carol.

I was never in the damn store to begin with, but I had $42,000 in the trunk and another $2,000 under the hood in coins and they were trying to find out where all this money came from.

I'm convicted at the preliminary hearing. Went to court for trial. Bingo! Game over. Divorce papers were in process. Mental cruelty was claimed because of my deceit and criminal activity.

I was actually glad the pressure was off. There was a lot of pressure behind my marriage. Gavin is my son and I love him. I love Carol because we were childhood sweethearts. There is always that feeling. The last thing Carol said to me on the phone was, "I love you and I'll always love you."

I was coming back from trial and went to see my mother. We were in a very emotional mood. I was sitting on the stairs in her house and we started to cry. She said, "What's going on?" I had a job, I coached a soccer team, a football team, a baseball team. I was an active pillar in the community. No one knew I was doing safes.

After my sentence I was sent to Drumheller and then to Collins Bay in Ontario. Collins Bay is a heavy medium. It's an old place. You're double-bunked. You've got no room at all, so you get aggravated very quick and learn that you have to watch the next guy to you all the time. You're living in a place where you're constantly looking over your shoulder. People got stabbed left, right and centre. Screwdrivers sticking out of heads. All kinds of blood, guts, teeth, eyeballs, ears. I became a cornered animal.

I spend 10 months in Millhaven. Millhaven is a trippy, trippy place. Dead guys. If you look in the wrong direction, at the wrong time, someone would say, "What the fuck are you looking at?" Millhaven is death. There are a lot of weird, dangerous people.

I lost Carol. Gavin and I kept in contact. I get a total of five years. I'm in Collins Bay from 1983 to 1986. That's where I ran into Daphne. She came up to see me with my sister. I'm vulnerable, I guess. I'm like a puppy looking for it's mother's tit.

Daphne is finally accepted on my list. Then we start a correspondence thing. The next thing I know I'm seeing her. Then we're kissing each other. Then I'm going out for parole. I get out of Collins Bay on May 7, 1986. Daphne comes to get me and I go to a halfway house.

I saw my father maybe six months after I got out of the halfway house. My grandmother is the first person I go see. I see her maybe a week after I'm out. I don't see her. I don't see my Nanny. I see a skinny, frail woman who says she knows me from church. Her and I used to go to church all the time. She weighed about 92 pound. She used to be a 5-10 woman, 130 pounds. She couldn't even butter her bread. That totally destroyed me. It just ripped me apart. She's dying of Alzheimer's. My grandmother was my rock. She was my whole world.

When I went to jail, in 1982, she was healthy. My grandfather had never written me a letter. I received a letter from my sister who told me she was sick. No one had told me she had Alzheimer's disease. When I got out and went to see her, it just shocked the living…it tripped every emotion in my mind. Of course, I was mad at myself for not being there for her when she was sick.

I was pissed off when I left the first time. I was very mad at myself for not being there for her because I wanted to remember her as she was, as being very stern, very gentle, very soft. A strong woman. When I'd seen her that way it just hurt, unbelievably. After I saw my grandmother I just tucked it away. I put it in behind the wall, along with everything else in my life.

That's the time when everything sort of piled up. I was terribly upset with myself because I wasn't there when I should have been. She had given me everything in my life. The only thing she really wanted was some support. And I wasn't there. I was in jail. That was a hard one to swallow. It still is *(suppressed crying)*.

Daphne was there when I first saw my grandmother. That's the only way I could get there. She drove me there. I didn't have a vehicle. After my grandmother we were supposed to go see her parents. I got along well with her father. Her father and I fished together. We went to her father's and he's having a barbecue. I tell him I'm a vegetarian. In 1986 I started weaning off meat in Collins Bay. I felt I shouldn't eat any more red meat. She knows I'm a vegetarian. When he says, "How do you like your steak?" I say, "I'm a vegetarian."

He looks stunned. "No, no. You have to eat."

"I'll eat some vegetables."

He looked all offended. She said to me, "You're really insulting him if you don't eat."

It's the first time we're here. So I ate meat which made me feel just bitter and frustrated as all hell because I had changed my mind to satisfy other people. That stupid wanting to compromise so it's no problem. I felt angry.

I went back to see my grandmother a week-and-a-half later. My grandfather and grandmother were having lunch and she couldn't put tomato on the bread, she couldn't put mayonnaise on the tomato, she couldn't even make her tea. I stayed through lunch. I was angry at myself that I hadn't been there for her. Yeah (*at this point he talks slowly, heavy emotions boiling the words, loosening them, making spaces, making them guttural, deep, heavy*). To tuck that away I needed some cement, I needed a whole truckload to dump that in the back. But it came out. My wall broke down over a period of time and she died in 1987, December.

I'm working for Underground Services. I'm doing the O'Connell Bridge in Ottawa. I run a six-man crew. I am operating a 15-pound jackhammer. It was all overhead work. You stood up and held that hammer above you all day long. And I could keep it there all day long. I loved it. Smash all that brick. This is the summer. I'm pounding out the jackhammer and living at the halfway house at the same time. I'm here for four months.

September, I get out of the halfway house. Daphne picks me up. When I first moved into my apartment, it was me alone for maybe two months. Carol gave me some things. I got a dog, Shimo. Daphne liked Shimo. Then I find out that Daphne is a teenage alcoholic and she's only 18 years old. I was 32 at the time. But it's enjoyable and the sex is great. Now she wants a cat. I don't like cats.

She was dumping all her problems on top of me. Talking about her father. Now her father wouldn't give her the money he said he would. She has a fight with her parents and doesn't want to go home. Can she stay here tonight? Next thing I knew all her bags are moved in. Once everything is in, what do I do?

She said, "I can't go back home."

I said, "Go home, you're allowed home."

"What will I tell them? I have to tell them what's going on."

"So tell them. Just get out. Go home." I said it so many damn times.

"Go home. You don't belong here."

She was a tidal wave that hit me. There was a bag here, a box there, dishes. Clothes started to appear here and there. Then the decor was changing. Things were added. I didn't have a coffee table. She said we needed one.

I said, "I don't have any money."

She said, "You have all that change."

I used to take all my change and throw it in jars. She counted it all out and rolled it. There was $400. The next thing I know she's fully moved in and I'm supporting her going to school. A one-bedroom apartment is not good enough for her. I ended up renting a $562 apartment. She just crowded every room.

I didn't want to do any criminal acts. I had a bunch of old friends coming and dropping off cocaine. We're tripping on coke, on mushrooms. She was 18 and exploring a little bit. I wasn't a big drug person. I never drank heavily before in my life. But I drank in those two years. Once my grandmother had died, that's when things started hitting home.

I was seeing my son every second week at the time. I wasn't on coke or alcohol when I'd see him. I was on drugs in between the periods I see him. She had to be there every time I saw Gavin. It was creating a conflict all the time. Plus I was having my own conflicts in life. This is when I went fishing with my brother.

I got out in May and she died in December. I go to the funeral. I don't let all my feelings out. I don't think anyone knew exactly what that loss was to me *(a lot of gulping and swallowing)*. Only me *(he's crying)*. She was my life.

The spring and fall always makes me think of my grandmother, those were her favourite times of the year. In the spring she would do her flowers. She loved flowers. I'd dig up her garden and turn it over. She'd plant the bulbs. We'd talk. In the fall she admired the colours. In the winter she used to go tobogganing with me every night. She used to skate with me. My grandfather never came.

I lost my friend *(a big gulp)*. A friend, my love. I'd say she was my connection to the world *(crying)*. There's a lot of pain that she's gone. Still today. Never said anything to anybody about the way I felt. When I saw she was dying and when she died, the booze was a suppresser, a tranquillizer.

After the wake I took my grandfather downstairs and we talked. He

110

told me what happened. They had separate cots in the downstairs bedroom. She came over to his bed, crawled into his arms and said, "Just hold me." She said something to the effect, "This is it. I'm dying. It's over." She was clear at the end.

The summer after my grandmother's burial I was in the boat with Don. I wanted to smash him in the head and couldn't figure out why until I was sitting there longer and had this vision of me being in the upstairs bedroom and him jumping on me and rubbing himself on me like a dog. Whoa, where did that come from? It was quite shocking and devastating for me until I tucked it behind my wall.

My father was renovating the house at the time my mother left. The upstairs bedroom was going to be theirs and then it was Don's. He was mad at me because I was in his territory. He was 12 or 13. I was six or seven at the time, still living at my grandmother's. This is where my brother pounced on me, rubbed himself on me like a dog and told me I was pregnant, then laughed. I was scared. What are you doing? I didn't understand any of it. I was just there for the weekend so I never breathed a word about this. I blocked it off. I never told anyone until I got arrested on this charge. Then I told my sister in the visiting room in Hull. She got a look on her face, sort of surprised but not totally surprised. She grinned in recognition. My automatic thought was that the son of a bitch had done it to her too. We quickly went off the subject.

The relationship with Daphne works when we're both high and I'm not apt to get high all the time. If I'm not high, it's a constant conflict. The only time we have any fun is when drugs are around. She liked to smoke and drink a lot. If I go out for a walk, it's always, "Where are you going?"

"I'm just leaving."

"I hope she's a good fuck."

I have no concentration. My mind isn't staying in one spot. I can't keep my mind still. I go to another company. Also working on a jackhammer. I could have gone all over Canada. It would have been nice. It would have been the first time, after getting out, I would have had something to look forward to. I went and talked to my parole officer and he said, "Yeah, I think it's a great idea. I'll give you the passes you need to do it."

I went home and spoke to her. She said, "What about Gavin? What about me? I'm going to school, how am I going to live here?" I ended up changing my mind.

I got a job as a night foreman. There was a 15-man crew. We were going to work on the Holiday Inn, doing underground parking. Now she doesn't like the idea of me working nights. Can I change that? Then all of a sudden this job wasn't good enough for her because I would come home with my boots and jeans dirty. Now I'm driving a truck and dumping off Pepsi and Ginger Ale. Most fucking boring job I ever done in my life.

I'm losing control of my life. I go to pick up Gavin at eight in the morning and she has to be at work for seven. She's got a car but she wants me to drive her in. I drive her in, then pick up Gavin. If Gavin and I wanted to go to a movie, we couldn't because I had to be there to pick her up. On the weekends I don't see Gavin without her. She's always gotta be there.

I had a good relationship with my son and probably still will when I see him some day. I don't know where he is. The last time I spoke to Gavin was on the phone in 1988, in Hull. He asked, "How long this time, Dad?" Those were his exact words.

Choking back my emotions from coming out and ruining the telephone call, I said, "I don't know. I just don't know. The one thing you can always be sure of in your life is that I love you. That you can be sure of. I may not be there for a while but I love you."

He was 11 at the time. Now he's 21. I know Carol's name is still my last name. I've got the numbers but I haven't built up the courage to phone.

Now Daphne wants to open a jewellery business. Silvers Original. I said, "Who's going to sell it?"

She said, "You could sell it."

"Yeah, I've done some sales, but…" I took it around. Some drinking started to take effect when I tried to drown the feelings coming up. Then I didn't want to come home anymore because it wasn't nice to come home. It was just like going home when I was a kid. You knew you were in trouble even if you knew you didn't do nothing. I'm in a relationship I don't want to be in.

Then finally I get rid of her. Daphne is gone. She's not involved in my life anymore. But I'm still all fucked up. The wall is coming down. All the things that ever happened to me in my life, all the rejections, the pain, the disrespect, not being loved and being called stupid and dumb, being dumped around when I was a kid, my grandmother's death, everything is coming up. Life is going to hell. My whole wall is coming down. Reality is kicking me in the face. I was seeing all these things in my mind, remembering all these things. I tried drinking them away. I tried partying them away.

Finally I went to the Royal Ottawa Hospital. I walked into emergency and said, "I want to see somebody."

Out came this girl. "What seems to be the problem?"

"I don't know what the problem is but I have no concentration at all."

"Are you afraid you might hurt somebody?"

"That's a good possibility."

"Are you on any type of parole or probation?"

"Yeah, I'm on parole."

"From where?"

"From a federal penitentiary."

"Oh, you have to see someone special. He's not available at this time. We'll call you back on Wednesday and make an appointment."

I went home and sat by the phone. It finally rang. That was June 7. They set up an appointment for me on October 23. I phoned my mother. I said, "I have a problem and need some help."

I don't call my father, I call my mother. She asked me if this has anything to do with Daphne. I said no. I said my whole life was coming at me all at once and I just didn't know what to do with it. I couldn't put anything into place. I need someone to speak to. She said it costs a lot of money to talk to somebody. Like a psychologist. I guess she figured that I wanted her to pay for it. She said, "I'll see what I can do." She didn't want to know anything about it.

I moved out of the condominium. I've got four bedrooms in that house with a freezer downstairs, a washer/dryer, a couch, chairs, a dining room table, a kitchen table, a bedroom set. I move all of that myself in my truck except the freezer and washer/dryer. I move out to my sister's place, Christine. She has a spare bedroom. All my stuff is going out there. I'm happy I'm making this move.

She said, "How are you going to move the freezer?"

I said, "I don't know."

She looked at Roy, her boyfriend, and said, "Go, help him."

This is on the long weekend, Labour Day. I'm moving all that weekend, doing 10 loads a day. I'm driving home in my truck. It's two o'clock in the morning. I'm not moving anything. I was at a bar with friends and coming home. I stop on the side of the road and start crying, hitting the dash and kicking the inside of my truck, freaking out. I can't understand why. Shimo is trying to lick my face. I have him with me all the time. I go home.

I laid down on the couch and Roy comes over that morning to move the freezer. He comes at 9:30 and I haven't really slept. Now him and I move the freezer. We make two or three loads that day out to my sister's place. An old friend of ours phones in the middle of the day and says, "Tell Bert I haven't seen him in years." He wants us to come over. We stopped over there for a couple of drinks. Then go back, do another load. Come back and have a couple of drinks. Then do another load. Then stop at six o'clock and drink right through to 11. Now Christine is calling Roy and I don't know he's supposed to be home. I'm in a good mood talking with Mike. There are a few people there. More come over with wine. He's got hash. I've got Moroccan in my truck. Shimo is there. He's running around chasing Mike's bitch. Everybody's in a good mood.

That day I probably consumed 16-20 pints of beer, a little shot of wine here and there, and a joint here and there. Feeling all right. We have Chinese food with Mike before we leave. I have a shower at their place. Roy doesn't want to leave. He wants to stay and have a few more beers. We're leaving now. We're going home. I'm plastered. He's plastered. I pull up and we unload the last load.

As I'm leaving my sister is pulling up in the driveway. Roy is in the house pissed. I can tell from her eyes she is very upset. I said, "Don't be upset at me. I didn't do nothing." Now I know that Roy was supposed to be home. We're supposed to have a barbecue. She had laid everything out on the table and we didn't show up. But I didn't know this then, so I kept driving. I'm in a perfectly good mood. Everything is fine.

I get to Hull at midnight, to a bar looking for Janet, a barmaid I know. There's no one in the bar. It's dead. It's the long weekend so a lot of people are away. I talk to Janet then say, "OK, I'll see you later." I had to go to Dion's to meet a friend of mine. Dion's is a little more crowded. I'm talking to this girl but my friend doesn't show up. I'm drinking Sambuca with beer chasers. I'm totalled. All of sudden I hear something like last call. Now I have to go back and see Janet. I stumble out the door and go down the street to the first bar.

The door is closed. They're not letting anyone in. I say, "Listen, I want to see Janet." The bouncer says, "Tuck your shirt in," and opens the door.

So I go to the bar at the back. I'm talking to her and she's half dancing with this guy in the bar. She introduces me to him and then he walks away. I'm still talking to her. Then he comes back and bang, the fight's on between him and I plus two other bouncers and the manager. They are fighting me. I haven't done nothing. I'm drunk so I can't really fight back to save my life. I'm sort of covering myself up. I got kicks and punches. My blood is being spewed all over. They're taking me to the door. I've got a white shirt on and it's all covered in blood.

I'm asking this guy, "Why?"

The guy says to me at the door, "Norm did it." They throw me out. I'm half-dazed.

All of a sudden the door swings open and these guys are coming out after me again. I booted it across the street. They grab a hold of me just as I get to my truck and start beating the shit out of me again. I got about eight or nine shots on the side of the head. He almost knocks me out. I fall down and get up. I'm all screwed up now because I don't know why this is happening. I can feel the tears coming down. I open the side of my truck door and they're all standing, yelling at me from the sidewalk. This is when I snapped. I'm crying as I'm driving down the main street. I felt the anger coming, the adrenaline pumping. The name Norm stuck in my head. I'm enraged now. I'm driving down the street, crying, and can feel the surge of energy come from my spine to the back of my head. I said, oh, no, no, no. I know it's something I'm not going to be able to control.

I didn't have any idea where I was, but I was wide awake and could hardly see. I couldn't see the street signs to let me know what street I was on. I had to stop the vehicle, get out and walk over to try and figure out what the sign said. I was heading back to my place. Instead I ended up at Daphne's place, all bloody, and scream through the window. I want to use her phone. She came to the door.

All I said was, "Look what they did to me, look what Norm did to me." I thought they had tried to kill me.

"He said he was going to get you," was her comment.

She started to move her hand toward my face and I knocked it away.

115

I said, "Don't ever fucking touch me."

I think that's when things connected. She had gone out with Norm at our break up in April of the year before. Her and I got together for a little fling shortly after that. Then I tried to throw her out with all the jewellery and she had said, "You'll be sorry." She had manipulated this idiot into jumping me in the bar. She had sicked this guy on me.

I went into the bathroom to take a look at my face. It was all swollen, huge. I had blood all over me. I snapped. I come out of the bathroom calling for a gun. I was going back to the bar to kill everyone. Then all of a sudden I tell her, "You're going with me." I take her out of the apartment.

I know my gun has been taken to my sister's. I boot it down the Queensway. I'm yelling all sorts of obscenities at her because now I've realized that it's her fault that I'm in this situation. I'm going down the Queensway from side to side and all over the place and she's screaming and yelling, I'm screaming and yelling. I'm dying that night. I'm telling her that all my belongings must go to Gavin and if she keeps anything of mine I'll come back to haunt her till the day she dies.

I'm driving out to my sister's place. It's three or four in the morning. There's no traffic. I see the little light come on. We need gas. I get to my sister's place and I call out for Roy. He comes downstairs and I say, "I want my gun."

He doesn't ask me any questions. He was looking at the side of my face which was huge. He brings my rifle down. I take it out to the Jeep and try to start it. It won't start. I'm out of gas. My sister's car is ahead of my Jeep Cherokee. I take a 50-foot garden hose. I slice each end off, shove one end in her gas tank and I'm sucking on the other. This is 50 feet long. I'm sucking on this, trying to get the gas out of her car and put it into mine. I don't have a set of Michelin lungs, so I can't get the gas. I have two gas cans that I've moved. I know they're there. I go into the shed. I'm crushing everything. I'm ripping, fucking mad.

I find the gas can. I pour gas in the Jeep. I've got the gun out of its case. I shove in one of my clips. I can't load the clips. She's loading the clips. I've left my sister's place. Driving down the highway I fire 10 rounds into the air. Then I point the gun to my nog and I'm yelling at her to kill me, to pull the trigger, just pull the fucking trigger. I lose control of the Jeep and go into a ditch. It's a four-wheel drive. I get out of the ditch, so my motor skills are working. We're back down the highway. I'm screaming and yelling.

All of a sudden she says the bar is closed so I'm all screwed up now. She says, "He's at home."

"OK, you know where he lives."

She tells me. Every exit I see I want to know if this is the exit I should get off at. I don't know my way around anymore. She has to tell me where to go. She tells me, "Go left. Turn that way."

I wouldn't have known what was right or left. I keep saying, "Are we there yet, are we there yet?"

We get there and she says, "He's not home." I went around the back. Took her out of the truck. This is 5:30 in the morning. I kicked in the side door to his house. We go in. I go to the end room and there is someone. I have no idea what Norm looks like. This guy there is not the guy I've envisioned in my mind who was pounding the fuck out of me before. He's sleeping. I'm making a lot of noise. First he goes, "Shhh." I take the gun and stab him with it in the mouth. I didn't scream the name Norm. It wasn't the right face to go with the name. I poked him with the barrel because he wouldn't wake up. I shove the gun into his mouth. As I'm pulling the gun back, he reaches up, grabs hold of the barrel. The gun is at hip level. Of course my finger is in the trigger cage of the rifle. I'm pulling and he's pulling at the same time. The finger came back, it's a semi-automatic, a .308 Winchester, and so it just went boom, boom, boom, boom. Four shots.

She's the one that says, "Let's get out of here." She rubs her prints off the door with the curtain. She testified to this in court. Prints were the farthest thing from my mind. I hadn't committed a crime that was preplanned. I don't know he's dead.

After we left his place, I drove to her house. We showered. After the shower I put the same clothes back on. I haven't slept. I drop her off at work and get in touch with a friend of mine. I told him I shot someone. He totally removed all evidence of any blood. Shoes, pants, shirt, socks. I guess you could say the criminal mind went into effect. He cleaned everything. I destroyed the gun.

That whole day I had no idea who was dead. She knew who was dead. When I got home she was at home. I found out I had killed Norm that night on the news.

She says, "Do you know what happened?"

I say, "No, not really."

I got arrested that night. They questioned her. She said she knew nothing. She said I came home at three in the morning and went to sleep on the couch. When she got up for work, I was still on the couch and I drove her to work. They kept me for 72 hours. I came into the house and she said, "I knew they couldn't keep you."

I was still dazed. The days moved on. All of a sudden she got the idea that she wanted to move out to the country. We go out and rent a place together. The day we actually rented the place and I put the cheque down is the same day I was arrested.

The only reason they could hold me was because they put me back in on parole violation. I violated parole because I moved without giving them notification. Now they can do an investigation with me inside. They're putting pressure on outside people for information.

I'm talking to my father this time. I just called him to tell him I'm back in jail. He said, "Yeah, the cops have been here."

He came to see me before the trial. I told him I was glad Nanny wasn't alive to see this part now. I tried to talk to him about our lives. I asked if he remembered slapping me around the kitchen? He said, "No, I don't remember that." I didn't get much of a response. He just wasn't interested in talking to me about that. But he came to see me every Wednesday, so I tried to get little things in here and there for that eight months.

I made two phone calls to my mother. She knew. It was in the paper.

I said, "I need you to testify to the fact that I phoned you."

She said, "I'll think about it."

Then I tried to phone after that and the number was changed. I talked to my lawyer and he subpoenaed her. She took off down south. She stayed there the whole eight months. My mother wouldn't come to the trial to testify because it was too much publicity for her good name. They would find out she has a son outside of the one she has at home.

They have no proof yet. But Daphne has talked. After they arrested me, she went to see two lawyers. I think she believed she could gain something out of it. You see, she wanted to write a book on her sexual experiences, like Xaviera Hollander. She had the photo of every guy she had sex with and how many orgasms she got from each one. I was in the book. I wasn't a violent criminal but I was still a criminal, so I think that was the element that excited her. The people I knew excited her even more. She went on a Witness Protection Program. She was supposed to be the big centre of attraction. She's playing a part. Daphne had her hair died, is wearing these glasses and she's like in a spy movie. She's testifying. It's exciting for her. She's changed roles. She's gone from my side to the other side because they have something to offer. They send her to modelling school.

Now there's a date for a preliminary hearing. I feel numb. My father was at my trial. My sister testified for me. On the 19th they take me to Hull and that's the day I was formally charged with first-degree murder. I was sentenced in March 1989. I'm doing 25 years to life. In April I filed a judgement for appeal.

When I was convicted I was sent to Archambault. It took me three months to see the psychologist. I see him twice a week for three or four hours a day. I have things I have to get off my chest. I needed to dump it out of my memory bank and put it out on the table. Once it's on the table I can root through it, put it in order. I want to try to straighten things out. Of course, I got teased by all the guys. "Where are you going? You nuts?"

I laid out my life to the psychologist and faced that I had taken someone's life. I feel devastated that I took someone's life. How could I have done that? Then I wanted to know how it developed. Where did all of this come from? How could I have been so angry, so out of control, that I killed him? I had to take my life and sort it out. I had no road maps. It's all turnpikes and off-ramps. Nothing was ever settled when I was a child. I had to try and settle things. Some parts I had to give up on like my mother. There's no more communication there and there never will be. I guess I could say I forgive her for not showing up and turning her back on me. I forgive her for it, but I want nothing to do with her.

I never used to say squat before in my life because I never knew what to say to people. When I was living at my grandmother's I was very talkative. When I went to live with my father, everything changed because you were scared to say something. How would it be interpreted? I just clamed up. I lived a functional life but always had an internal conflict. I think the real me was trying to get out but the other part was just more powerful because it stopped me from feeling. I was very insensitive in my life. I used to think I'm so much like my father and I was like him. But I was very sensitive. Carol knew who I was at

119

one time because when I first met her I was living with my grand-mother. She knew I was there, she just didn't know where I had put myself. I was trying to figure my life out.

The psychologist isn't saying anything. I'm sort of talking to myself but only with a person in front of me. There were quite a few emo-tional sessions when I got into my grandmother, my sister, my father. I'd ask him, "What would provoke or possess a person to do this sort of thing?" Now I'm trying to justify everyone's actions, find a good reason for what they've done. I had to figure them out. I'm blaming me for their actions, but I can't do that because that's what I've been doing. This is what happened. Accept it.

I go from kindergarten right up to present day. Takes me almost a year. But when I terminated it I was at peace with myself. I felt life was gorgeous, beautiful. All of a sudden you can handle pressure. Your day is done and you've accomplished something even if you just cleaned the toilet in your cell. It's done. You feel great.

I'm recommended by the Correctional Officer to come to Federal Training Centre. I get transferred all right but I go to Donnacona. They figure I need more time in a maximum. In Donnacona I didn't care if you liked me or not. Anything I do from now on has to be for me. That was in 1991. I've tried ever since then to take responsibility for what I've done in my life and let people have responsibility for what they've done. I want to be burden-free. It took me almost a year to put it all out on the table but it's taken me 10 years to put what I have together today.

I went to school in Donnacona. I did my math. When the guy sat me down and said, "Divide this," everything started to come back. It was all in there but it just wasn't put to use. I finished my high school. Going to school gave me confidence to know I can accomplish things. It's given me the problem-solving which I never had. I would step over the problem so the problem didn't exist. School has matured me.

I have a better idea of myself. I know I'm stubborn. Even in the welding class, I was welding and I'd do it my way. My teacher stopped me and said, "I'm the teacher, this is the way it's to be done and this is the only way to do it. You do it my way." I had my own idea of how it should be done. I didn't know how to do it but I was trying to do it my way anyway. It took another step in my life to say, OK, he's the teacher. I'm supposed to learn it, I'm not supposed to teach him how to do it.

I won my appeal in 1991, almost 1992. Then I became a remand again and went to Parthenais Detention Centre in Montreal. I have no sentence anymore, I'm not a federal case. I'm lined up for a new trial. I wrote journals at Parthenais for two-and-a-half-years. I wrote out everything that ever happened to me in life. I'm writing, reading, exercising. I read some 180 books in Parthenais. I read my first book there. I read every night. I never even read the newspaper before that.

I'm talking to a black fellow from Philadelphia. I talk to him about my father kicking me around, calling me a dunce. Jay was looking at me, "You're no dunce, you're not stupid." He was an older man. He was intelligent. He had grown up with the Black Panthers in Philadelphia. He talked about his mother. His mother used to hit him with a little stick. She used to shake it at him. We got personal. He talked to me about where he grew up, what jobs he had. We talked about reality.

My understanding has come very gradually, since 1992, when I started writing my diaries about who I was. After this crime I thought I was insane because of what happened. I thought maybe I had multiple personalities. Where did I find all this sensitivity from? I never cried in my life before. What am I? Who am I? Multiple personalities or just one person?

When I looked over my diaries I saw that I was quite sane. I just didn't get a lot of the attention I should have gotten when I was little. I began to understand why I did a lot of things. Why did I cause a lot of trouble in school? I needed some attention. I was very agitated all the time and I was very quick to react. I'd sucker you. I'd give you an uppercut, left hook, or a right jam.

Now I don't dwell on my past. I've dealt with it. It's finished. It exists as a memory because it'll never go away. That's the thing you have to accept, you can't shut it out. Now when it comes back I can chuckle, I might shed a tear, but most of the time, yeah, that's life. I've lived it and gotten through it. Now I have to move on. It's taken me 43 years to learn that.

I talked to the psychiatrist, then to my Correctional Officer, then to me in my head, then to Janet, a volunteer, then to the pastor here. Now I don't need people around me. I can be happy with me, be alone and it doesn't bother me. I don't need the money to attract the friendships. First time in my life. The dream of having a mansion with a Jaguar and a Corvette is all over. I thought it would give me status with my mother.

In June of 1994 I went back to trial again. It took three years to get the second trial. Christine testified to what life was like for me growing up. I was always the rejected one, no one wanted me. It was very emotional for me to see her up there because I knew she was hurting. I didn't want her to testify. At the second trial I got second-degree murder and 10 years. I have one year left. It's ten life.

Now I'm sent to Cowansville. Cowansville is where I finish my secondary five. My English and Poetry. On November 7, 1996, I go to minimum. I learned how to budget my money in here. I've had so much of it and spent it so crazily. I needed three pairs of running shoes and I bought them over a period of six months.

The murder actually made me grab a hold of my life and say, look, this is what you were. You've got to put away all these stupid ideas that you've had, that people have given you, if you want to have any kind of life outside after this sentence is finished.

I want to put dreams away, the dreams and fantasies I had as a child. There is no perfect life where nothing ever goes wrong. Before, when everything had to be so perfect, when something went wrong I was devastated, angry.

Before the murder I wasn't happy with myself. I wasn't at peace with myself. Now I live my life to the fullest and accept the consequences. You can live your life to the fullest without being against the law.

I wish the murder had never taken place. I could say I was mad at him before. I'm not mad at him anymore. I'm also not mad at myself anymore. I've come to peace with it. The first thing I had to do was try to forgive myself for the murder because I never meant to kill him. I never meant to kill that groundhog when I shot him out in the field. But to take responsibility I have to stand up and forgive myself for that action.

If I could give his family some comfort and say I wish it had never happened, I would see them. And yes, I wish it had never happened. His daughter was six at the time of the murder, so I know what it is for her not have a father. I know what it must be like for Gavin, even though I am not dead.

I say a prayer for his daughter, his mother and his father every night of my life. I say a prayer for him and his soul. I've done it since 1988. First it just started as a thought. I don't always kneel down and pray; sometimes I pray in bed, lying down. What difference does it make? I can be sitting on the toilet and pray. How can I ever make up for it? Well, I can't. I feel the only way I can actually do anything is to say a small prayer.

I think it probably came from my grandmother. I always said my prayers when I was a kid. I didn't continue to pray when I went to my father's. Being there sort of destroyed everything. It started again in here. My son Gavin is the first prayer. I say a prayer for my grandmother. My prayer for her probably prompted me to pray for Norm and his family. Now my list has grown for health and happiness for a lot of people.

Would I have taken my life apart like I did, and try and restructure it and rebuild it and find out who I am, had I not committed the murder?

The loss of his life has given me my life, has made me realize that life has to be lived, has to be enjoyed. Taking a life has given me a greater vision of what life could be. I would say that the loss of his life and me being responsible for it has given me a sense of responsibility to live my life to the potential that it has.

I really have to say that my life is coming together. It's a long way to go but it's coming. I feel happy.

MARY

A parole officer puts me in touch with a halfway house and tells me there is an Inuit girl from northern Quebec staying there for a few months before her trial. She would be an interesting subject to interview and it might also be good for her to tell her story. She is lonely, knows no one in the city.

I call her. Yes, she wants to talk. Wants her story known. She said, "I don't want anyone to live through what I went through."

Over the phone there is a sweet, light, little-girl quality to her voice. In person Mary (32) is shy, almost retreating. About 5-2, she is attractively plump, soft, with rounded features, inviting curves. Her voice has a caressing, tender sensuality about it. At the start of the interview she is reserved with a bashful smile. There is an underlying tense nervousness to the seemingly calm welcome. It's not easy for her to talk, to reveal intimate details about her life, but she's resolved to do it. I am so surprised when at intermittent times during the interview a light, carefree giggle bursts from her, illuminating her entire being. It's a shy giggle that glitters, seems to float on sunbeams. There is an airy lightness to it, filled with the purity of joy that makes her story even sadder. I could see the potential for her to be a carefree, generous, happy soul.

The interview spanned a two-month period. Sometimes it was hard to see her: she became so depressed, being away from the North and her children, that she had tried to commit suicide. But she was determined to finish the interview, determined, though scared, to go back to her hometown up north for her trial.

I come from Great Whale River, in northern Quebec. I never went to jail before. When my husband died I kept on going to jail because I broke my probation. In the past two years I've gone to jail 11 times. I was drinking and I wasn't allowed to drink. But I was lonely. I was living with my parents till I was 17. Then I met my husband. I was with him for 13 years.

He died the night he tried to kill me. I stabbed him with a knife three times on his upper arm. He wouldn't stop. If I would have wanted to kill him, I would have done it on his stomach or chest. I called the nursing station and they never came. They said I called six times. I went to neighbours and they couldn't come right away. I went outside to look for a person to help and no one was around.

After I got knocked out I said to myself, I have to save myself because I was really afraid he would kill my kids, too. Even to their face he says, "I can kill you." Everyone knew he was violent but no one did anything. Once he went to jail for beating me up and when he came back I really got it.

I used to say to myself, how could my mother take it, my father beating her? How come she's not just leaving him? I said to myself, I would never marry a man like this. I don't want to be like my mother. But I was the same. I married a man just like my father.

All I remember is my mom getting hit from my father all my life. He even tried to kill her. They were drinking and drinking. My mother didn't want to drink anymore but my father used to force her to drink.

I'm the second youngest. I have four brothers and two sisters. We always had to say yes to him. We had to go home at nine or 10 o'clock because they were going to the bar. If my sister and I are 10 or 20 minutes late, we'd get it. We had to be home to babysit our younger brother, the boy my mother adopted. He killed himself as soon as he turned 18 while he was in prison. When he broke up with his girlfriend he got mad and my parents were afraid of him now because he was bigger. My father used to really beat him.

My older sister, who is a year-and-a-half older than me, was my best friend while we were growing up. She used to get it a lot. My father used to say, "She's not my daughter." He was sure I was his daughter, but he still beat me.

Two years ago my sister finally remembered that my father was sexually abusing her when she was a little girl. I remember my father used to go to her room after she had passed out drunk. When I was 12 years old I walked into the room and her pants weren't on. I tried to put them back on. As a teenager she used to drink and just pass out on the bed. All of a sudden her pants weren't on anymore. He used to say, "My

126

daughter took her pants off again," but he was the one doing that. When my sister was drunk she would say, "Watch my father, don't let him come to my room." But I can't stop him.

My older brothers and sister, who is nine years older than me, hardly saw us getting beaten because they went to high school in Ottawa. That's why my father could get away with it, beating us up and even my mom, because my two brothers are not there anymore. But when they were small I think they were afraid of my father, too. My mom told me that he beat up everyone, but when my two oldest brothers got bigger he stopped hitting them because they were too big and they could hit him back. I used to tell my oldest brother that my mom got hit from my father. And my mom says, "No, I don't, we're OK."

One time they came from school for the Christmas holidays and everyone got drunk except my second-oldest brother. He came in while my mom was really getting beaten and he almost killed my father. That was the first time he ever saw my mom getting beaten but he had been hearing about it. My mother always denied it because she was afraid they could do something to my father. When my brother came in while my mother was getting beaten he said, "I can fight back, why don't you fight me?"

My brother was hitting my father and all my father said was, "Stop it, stop it."

"You don't stop while you beat up my mother. Why should I stop? Why don't I just kill you because I've been hearing my sisters tell me that you beat her all the time. You used to do that to everybody. You still do that?"

He tried to kill him with a stick but my mom stopped him. Then my brothers had to go back to school.

I used to look at my mother really having a hard time. It's so cold in the north and in the winter time he would kick her out only in her pyjamas so she could freeze. Not even socks. One night it was 11 o'clock. My sister and I are coming home and I said, "Can I smoke first before we go in?" I used to hide my cigarettes under the house. I was trying to find them and could hear somebody moaning under the house. I said to my sister, "There's a little puppy." She started to ask the puppy to come out. But my mom came out from under the house with only pyjamas and no socks. That really scared me. We asked her how long she'd been out. She said she didn't know.

My mother tried to stop my father beating us, but he never listened to her. She even cries when she sees us get beaten up. Sometimes when she is saying too much, he turned on her: "You're letting this happen!" Blaming her. But she tried to protect us.

One time she even had a gun on my father, to try to stop what he was doing. "If you touch my children ever again I'm going to shoot you. I can't look at my children get beaten up from their father."

I was about 14 or 15. But he still continued to beat us up. My mother was afraid of my father. She used to have to say yes to him, too. He says he's the man of the house. One time my mom went away to have a baby on a little island in Moose Knee. It was pretty far away and we all stayed home. One night I heard my father talking to my mother on the phone: "If you don't come home early, if you don't have that baby early, I'm going to burn the house down and kill my kids and take one of them with me." That was me. He thought everyone was sleeping. I was maybe 10 or 11. I was planning to save my sisters if he's going to do it, so I didn't sleep all night until I hear him snoring. My mom got the baby the next morning.

I started drinking when I was 12 years old. I used to steal my parents' alcohol, have a little shot and put it back. I got high but I couldn't get drunk. I was scared of my father. But I got drunk inside the house when I was 14. I was stealing some alcohol from my older sister. Then I didn't remember anything. I woke up. All vomit and everything. Disgusting. My father saw. My sister told me that he beat me up while I was drunk and he let me stay in the room all by myself in my vomit. The next morning I really got it. He beat me with a stick.

My sister and I used to hide a lot. We had two hiding places where no one could find us—over the furnace inside the house and under the roof. We could see people passing by but they can't see us. Later I was the wildest of all the girls. I was going out of the windows and my parents didn't know. My sister couldn't do it because she was too afraid they might find out. I walked around, went with my friends, then came back through the same window and he never found out. I had my own room. I could lock it. So I used to take risks. I said, OK, it's one beating, I'm used to it and I'll get over it.

I wanted to be bossy maybe because I was looking at my father being bossy. In school I could go to another student and be bossy on them. I got into trouble with my principal all the time. I didn't care about anything. My principal asked me if I had ever seen anyone hitting someone. I didn't say anything. I was scared of my father because if I tell he may turn on me. I was like my son but I never used to break anything. I could get mad easily. If the principal is trying to talk to me, I ran away from him because I knew he's not going to hit me. He's not my father.

I had a boyfriend when I was 13 and used to go to parties with him. But sometimes I used to get into fights with girls. There was a lot of fighting going on because the Cree and Inuit used to fight a lot. We were fighting for our land. We didn't want them in our community. They would come to our dances and had a really hard time because we didn't let them go in. They'd have to come in a big group. They used to beat up our people so we paid them back. But right now we're starting to be friends. People are even starting to get married.

My father doesn't like it when my sister has a boyfriend. He is still fussy about my sister, the one who is a year-and-a-half older than me. Even today. When she goes out and stays out late, he gets mad at her. Jealous mad. She's still having a hard time with my father. She's not married. She finished school and got pregnant right away by her boyfriend while she was in Montreal. My father stopped with her when she started getting bigger.

When my parents aren't home I used to cry to my oldest brother on the phone because he was my favourite brother. He's 14 or 15 years older than me. I used to tell him, "It's hard, I don't like it, my father is violent, he beats us up." I'd ask him to come home because I am tired of being hit. So one day he quit school and finally came home. I remember he came home with candies for us and it was so nice. It looked like everything started to change. There was still drinking and they were still arguing but my mom was getting less hit. My brother goes out for the weekend to parties with friends, so when he's not around my mother is still getting hit but not on the face so my brother wouldn't see it.

One day, after my mom got really beaten up and she's just lying down in the morning, I said to my father, "I want to get out of here. I want to go and live with my aunt." I was 14 then. I said, "I don't want to live here anymore. I'm tired of you guys being drunk and fighting."

He didn't say anything for a while. Then he said, "I don't want you to go."

I said, "No, I'm tired of being here. I want you to pay my way to my aunt because I know she really loves me when I go see her once in a while."

My mom had to come out from the room because she was hearing what I was saying. She said, "Look what's happening. Our kids want to get out of this house because you're violent." She said, "I want to break up with you. I'm not going to lose my kids."

The next morning my mom woke me up at six o'clock saying, "Your father is leaving. He's not saying where he's going but he's really dressed up and he's walking somewhere." I thought he was just going hunting. It was nine o'clock and I was about to leave for school. She said, "I don't want you to go right now. I'm worried and need someone here with me. Your father is walking somewhere so he could disappear and kill himself."

When it got dark I told my mother to tell someone. The cops and people were looking for him all night and couldn't find him. The next morning they couldn't find him. In the afternoon they couldn't find him. In the evening they finally saw him. He was still walking. He said, "Leave me alone. Let me just walk. I don't like my life anymore." But they couldn't let him go because he was walking nowhere and it's so cold out. It's winter. They finally bring him home. When my father came back he promised he wouldn't drink.

Ever since then both of them stopped drinking. A year later my mom said, "Thank you. You were young, I don't know how you did it but you had the guts to say you don't want to live here anymore."

I stayed home. I was happier with my father because they didn't drink anymore. It looks like everything is back to normal. But I don't know what normal life is (giggle). He was still telling us what time we should be home and hitting us if we're late, or if we do something wrong he beats us, me, my sister and brother.

I didn't go to my aunt's but I still wanted to go. I used to sleep somewhere else and not go home for days. I used to run away once in a while because I was too scared to go home. So he looks for me and finds me. I go home and get beaten up.

As a teenager I used to go to parties, bars. I used to go to bars even when I was 16. They used to think I was 18. I looked older than my age. I used to pick up guys and sleep with them. I don't know why. I needed someone to love me because I never had it. I needed someone to care for me so I used to fuck around a lot, not knowing what I was doing.

The next morning I'd just forget about them and go to another guy. No wonder girls didn't like me when I was growing up.

I was sexually abused when I was seven years old by a neighbour. My mom used to tell me to go clean up his place because he couldn't do anything much for himself. He had a problem with his leg. One leg was shorter than the other and he walked very slowly. He was kind to my family. He brought things like food. So my mom wanted us to help him but she didn't know what was going on. I never told her. He said at the beginning that he wants to touch my thing, down there, my vagina. I said "Why?" He said, "Every girl does that." So I didn't know. I thought it was true. And he used to fuck me. It hurt. I'm just a kid. I tried to tell him it hurt me but he said, "It does happen that way. You'll feel better afterwards." And it was true. But I felt uncomfortable. It went on till I was 12 *(crying)*.

But when I was in school and found out it shouldn't be that way, I felt bad. They said a man shouldn't touch a woman, a little girl especially. I thought, oh boy, what did I do? Looks like it was my fault. I feel responsible. Then I wouldn't dare go to his place anymore. I used to pretend to go there.

I started drinking when I was 12 years old because I felt like a slut, a tramp. I used to be ashamed of myself. I felt different from other girls. I felt like everybody knows but nobody knows. I felt like I'm bad, like nothing. I didn't care what I was doing, like going out with all different kind of guys. And I didn't like that at all. But then I had a boyfriend. It stopped me for a while. Then I got pregnant with my older son when I was 17 years old. A little later I met my husband. And I felt good about myself. But I never told my husband because I was so afraid that he may say it's my fault. Just like when I got raped and he beat me up for that. I wanted to tell my mother but I couldn't. I carried that secret of what he did for years. When our neighbour died five or six years ago I felt relieved and then I finally told my sister about it.

I had to get away from that house because I was getting fed up, but I loved my mother very much. She was so close to me, she could tell me everything. She still does. A year ago she even told me that my sister, Eve, has a different father. I asked her who the father was, but she said she'll tell us one day when she's ready.

She told me that she got raped. That's how she got my sister but she doesn't want her to know about it. I told her, "You have to tell her the truth." She did. We can talk about everything, me and my mother. I used to talk with my sister, Eve, but she's changed now. She's jealous of me. She says that I'm pretty and she's ugly. Every guy likes me and no one likes her. Last year she even tried to ruin my face.

My youngest brother was five years younger than me. My mom adopted him as soon as he was born. Levy was my mother's sister's son. She wasn't married and she wasn't working, so my mom said, "Give him to me and let me raise him." My father beat him, too. Levy became violent and my parents started to be scared of him. He was breaking things and talking anger to my father. Saying he hates him, that he can fight him someday. My father put him in reform school when he was 17. The cops didn't want to take him because he was not doing anything. He was just mad. But my father says to the police he's afraid of him. So the police forced him to go. He was mad at my father, even my mother. They let him go there and he never came back. He came back when he was dead.

Just before Levy went to reform school he took care of my kids when they were very small. My boy was two years and the other one was almost four years old. Every time I went back to my mom's town, he was always there for my kids. He wanted to take care of them. He loved them. He used to even let them be on his back, carrying them. I miss him. He used to call me when he was down. I used to try to help. He only had three months left of reform school the night he committed suicide. That night he tried to call me but I wasn't home. After he died my husband said, "He tried to call you last night and I forgot to tell you." I felt so bad.

Every time he had problems he called to say he wants to live with me but my husband didn't want him to live with us. I wanted him very much to be with me. My husband I think was afraid that if he sees the way he's treating me, my brother would beat him up. He was afraid of all my family because he knows he's doing something wrong. He didn't want to talk to my parents. He didn't want to have anything to do with them. I really had a hard time when I wanted to go home.

Eve and Levy, when I wasn't there anymore, started to be so close to each other. They became best friends after I got married. She used to call me and say, "My brother and I are so close to each other now." I used to be happy for her.

Levy hanged himself. I was very angry when I found out (crying). I started to hate my father more for what he used to do but I couldn't show it to him. I'd talk back to him. I used to snap at him. When he would talk to me, I'd say, "What do you care? Don't talk to me."

My father is still strict. My mom told me that he used to get beaten up from his mother a lot. That's how he got angry. I heard my grandfather died right after he got my father. My father has two brothers and one sister. He's the second oldest. I think they have different fathers. I heard that my grandmother really liked white people. When an Inuit woman is fooling around with too many guys and white people, they threw them out of the community. They're ashamed of them. They left them across the river. They had no husband, no one to take care of them. Their children went with them. They had a tent. It was summer time. When it was starting to get winter they let them come back.

My mom said she had my brother, her first child, when that happened to my father's mother. My mom got married when she was 14. My father was maybe 16 or 17. I remember my mom telling me that my father felt sorry for his mother, so he went there with her. His oldest brother and his sister were there, too. They helped her.

Later, when I was already married, my mom used to take care of my grandmother because she was too old to take care of herself now. I tried my best to stay away from my husband, so I stayed at my parents and she was there. Every time I went home she used to be so happy. My mom said, "I see some change in your grandmother, she's more happy when you're here."

I used to say to my mom, "Wife, do you want to dance?" We danced to the radio and were happy. Then I had a call from my husband that he's going to kill my kids if I don't go home.

I called my mom a week later and asked, "How is my grandmother?"

"She's been asking for you and she doesn't want to do anything anymore." I had to come back to see her a month later. She was still asking for me. She lost her memory. "Where is Mary? Where is my grandchild?"

"I'm right here."

"Where is Mary?"

My mom said, "All of a sudden she changed while you were not here."

My mother told me that her father died when she was less than a year old. Her mother died when we were babies. I only saw her picture.

133

I was named after her. Maybe that's why my mom is so close to me. She calls me mother sometimes. And I feel, oops, here she comes, she needs to talk.

I'm happy my father is not the same anymore. My mom is the boss now. She can say anything she wants. She can get mad at my father. Maybe my father knows that we love my mother very much. Maybe we're adults and he's got lots of grandchildren. I've got my 15-year-old son and he's very tall. My brothers have kids. It switched. When I hear my mom talking to my father I think, what's going on? She stood up for herself.

My mom never talked about sex, nothing. I got pregnant when I was in Grade 9 and stopped school. I met a boyfriend at the parties. He was about seven years older than me. I didn't have my period for four months and I didn't know what was going on. I told my sister that I didn't have my period for a long time. She took me to the nurse. She was there for me. My mother was upset that I got pregnant too early.

My parents said they were going to keep it but I wanted to keep it. Both my mom and my father said I'm too young. That really hurt me. They said, "You don't have a husband and you're not working."

I finally had a son in the hospital and went home. I used to try to take care of him but my mom doesn't want me to. I say, "Can I sleep with him for one night?"

She said, "What if you're moving around too much? You can crush him, or something may happen." He slept in my mom's room.

When I'm holding the baby, she says, "Give it to your father."

"How come I can't take care of him?"

She said, "You're young. You have other things to do. Just treat him like he's your brother."

"What? He's my own kid."

I had an argument with my mother about my child. She changed the subject. I started to drink more and more. They didn't care what I was doing as long as I didn't take care of my baby. I tried to commit suicide two months after my baby was born. I cut both my wrists with a knife when I was feeling high. I wasn't even looking. I was just slashing and slashing. Then I tried to poison myself because the cutting of the wrist didn't work. I was bleeding and went down to the kitchen to look for something to poison myself. My parents were sleeping. In a cup I put all different kinds of soap, Javex, a little of everything. I drank it and went back upstairs. I was in my room and my stomach was starting to hurt. I was groaning and my mom came to my room. She didn't notice my wrists because I was turned to the wall. I said, "I'm having a stomach ache."

She went out and came back again. She said, "Are you really that sick? Can you look at me?"

I said, "No, I don't want to move."

She said, "Can I see you, please?"

I said, "No."

She said, "I saw some blood. Are you bleeding? Let me see your face."

I turned to her. She said, "You look so pale. Can you sit up, please?"

I said, "No."

"Sit up!"

So I had to and she saw I was all bloody.

My mother and father took me to see the nurse. They pumped my stomach and then asked why I did it. I just said, "I didn't want to be alive anymore." After that the social worker started to see me. That's one of the reasons I left town, because I didn't want to be taken care of by social workers.

Also, I got really angry with my parents. I'm seeing my baby and I can't take care of him. I can't even hold him. I said, "It's about time I leave this town."

I went to a music festival up north. It took four hours to get there by plane. It was almost near James Bay. I enjoyed it. They did throat singing. Women had to do that. I can do that. All my sisters were taught by my mother and she learned it from her mother. My mom started to teach us when we were very young. It's difficult to do. We have to have strong throats. We had to learn that because it's our culture. You sing inside the throat. I'm one of the best in the family. We used to travel for that. My mother used to play guitar and we used to sing. We recorded our music and the singing. She wanted me to be a singer. I really wanted to continue but Luke, my husband, didn't let me. I felt bad about it. My mom always said, "Don't forget it." Every time I'm home I practise. We all practise.

My mother sang professionally for a while but she stopped because she was bruised most of the time. She couldn't face people with a black eye or a bruise on her face. When my father broke her guitar she even stopped singing at home. She was crying. My brother bought her a new one but she hardly does it anymore. I think my father told her to stop. I felt bad because every time she sang I felt wonderful because I knew my mom can do something while she's getting beaten.

I taught my daughter to sing. She was here for one month and said, "Let's do that, Mom." So we did. My mother is teaching her right now. It could be very nice if you hear two people singing and each is singing something else and it's mixed.

I used to look at my mother singing and I used to say, "I'll be a singer some day." I wanted to be a singer but my husband didn't want me to because he said I'm going to travel a lot if I did that. So I never did. I still sing sometimes at Christmas and people like my voice. Even the bands wanted me to join them but I said no because I was thinking about my daughter. She was still too young and I didn't want to leave her. She's three years old now.

I stayed with my aunt up north after the music festival was over. One night I wanted a pop. I didn't want to go alone and her 13-year-old son came with me. We went to the poolroom and that was the first time I saw Luke. I liked him. He was handsome. He was working as a cashier.

There was no one there, so he asked me if I wanted to play pool with him. I said, "Yeah, why not? But I'm not good at it."

He said, "I can teach you."

We played pool. He took me back home. "Can I give you a call tomorrow?" He called me and said he was working that night and I could go there to play pool with him again. I liked him. He was real gorgeous. Everyone liked him. He was kind and he gave me attention. I didn't get attention for a long time because my parents were ignoring me.

One night I went to the movies with my aunt and Luke was there. We went into the theatre together. He said, "Do you want to sit next to me and watch the movie?"

I said, "Why not?"

My aunt sat with us. I was nervous because I liked him. After the movie he said, "Can I give you a ride home?"

I said, "My aunt is with us, I have to walk with her."

My aunt says, "Go ahead, have a ride."

I went home at 12 o'clock. We started to kiss around and began to go out. I stayed with him for Christmas, on December 23, 1982. That was the first time I slept with him. A month later I got pregnant. That first Christmas I spent with my husband at his parents' house was a lot of fun. I felt welcome. I started to live with him and his family.

The first time my husband beat me up was at his parents' house when they weren't there. I just looked at him and asked, "What's going on? What are you doing?"

And he stopped. He said, "I didn't mean to do that. I was mad because I thought you were fucking around with another guy."

When we had an argument I moved to my cousin's place. He thought I was going out with another guy while I was sleeping at my cousin's. When he called there and found out it wasn't true, he said he was sorry.

When I had my first son we got our own house. He was kind and caring but after a year he started to change. He hit me, saying I go to my parents' too often. When I called him from my parents' he said, "Come home tomorrow. I want to see my son right now."

"Why?"

"Because you're leaving him alone."

He had called while I was out. I said, "He was just sleeping and my mother was here. I went to the store and visited my best friend."

"Come home. I don't want anyone to babysit my son." He hung up.

I said, "I'm not going home. I'm not ready." I was going to be here for two weeks.

I saw my first son when I was home. My mom doesn't mind me taking care of him anymore. I could hold him. We could go out together. He was so cute. I had told my husband that I have a first child and he's with my parents. But he said he's not going to take care of someone's baby. That really hurt me. He felt ashamed. Don't ever tell anyone that you've got another child. He hated my son. He didn't even want me to mention him.

The next day Luke called and asked why I hadn't taken the plane. I said I want to stay with my parents. He hung up on me. Two days later he called again. He said he was going to commit suicide.

"Why?"

"Because you're not coming. You're leaving me. I'm going to kill myself tomorrow if you don't come."

I thought, so you really miss us. OK, I'll go home. It looked like everything was normal. When I was inside the airport he hugged me and said, "I'm happy you're home. I missed you so much." After we got home he started getting mad. He said, "How come you didn't want to come home? Were you seeing another man? How could you do that to your own son?"

Boy, did I get it. He punched me and punched me. Pushing me around. That was the first time he hurt me. I was very surprised.

"What's going on?"

"Everything is your fault." But he said he'd never do it again.

When I was two months pregnant with my second one we got married. At the beginning I tried to open up to my husband. I tried to tell him how I felt. He didn't care. Then I said, that's it, he doesn't give a shit. He doesn't want to hear about it. He gets mad about it. He beats me up for it. I just closed up. I talked to my mother instead.

When I met him I only knew that he was taking grass. I can't smoke that much because I get a headache but he had to have it every day. I even had to go out and buy it for him. He kept on saying, "I'm going to stop, I'm going to stop." But he was beating me up. He doesn't want me to talk back. He just wants me to sit there and listen to him but it was getting worse and worse.

I asked my mother-in-law if she ever got beaten by her husband. I didn't know how to tell her that I was getting beaten up. She said, "No, never. He never laid a hand on me." I shut my mouth. I didn't tell her that I'm getting beaten up from her son. But I heard from his aunt, his sister, his brothers and even Luke told me that his mother used to get beaten up.

A couple of months later I told her, "Your son is beating me up."

She said, "It's your fault because you're a woman."

I thought, I shouldn't have told her. I can't talk with a person like this. I told my mother that I tried to tell his mother and she said it's my fault. My mother called my mother-in-law.

She said, "Your son is beating up my daughter. Don't say it's her fault. Tell him to stop."

My mother-in-law was really mad. She came to our place and told my husband *(crying)*. When she went home I got beaten. He said, "Don't ever let my mother know that I'm beating you up."

I'm trying my best to be a good mother and a good wife. I don't fuck around. I try my best but he had a drug problem. Cocaine and hash. He was a drug dealer. Before that he was a policeman. He was still taking drugs, but he didn't deal. He started dealing five or six years into the marriage to support his habit. People came to the house to buy drugs and he gave it to them in front of the kids. I said, "I don't like that. I don't want my kids to know that you're dealing."

He was starting to say that he can kill his sons and kill me. The first time he said that was when my son was six years old, my first son with him. When he's mad he says he can do anything he wants to do. Everyone was afraid of him. He can go to a person who got him mad and threaten him with a shotgun or beat him up with a stick.

When I went to my parents with our second baby I stayed away for a year. I came back because I answered the phone accidentally and he let my son cry. He said if I don't go back he was going to kill him and then kill himself. I said, "That's crazy." I went to a social worker in my hometown and had her call him. She said he can do what he said. There are guns in the house. They were on his side, telling me to go back. I had no choice.

When I went back, the social workers there were helping me, they were telling him not to hit me. He agreed and he didn't beat me for maybe two months. After that he started to get jealous—who did I go with when I left him for that long? I used to get beaten up for that for a long time. And I can't talk back or he gets really mad.

He used to say that he's going to change. He even put a gun to his head when I said I had enough. I'm tired of my face being swollen all the time. I'm tired of having black eyes. He said he was going to kill himself. I said, "That's it. I'm fed up. You can keep the kids as long as they're safe." But he wanted to kill himself. I had to be awake all night talking to him.

Then I started to talk back, saying, "Why are you doing this? What am I doing wrong? How come I'm getting beaten up?" He got quiet. I was sitting at the table trying not to look at him, trying not to be near him because if I'm near him he's just going to lash out at me. Then he went into the bedroom. I heard a gunshot and got really scared. I thought he killed himself. I called his name. He didn't answer. I was scared to go upstairs to the bedroom. I looked at the guns, he had a lot of guns, and there was one missing.

I went to my neighbour's and said, "Go see my husband, because I can't go there."

They called the cops and a cop went to see him. He said, "He's OK. But he's holding a gun. If he wants to kill himself, we can't stop him." He left.

Luke called me to go upstairs. I had no choice but to go. He pushed me away. "Why did you let people come here?"

"Because I thought you were dead. You didn't say anything."

He stopped for a while. I said, "Why do you have a gun?"

He said, "I'm going to kill myself." I got really scared. Then he said, "I'm going to talk about what I've been doing wrong." He's going to confess to me. He said, "I'm sorry I've been beating you up. I'm sorry I've been going out with all different kind of girls when you're away."

I thought, oh boy, I never knew about that. I had suspicions but I never said anything. They always call me. "I've been bossy to my kids. I've hurt them."

And he was afraid to tell me one thing. He kept on saying, "I want to tell you something." But he let me wait and said nothing.

Then he wants me to talk about the bad things I did too. What am I going to tell him? I've been honest with him. I said, "I don't have anything to tell you." But I've been telling a lie sometimes just to save myself, that's what I told him. He said he wants more than that. I told him that sometimes I didn't want to come home and stayed out later because I know we don't have money and he doesn't have drugs and sometimes I get scared. I stay out, near the doorway, praying *(crying)*. Even when it's winter.

Then he said he tried to let me kill myself. I thought, that's what I've been doing, trying to kill myself. When he really beat me up I took a lot of pills. It used to be so scary. His uncle used to find me and take me to the hospital. In the hospital they pumped my stomach. Then I had to go back home. Sometimes after he beat me up he held a gun to my face and said, "Let's die together." He's driving me to hate myself like I'm no good, I'm fat and I always do something bad. When we have a big frozen fish he has to cut it with an axe. While he cuts it he says he could do that to a person. Wham! Smash a person. Cut them into pieces like the fish. I know it's me he's talking about.

The nurses were telling me, "We can help you if you want help." I keep on going there having bruises. Twice I was afraid that he had cracked my skull because it was really hurting. I went to the nurse for X-rays and surgery. Another time I thought my arm was broken because he was really pulling on it. He made me lie down and tried to choke me with his feet while pulling my arm. He did that a lot.

Sometimes he is already mad when he gets into the house. I am really scared about what's going to happen. I try to cheer him up. But he says, "Leave me alone." I try to do that. Then he says, "Mary, make me tea." I make him tea. Then I would go out of the room so I wouldn't disturb him. He says, "How come you're not staying with me? I just came home."

"You said you wanted to be alone."

"Now I need someone to be with me. I want you to stay in the room. You don't care about me."

"You told me to leave you alone so I went out of the room."

If I don't say yes when he wants to make love, he's going to beat me up. If I'm not in a good mood, I try to say, I want to sleep, I'm tired. He pulls my hair and tells me to get out of bed. He says, "You're tired, get more tired." He gets me out of bed and tells me to go to the living room. I go to the living room and sit there, scared, waiting for him to come or just waiting to see what was going to happen (*crying very hard*).

Sometimes while my kids were out he closed the door. I say, "I have to take care of my son." I tried to be nice with him so he wouldn't get mad.

He used to tear my clothes off. He asked me who did I go with. "Who are you seeing?"

I said, "What do you mean?'

He says I'm fucking around with someone. But I can't go out because he's telling me not to leave my kids. I have to carry my kids every time I go out. My mom used to say, "He's going to change someday, like your father." I stayed with him because my father changed.

I had four children with my husband. I had to let one boy go because he said he had enough boys. I said, "I can't give away my son. I already did with the first one."

He said, "No, three boys in the house, that's too much."

In my mind I thought, you're afraid of them. When they are old enough they could beat him up because he let them see me get beaten up. But I had to give my son up for adoption eight years ago, as soon as he was born. I didn't want him to go (*crying hard*) but I had no choice. I wanted to run away with that baby but I couldn't because my boys were with my husband. I gave him to my cousin. My cousin really wanted a little boy so he's being taken care of very well. He lives in my old hometown. He knows he's from me.

My husband told me I had to give him up before I gave birth. I used to try and say, "It's a girl," and my mom said, "It's a boy." If your lips are blue it means you're going to have a boy. If your lips are pink it means you're going to have a girl. If the baby is all around your stomach it means it's a boy. If it's pointed it means it's a girl. My mother said, "You have too many kids and your husband is violent."

I said, "I want a little girl. I don't care if I die having a little girl, as long as she's almost like me." Then later I had another child, a little girl. When I finally did I said, "That's it," and had my tubes tied. And she's like me.

Everyone knew that I was getting beaten up. He took me outside, pulling my hair, tearing my top off, beating me, then took me back in. People could hear I'm getting beaten up inside the house. They were afraid to be friends with me because my husband was so violent. The community pressed charges against him for beating me up. The cops came and he got arrested. He was in jail for four days and all his family turned against me.

Even his sisters were saying, "You let my brother go to jail!"

My mother-in-law said, "You little girl, you let my son go to jail!" Everyone blamed me.

His father didn't know for many years that I was getting beaten up. The mother knew but she never told her husband. He finally found out because I'm not going to his place for quite a while because I'm all swollen. When I don't have a black eye I usually go to see his parents almost every day. Sometimes just for a few minutes. But when I have a black eye I go there once a month. He tried to ask his wife why I wasn't coming and she said, "Maybe she's just feeling sick."

One day his father came to our house. He just went to the porch and said, "Mary, can you pass me some tea?"

He didn't come in. I'm all swollen. What am I going to do? He said, "Mary, can you pass me some tea, please, if you're OK?"

I passed him the tea and he said, "Oh my God, that's why you're not coming. Who did that?"

"Your son."

He said, "Don't ever hide this from me." He apologized for his son. Later he called Luke to go to his house with me. I was ashamed of myself because I was swollen. After we eat I went to another room to smoke. Then I heard yelling. His father is saying, "I'm going to hit you and hit me back if you want to. I want you to know how it feels getting hit. You've been hitting your wife, that's why she doesn't come. But she liked it here. I went to your house for the first time and I have to see your wife with a black eye, all swollen. That's not respecting your wife."

He hit him with a stick. Before we went home his father talked with us. He says, "Try to work this out. We love our grandchildren and want them to have a nice home."

When we went home I got beaten. He was really mad at me saying it's my fault that he got hit from his father for the first time. He was choking me and my son was standing there crying, "Mother, mother!" It was awful. I thought, boy, he's getting worse, so the next day I called the social workers. I had to make a collect call because he's going to look at the phone bill to see where I've been calling. I had been making collect calls to my parents because he's going to get mad that I've been phoning and talking to my family, my friends.

I used to look at my mom get beaten up. Now it's me. I thought women had to be like this. But about five years ago my mom told me that not everyone gets beaten. I was thinking it was all my fault because he's telling me that it's my fault. Now I know that a person mustn't get beaten just because she's a person.

When the house is not clean he throws everything, telling me to clean up. No wonder when my son is mad he throws everything. He got it from his father. Now he's 13 and he's in a group home. They're trying to make him better. My son is really having a problem because he used to look at me getting beaten up. At school he even drew a picture of a pregnant lady getting beaten. They asked, "How come you draw someone hitting the stomach of a pregnant woman?"

He was getting violent in school and the teachers asked me if I'm getting beaten up by my husband. I said, "Yeah, but not that much." If people get involved I'm going to get it and I don't want that. I was ashamed too of what was going on. When I have a bruise on my face I don't go out because I don't want people to see me like that. But I did go out one time. I said, "I've had enough. I miss going out." I went to the store.

Later Luke asked me, "You went out like this? What are they going to think of me?" All he cared about was himself.

One time we ran out of cigarettes at 11 o'clock at night. It was winter and I had to walk very far with my baby on my back in a stormy night to buy cigarettes. The snowmobile is just sitting there and he doesn't want me to use it *(crying)*. I had to walk in the soft snow. It went up to my thighs and I had to come back the same way. It took me almost two hours back and forth. I was freezing. And when I arrived he said, "How come you took so long?"

When I went to my hometown I used to drink a lot. Sometimes I didn't go home. I just stayed with friends or the person I felt comfortable with. My mother understood. My father used to tell me not to do that because I'm married. He thought I was fucking around because I was sleeping somewhere else. I sometimes just used to say, "Leave me alone, just leave me alone."

But I used to talk to my mother. She said, "Go ahead, go out, as long as you come back safe."

I drank to forget. My husband used to drink but stopped because he knew he could kill me when he was drunk. Every time he's drunk he beats me up. The cops told him one time, "You've got a drinking problem and you could kill your wife when you're too drunk. Look at her face. Look what you did. You're lucky she doesn't want to press charges." If I do, I know when he comes back he could just kill me.

He used to say, a year before he died, "I don't give a shit anymore. I can kill anybody. I'm tired of my life."

In my mind I'm thinking, I'm the one who's really tired. I couldn't even have friends. But I have one good friend, Jesse. He used to tell me, "She's not good for you. She's not going to let you do your things."

When my sister wanted to come and visit he said, "Why? What does she want?" She stayed with us for two nights and then my husband kicked her out because she was drinking. After that she never wanted to come back to the house. She was scared of him.

I told Luke, "She's in trouble, we have to help her."

He said, "It's not our problem. It's her problem because she's drinking."

He doesn't mind when I drink because I don't do anything when I'm drinking. His sister was at my place. They were smoking and I smoked a little bit. We finished our drink and I wanted a little bit more. His sister said she had a little bit at her place. I said, "I have to ask my husband if I can come." He didn't mind so I went to his sister's house. I was drinking 94 percent alcohol but I added a lot of water.

Later I called my husband and said, "I'm going gambling because I'm not that drunk."

He said, "Don't get too drunk."

We went gambling. A lot of people were drinking that night. Jesse and I went to get more alcohol. She was my best friend. She started to be my friend because she got beaten up too and we used to talk about it.

One night she ran away to my house because she got beaten up by her boyfriend and slept there. My husband was camping with my older son. I felt comfortable with her. She had the same experience as me. She was pretty young and had three kids from her boyfriend. I said, "If he does that you have to stop getting pregnant. I don't want you to end up like me. Get away from him." She's not with him anymore. She listened to me.

So Jesse and I went back with the alcohol and I started to drink more and got drunk. There's one girl who really hates me because her brother raped me and he's in jail for that. The family hated me so.

Three guys raped me while my husband was camping. I was smoking outside. It was one o'clock at night. We don't smoke in our house because I have kids to take care of. I was smoking outside and one guy kidnapped me. He pulled me by my hands. I yelled, "Help!" No one came. I screamed, "Leave me alone!" But he was too strong. He took me to his cousin's house. There were three guys. They were drinking. They beat me and raped me. But two of the guys couldn't do it because they were afraid of my husband. The guy who took me was beating the third guy to rape me. He forced him. He didn't want to do it. I couldn't get out for seven hours. They were looking for one more girl but couldn't find her.

I managed to escape and went to a neighbour. I was all bloody. They opened the door and said, "But your husband isn't here!"

"Someone else did it to me." I had to go to another town to the hospital because I couldn't see, I was so swollen.

My friend was inside the house but she didn't hear anything because she was listening to music. She babysat till seven o'clock in the morning. She was worried because my husband was only coming back later that day. And I was so happy that he was coming. My husband came and said he supports me. My mom even came because they were

145

really afraid that I may die because I got so beaten up. I had to open my eyes with my fingers to see. I stayed for a month at home with my mother to recover. I said, "I'm tired of being beaten up. My husband beats me and now this."

My husband changed for almost five months. He never hit me. He said he was sorry but later he started saying it's my fault. "Why were you out?"

The guy who kidnapped me and beat the guy to rape me beat up his father too. His father is not normal anymore. He got brain damage from his own son.

I went back home. Finally I started to go out. But it was scary going out alone. His family started to say dirty things like, "I'm happy you got raped." Saying I'm lying I got raped. I used to say to them, "Ask the nurse, they know I got raped." I decided to tell my husband what's going on with that family and he talked to them. They stopped for a while. But then they started saying to other people that I didn't get raped.

This guy who kidnapped me is still in prison. He has four, five years. The whole family is mad at me and the sister is jealous of me. I tried to ignore her. I always tried to ignore them, even if they're saying bad things. That night, at gambling, I finally said, "I'm tired of you telling lies about me to people, saying that I never got raped. How would you feel if you got raped? How would you feel if you got beaten up?" I punched the sister right in the face. I couldn't stop hitting and punching her.

They took her out. Then I went out. I said, "I'm going home." But they were waiting for me outside, the sister and her mother. They were drunk. They started fighting me. I went inside to call my husband. But the line was busy and busy and busy. I went to another house. Those people were drunk too. I tried to call him and call him so he could come and get me. Now there were three people and his mother out to get me. The woman whose house I was at wanted to take me home but the snowmobile wouldn't start. I had to walk back home.

When I got home my husband took me right away and POW! While I was trying to call home, the sister of the guy in jail called Luke saying that I was fucking with her boyfriend. That got my husband real mad. He said, "This time I'm going to kill you!"

I tried to explain to him what had happened but he didn't listen.

He pushed me down on my belly. He laid down on top of me and had his feet to my throat while pulling my arm. I lost consciousness. He thought he had killed me. I finally woke up. I thought if he kills me, he could kill his kids and himself.

He took the telephone and started knocking me over the head. I have a lot of stitches there. I've had a knife with me for a long time but didn't know how to use it. Once he stabbed me in my legs but it didn't hurt because I was too scared. A day later it started to hurt. So I thought, it's not going to be any good if I stab him in the leg to try to stop him. I stabbed him on his upper arm but it didn't stop him. He really wanted to kill me. He was trying to choke me so I tried to stab him on his shoulder and that worked. I stabbed him twice on his arm and once on the shoulder. He went backwards and let me go. I went out as fast as I could. I yelled for people and no one came. I went back in. There he was and the knife was still in his shoulder. He told me to go to him and I said, "No." He said, "Come here!"

"No, I'm not coming."

"Come here!"

"I'm scared of you, you can kill me. You have to go to the nurse now because you're bleeding a lot."

He said, "What do you care? If you care for me, come here."

He was still holding the knife. I know he can stab me with it so I said, "No way."

I called the nurse. I was panicking. He is bleeding a lot. Then I dropped the phone because it looks like he's starting to get up. He said, "Mary, look." And he put the knife deeper.

I said, "Oh my God, don't do that!" I went to him and took the knife out because I could see a lot of blood coming out and got really scared. I was trying to get to my kids because I could hear someone crying. My kids were in the room off the hallway and my husband was in the hallway. The door was locked and I finally opened it but my son was too scared to get out.

I went to call the nurse again. I yelled into the phone, "When are you guys coming?" I hung up. I was panicking. I noticed that he was getting weaker and weaker. He fell down. I tried to carry him but he was too heavy. I took his leg and pulled him. I put him on the couch. I found myself outside again trying to look for people and to see if some-one is coming.

I thought, I'm going to have to do it myself, take him to the snowmobile and take him to the nursing station. I tried that but he said, "Leave me alone."

I finally took him to the doorway. I realized my kids were looking. I said, "Please go back to the room." They were crying. I took them to the room. I'm in shock.

I call the police in my hometown and say, "I stabbed my husband and he's dying. I killed my husband." I felt that it was my fault because I put the knife in. I said, "No one's coming, no one is helping me!"

He told me to be calm. He knew who I was. After that I went next door. I said, "I need help, my husband is bleeding to death and I can't carry him by myself."

My neighbour came to the house with me, then went out again. He said he was getting help. I started to panic. I could see the blood all over and thought, it's too late. I locked the door. I was afraid that the neighbour was going to Luke's parents for help. If his parents see him like this they'll be really hurt.

My husband said, "I'm sorry, Mary, what I've been doing to you."

I said, "Don't talk about it right now. I want you to be alive. Think about being alive."

When they start to apologize, my mom used to tell me, that means they're dying. I am thinking, oh my God, he's going to die. I said, "Stay with me!"

He's saying, "I'm sorry." He asked for his son and he apologized to him. I thought, I don't want him to see this. There was blood everywhere.

Suddenly there was a knock on the door. Finally! I checked who it was. A cop. I opened the door and said, "At last!"

"He's dead."

I said, "I can't be alone right now."

He asked me where he can take me. I said, "Not here, I can't be here." They took my kids somewhere. I was panicking, moving around. The policeman, an Inuit guy, took me to the police station. I was all bloody, even my hands were bloody. They didn't have water and I had to leave my hands bloody the whole night. The next day they took me away to jail. That was the first time I ever went to jail. The jail cell was so dirty. The pillows, oh my God!

The Inuit policeman was trying to help me. He told me, "Don't say a word to them because we can see you got really beaten up." He was saying this behind the other policemen's back. He knew me. All the other policemen were white except for this one guy.

They were forcing me to tell them what happened all day long. I said, "I'm not going to talk."

They said, "On the phone you said you killed him."

"I'm not going to talk." The Inuit policeman called a lawyer for me.

When I was in jail I thought, why didn't I get killed instead? What am I doing here? I planned to kill myself. I didn't care about my children because I knew they were safe now. But when I told my lawyer the whole story he said, "You're going out soon." I thought, why should I kill myself?

His mother came to see me in jail and said she is there for me. She said she'd take care of my kids while I was in jail. I believed her but soon after she started to hate me, setting my kids against me. She started to say I'm a murderer.

I spent 16 days in jail. Then I was allowed to go back to my hometown. I'm not allowed to go back to my husband's town. But my kids were with my mother-in-law. She didn't let them come back with me. I had to fight for them. The social worker couldn't do very much because, she said, I'm charged with murder. But my lawyer helped. My daughter finally came to me.

My daughter was so afraid of my husband. When she was only one or two months old, every time he is holding her she cries. He couldn't even babysit her. I said to my mother, "My daughter reacts to her father as if he were a stranger but he's her father."

My mother said, "When she was inside you she knew your husband was beating you and yelling at you. She could hear him say, I can kill anybody. She knows the voice and is scared of it."

The one who is adopted by my cousin was afraid of my husband, too. When he was one year's old we went to visit him. He was throwing sand and rocks at my husband, yelling, "Don't touch me!" He was mad. Luke just left, went into the house. He reacted that way to me, too. He was scratching me. I said, "Why?" He stopped when I started to talk. He recognized my voice and hugged me. That made me feel so good (crying). Now he's nine years old. He comes and visits because we live in the same town. He knows I'm his mother.

I'm still fighting for my other two boys to come back to me. My mother-in-law said I killed her son, so my sons are going to replace my husband. And she said I could kill them. I was a murderer. I got really scared that I may not have them back anymore. I was crying and crying, asking for my kids, saying, "At least let me see them. I miss my home, I miss my kids, I miss the way it used to be, even if I got beaten up." I tried my best not to let my kids get hit *(crying)*, even go there to stop him so he can turn against me instead of hurting my kids.

My kids came when I went to court for the first hearing in my husband's hometown. I took them home to my mother-in-law's after court. I thought, boy, what's going on? I was ashamed of my own kids. The way they were dressed. Their clothes were old, with holes. Before they had new clothes and new jackets. And she said she's been taking care of them! The clothes my younger son was wearing was from the 1960s. Even the colours are not the same any more.

I said, "Where are your clothes?"

They said they took them.

My mother-in-law, sisters-in-law, his family took everything. I had a washing machine, a dryer, a snowmobile, beds, my kids' things, my things. I told my lawyer and he said, "She's the mother." The lawyer couldn't do anything.

I didn't have any clothes when I went to jail, so my mother was in my husband's hometown getting my clothes. She went to my house and his whole family was running around getting this and that. She thought, "Are they greedy! My daughter lives here."

She started to cry because she saw my oldest son crying, saying to my mother, "They took my hockey stick. I want it back. I got it from my father."

My mom said, "Where is his hockey stick?"

They said, "We don't know."

He said, "They took my tape recorder. I want it!"

She said, "Don't take my grandson's things." No one listened to her. They took everything. My mother-in-law was in charge. Jesse was there because I told her, "Don't let them take my jewellery because I want to have something to remember my husband." They told her to get out.

My mother brought me a few things that were old, things that I used inside the house. She said, "You can start a new life. You can have anything you want. We can pay for them."

I said, "I need something to remember my husband and my kids need something." They didn't even give me a picture of my husband. Nothing.

I always say to my kids, "Just remember your father, he didn't mean to do bad things." *(crying)* I don't want them to turn against their father. I want them to forget what he used to do. I want them to remember the good times. But it's hard. Even on Christmas I got beaten up *(crying)*. Everyone is having a good time and I can't get out because I'm swollen.

My lawyer was saying that we're going to court for my kids. He told my mother-in-law that they're not going to win because I'm the mother. She said to my sons, "Go to your mother now." They finally came. It took me four months to get my kids back.

When my kids came back to me they were scared. They changed. I asked, "What was your grandmother saying about me?"

They used to say, "I don't know." Because she didn't want them to tell me.

One night we were talking. My oldest son asked, "Mom, are you a killer?"

"What do you mean?"

"Are you a killer? Because my grandmother said you can kill us."

"I would never hurt you."

He said nothing. I said, "Do you remember that I always protected you?"

"Yeah."

"Do you think I'm still the same?"

"I don't know."

"Do you think I don't love you?"

"I don't know."

"I love you. I'm not a scary mother. I don't hit you. Do I hit you?"

"No.

"Then why are you scared of me?

"Because my grandmother said that you're a bad woman and can kill anybody."

"Do you think I could kill you?"

He smiled and said, "No."

I started to hug him and he cried. He really cried. "His younger brother was sleeping. I asked him, Does your brother think that I'm a killer?"

"Yeah."

It really hurt me. I couldn't sleep all night. I said to myself, I will never let them go back there again until she says it was an accident. I told the social workers what my mother-in-law was saying about me. They didn't believe me. I told them to ask my kids. My son didn't want to tell because he was protecting his grandmother. When I told him, "Tell them what she's been telling you because it's not right," he finally did. But I still had to let them go there again.

Two years ago I moved into my sister's house because I couldn't live with my father anymore. He tried to control me like a little girl again. My sister had her own house, but she moved back to live with my mother and father. She felt safer there because she had a boyfriend who was violent. My father said to me, "You can have Eve's house now."

But I'm scared of my sister now. She's violent when she's drunk. When she found out that she was abused by my father she changed. She tried to kill me with a rock two years ago when she was drunk. Banging on my head. It was hard. Right after my husband died, so it really destroyed me. I thought she was there for me. She was my sister and friend. But she exploded. Eve beat me up in my house and outside too. I tried to go to my brother's because he was close and he called the cops. The police came and asked my sister to go with them. She told them I murdered my husband. I planned it. I was so pissed off when my lawyer told me.

She tried to destroy me. My mom knows that she's very jealous of me, just because I'm prettier than her. Just because guys like me more. She gets mad very easily when my father wants to help me. Maybe she's mad at me because my father didn't do anything to me when I was a little girl. I'm not close to Eve anymore but I would love to be (crying). I miss that. I lost my sister.

She went to a social worker. She felt very bad for what she did. She blamed it on my father sexually abusing her when she was young. When she was beating me up she remembered it and thought I was my father. But she knew who I was. She said, "Mary." Maybe she had a flashback for a while. She apologized to me a lot of times. But I'm scared to be with her now after what happened. Every time she's kind of drunk I tell her not to come in. She said she was going to get help with her drinking, but she never did.

I have a boyfriend now. At first we were just friends. We met a year ago. I drank with him a couple of times. My sister had four boyfriends, including him. I liked him. But I didn't want to hurt her so I backed off but we were still friends. One day I said, "What would you say if I go out with him?"

She said, "I don't care because I don't love him and he's just an asshole." I thought, he's not an asshole to me.

He only drinks on weekends. On weekdays he doesn't. He works. He's more caring when he drinks. More talkative, saying, "I care for you." I have never seen him being violent. He did get angry one time because I was drinking too much and didn't take care of my kids. He said, "I'm tired of you being in jail. When are you going to do something about it?" When I was in jail I finally realized I was doing something wrong.

I was more open with him. He wants me to come back there and try to work on my problem. He knows how I feel. He's the only man I ever told how I feel. He listens and cares. He can hug me for that. That's nice. I never had that. He's 29. I'm 32. Everybody in the family likes him because he's understanding. He doesn't go out when I'm walking around worried. He asks, "Want to sit down and talk about it?" And I feel better after that. When he sees I'm better he goes out. He lets his job go second and lets me go first. That's nice. He's a ticket agent for Air Inuit. My daughter really loves him. He loves my daughter and my boys *(light laughter that seems to float up from her throat and chest)*. I miss getting up in the morning and hearing laughter. He lives with his mother. He comes and sleeps at my place but not every night because I need my space. But he calls every night. I'm scared to live with a man again. I'm scared because of my past. I'm afraid I may meet a man like my husband. The first time my husband was very kind. If we start a real relationship I'm afraid he might turn out to be like Luke.

But Luke was a good father. He tried to do everything for them, taking them camping and hunting. They really liked it but he couldn't do it every weekend because he was on drugs. He didn't do it very often. He went alone with friends. But he had to take his older son camping and hunting. He had no choice because he was afraid I could run away with the kids and I tried that twice. He came back when I had everything packed. On Saturday we can fly out because there is a plane on weekends. He left on Friday, after work, with his friends. He's supposed to come back on Sunday or Monday morning. Before he comes back I pack everything. He came back the next day, on Saturday, while

I was packing. I don't know why he came back. I put everything back as fast as I could, but I was too late. He asked me, "What's that for?"

I said, "It's just there."

He was taking his clothes off and my son said, "Are we leaving, Mom?" He said it in front of my husband. He was only five years old. So my husband started to be suspicious. That's when he opened the luggage. It was full of clothes. He was really mad but he didn't hit me because I had my baby on my back. He kept on telling me to take the baby off my back. I said, "No." I know he's going to hit me and I was shaking, trying to get away from him, not to be near him. I'm looking at the plane. I could see it from my house. I said if I don't go, I'm going to get beaten up.

My husband lay down. He took his socks off. I was looking at the snowmobile and could see the keys. I left my oldest son, just took diapers because I breast feed and ran out with my two-year-old son on my back as fast as I could. I took the snowmobile and didn't take my gloves or anything. I went to the plane and made it.

We had to sleep in one town overnight. The next day I was walking to the plane and could hear a snowmobile coming toward me. I said, "Please, don't let it be him."

He stopped right in front of me. I still had to walk 20 more steps to the plane. He said, "Can we talk?"

I said, "No, because the plane is there."

He said, "I don't want to be mad while you leave. Can we talk?"

I said, "We can talk here because there are people around but I'm not getting on the Ski-Doo."

He said, "I want to see my son before you go."

I let him see my son but he took him. I know if I go back I'm going to really get it. I thought, I'll just save myself because he never used to beat his sons up badly when they were little. He was just really bossy, you have to say yes and don't ever touch my things.

He said, "You can go tomorrow. I'm not going to be mad, I just want to talk."

I said, "I want to go right now."

He said, "You can go tomorrow with your son but I don't want you to leave while we're mad at each other."

I said, "You're the only one who's mad, that's why I'm leaving."

He said, "I'm sorry. Can we talk?"

154

I had no choice because I started to get worried about how he's going to go back with my son. He's driving a snowmobile. So I followed him and he didn't hit me.

He let me go the next day with my son. He said, "I promise I'll change, I'll do my best."

My mom told me, "Don't go back there until he's really changed. Teach him a lesson. Just stay here and don't take his calls." I didn't take his calls for a long time.

One day my younger son fell asleep with his clothes on. I tried to wake him up. He was deeply sleeping so I decided to take his pants off.

He said, "I thought you weren't going to do that again."

I said, "What are you saying?"

He looked at me and said, "Oh."

I said, "Are you OK?"

"Yeah."

"Did something ever happen?"

He said, "No." I got suspicious that something was going on. He was even starting to sleep outside, never wanted to come home, was sniffing gas. My husband used to have a tent beside our house and he used to sleep there. Luke didn't care. I had to look for him. I said, "What's going on?" I thought he didn't want to see us getting beaten up. But sometimes I got really curious, like when I go home and he's there crying.

I was really suspicious. I tried to talk to him, saying, "I'm with you. Tell me what's going on." But he never told me anything. So I told my husband to talk to him. He said he wants to talk to him alone. He closed the door and I couldn't hear anything. Later he said, "Maybe he was just dreaming." I believed him for a while but I wasn't too sure. It really hurt me when he was just sleeping outside *(crying)*. He's only nine years old.

When his father was going camping he never wanted to go. My husband was always only taking one son at a time camping. "The next time you're going to come," he'd say. "The next time it's your turn." He couldn't take all of them.

One day my husband said he's going camping tomorrow and asked my youngest son if he wanted to come. He said, "No." I thought, that's strange. Arley really wanted to go. It looks like nothing happened to the older one.

Arley, my oldest son, when he's hitting his brother he really hits him. He can't control himself. Arley is like a man when he fights, he's like his father. I can't let them be together because I'm afraid Arley may hit him so badly he could hurt him. Maybe because they used to see me get beaten up. I told the social worker about it. They're not together anymore. Arley is in a foster home. He's 13 now.

After my husband's death Arley started to fall apart. He didn't care because there's no one to be scared of anymore. He says, "That's the first time I feel at home."

I said, "What do you mean?"

He said, "No one is yelling, no one is getting mad, you're not getting hit and that's nice."

I said, "Yes, it is but I still miss your father. Do you?"

He said, "Yeah, I miss him."

I said, "Do you want to talk about it?"

He said, "No." He never talks about it. I always try to talk about Luke, trying to make him like he was a good man. Arley knows everything that happened and he's having a real hard time now to control his life.

He was getting violent. Everyone was complaining, the school, my mother-in-law, my mother, the social workers. Everyone was saying he has a temper, he can't control it, he wants to hit someone badly. The social workers were telling me we have to do something before it's too late. They convinced me to finally let him go to a foster home. I had no choice. I used to say to myself, I can fix my son. But I couldn't. One of the social workers said I was protecting my oldest son like I used to protect my husband. She made me see.

My mother used to say, "Look at your son beating up his brother."

I used to say, "Oh, it's just boys."

But in some ways I knew something was wrong. He beat up other boys at school and even his teacher. I thought he would never hurt me. But he tried. He even said, "Why didn't you die that night?" It really shocked me. I couldn't sleep at nights because he ran away and had the key. I was afraid he could come back any time and kill me. My own son.

Arley tried to commit suicide about a month ago. They told me that he was threatening to kill himself all the time. Sometimes he can't control himself. His own father used to hold a gun to his face and say, "I can kill you. I'm going to kill you someday." My son even said that to one of the staff.

156

He said he's tired of being there. Tired of not being with me. He asks, "Are you going to be home when I go home? Am I still going to have to go back to my grandmother or the other grandmother? I miss being with you, to have our own house like we used to. How come we can't be a family any more?" He was moving a lot. He went to my parents and to my mother-in-law's. When he gets out of juvenile detention he says he wants to stay in one place.

Maybe my mother-in-law felt bad that she wasn't taking care of the grandchildren so she said, "I want to see them." Arley went there for his birthday from the foster home and he's back. I'm scared to ask him how it was. I don't want to get hurt. I'm waiting for the right time. I can't do anything much while I'm here. I'm still afraid that my mother-in-law says, "Your mother is stupid and she's in jail because she's dangerous."

I have to be here for six months. Then I'm going to have my trial. I have proof that I was getting beaten up but they don't really believe me. I'm tired of this. It was an accident. Jesse is going to testify for me and I'm happy for that.

It's almost two years now and I haven't had a trial. Three months after I was released I went back in because I started to go to bars and I broke my bail conditions. I didn't want to face the pain of being sober. They gave me chances, saying she just lost her husband. I still had conditions like not to drink, not to go to the bar, not to go to my husband's hometown, go home at 10 o'clock. The police call or they go to check up on me. Could you be home at 10 o'clock when you have kids and they are out and you have to look for them? Then you have to leave at seven in the morning and go to the police station twice a week. I was doing that but I didn't say yes to them about drinking. I don't do anything while I'm drunk. They think I can kill someone.

I said to myself, after I see my kids I'm going to kill myself. I started drinking so I would have the guts to kill myself. I even said to myself, people die from drinking. I passed out. I tried my best not to wake up. But in the morning here I am again, still alive.

Every time I start drinking I took my daughter and son to my mother. I didn't want them to see me drunk. My mother understood. She always used to say, "Every time you drink call me." I'd call my mother and she'd come for the kids. Her house is within walking distance. Or one of the family would come and check to see if I was drinking.

I was trying to kill myself because I was fed up with my nightmares. I couldn't take care of my kids because I was haunted by him. He was trying to kill me in my dreams. I had a dream two days ago that he's after me with a knife. He said, "You have to die." I sometimes wake up as he's about to stab me. He's still out there in my dreams, beating me, pulling my hair. I've been fighting for my life not to follow him. Can a dream kill you? How come he has peace now and I'm still suffering? Sometimes I get really mad and say to him, "Why did you die?"

Everything changed in one night, one single night. I lost some part of my life. I loved my husband, I really did, but I was mad at him because he was beating me. When I think about the past, I think, why did I let him do that? I'm smarter than that. I always had a black eye. It was hard. I still think about him. I want to let it go but my mind is replaying it over and over again.

For two years I had to go back to jail 17 times because of the drinking. For two years I've been leaving my kids behind. Two years is a long time for them. I tried to commit suicide twice. I first slashed myself. I was in my jail room. But the knife wasn't good enough. I only had a plastic knife. Nobody found out. The second time I tried to hang myself. Then I stopped. First, I wanted everyone to know that killing myself was my fault. It was no one else's fault. Like when my little brother killed himself, my parents blamed themselves. I didn't want anyone to blame themselves. It's my own choice.

My kids are with my mother now while I'm in Montreal. They say I've been drinking that's why I had to come to a halfway house in the city. Just because I saved myself, here I am. I can't see my kids. I even say to myself, why didn't I just let him kill me.

Sometimes I still think about suicide but it's getting less. I drink because I feel lonely. My mother and father aren't enough. Why should I fight for my life when I don't have any more dreams? I used to have dreams. I wanted all my kids to be with me. I want my son to have a family of his own and not beat them up, to be a good father, a good husband. I wanted to be a grandmother, take care of my grandchildren. But I say, how can I do that? People still think I'm a killer. Inuit people. Everyone knows everyone even if they're strangers. But it's getting better. I say, let them think what they want.

I've been doing therapy and I have to go to AA meetings three times a week. In AA I don't talk. I hear other people's problems so I feel

I'm not that different. I see myself in their stories. I have a few numbers just in case I want to drink. I call them first. But I've been thinking, no, I don't want to touch it again because it hurts me. That's why I'm here. When I'm drinking I do things I don't want to do, like talking to people. I go to people and say hi, hello. I go to strangers in a bar and talk to them. I don't do that when I'm not drunk. They come to me instead. I don't go to anybody just like that. When I get drunk and talk to a guy, I almost go to bed with him and I feel bad about it. I used to do that when I was a teenager. I didn't like it at all. I'm more like a woman now, I hope *(light laugh, a delicate giggle that seems to spring from her in a joyous wave, a melodic flow).*

I was drinking a lot. I'm getting better and better. I'm stopping. Let me just be myself, not to be scared of anybody who's coming. When I go out and hear someone walking fast behind me, I have to check. I have to look right away because I get scared. It still happens. When someone is running behind me I get frozen.

I have to learn to forget about my past. I want to start a new life. I want to like myself. When I was growing up I learned not to talk about the past, to hide it inside. Now I can talk about it. You can commit suicide over the past if you don't talk. I almost did. I didn't like myself at all but I'm trying to like myself now. That's the only way I can be happy.

I want to start a new life. Be a mother. Try to work. I'd like to help other women who are getting abused. If someone is like me, don't feel that you're alone *(crying)* because I felt that way for a long time. It's hard to just come to a person and say, "I'm getting beaten up." I'm starting to learn to talk to other people about how I feel. I feel better when I talk about myself. I didn't know how to trust. I'm still working on it. It takes time.

My court worker is trying to let me go home when I have my trial. I'm going to court February 3 in my hometown. She wants me not to come back because she knows I have to take care of the kids. That's why I'm doing the therapy, to stop drinking, to help myself. When Arley leaves the foster home, I have to be there because I want him to know his mother cares for him. Before I wasn't paying attention to them because I had a drinking problem. Finally I'm waking up.

Going to court will be scary because I'm charged with second-degree murder. At the beginning I was charged with first-degree murder but they changed it. Now they want to change it to manslaughter but my lawyer doesn't even want manslaughter. He says it was clearly an accident.

I'm going to have my trial for one week. What scares me most is how people will feel about me because they're going to hear my story. Maybe they're going to be afraid of me. Wouldn't you be ashamed when people hear that you've been beaten up and you stayed with him all those years? I feel dumb but I know I couldn't get out from under. Everybody is telling me that just makes me a strong person but I just feel depressed about it. Maybe if I get to know myself, I might like myself. I know I couldn't be sitting here talking about getting to know myself if my husband would not have died. I want to believe in myself. Before I never had time to think about myself.

Now I'm getting stronger everyday. But sometimes it comes back. It's hard to be happy. I slashed myself again because when I'm sitting by myself, when I think about what my husband used to do to me, it hurts. I want that nightmare to get out of me. I still have flashbacks. Right now I'm angry with him for having died but I can see a time when the anger will be less because I have to give him peace too.

I want a normal life. I'd like to be a normal person, a normal woman. I'm starting to know what a normal woman is. I didn't know. My mother has a normal life now. I want to be responsible for my kids. I want to be responsible for myself. I want to sing. To sing in public has been a dream of mine. I used to look at my mother singing in public and used to say, "I want to be like her."

When my mom used to teach me about our culture, I used to feel good about myself. When she's cooking Inuit food, I used to be proud of myself. She cooked fish or seal, geese, caribou. She would boil them or fry them, mix in blueberries. It's delicious. I went picking berries with my mom a lot. I miss those old times. I can make them happen again.

I thought, I can fight to be happy. I can try that.

Mary was acquitted at her last court hearing.

RORY

I got his name from someone I had interviewed for A Good Enough Life, *my book on the terminally ill. She had met him several times at an Alcoholics Anonymous meeting and thought he would be ideal for me. She described Rory (60) as a therapist, someone who lived in the country and ran a home for boys with drug and alcohol problems. I called him. He sounded friendly, professional, and was willing to participate.*

The first interview took place one summer day. He arrived at my house almost an hour late with a cellular phone in hand, wearing shorts and a thick white bandage around his calves. He said he had just come from the emergency ward of the hospital. A friend of his had brought over a motorbike. He was experimenting with it, driving around in circles and fell. The bike fell on top of him, burning his calves. He was clearly in pain as he tried to find a comfortable position on the couch but paid it no attention.

He was short, solidly built, in shape, with a strong handshake and a deep resonant voice. Unperturbed by his accident, he was in good humour, confident, open, full of energy. A man with a purpose. Ready to offer himself.

He showed up the following week for the second interview. I was concerned. The material he had given me the first time was very disturbing. The pain and turmoil within him were palpable. The assured veneer was cracking before my eyes. This was a man who was being torn apart inside. He was waging an inner battle. As he answered my questions, mangled and torn pieces of himself came to light.

Before he left I said I would leave it up to him to call me for the next interview, if he was willing to continue. I walked him to his car. After I thanked him for being so open there was a moment of silence. I felt he wanted me to give him a goodbye kiss, a hug, and he was wondering if I would dare after what he told me. I moved close to him and gave him a hug that lasted a few seconds, then I moved away, incredibly touched by the realization of what this meant to him.

161

He smiled, clearly grateful, and left.

I never heard from him. This is the only portrait made up of two interviews, the only one I could not complete.

A few weeks later I read in the newspaper that he had been arrested for robbery.

I communicate spiritually with my god at least two to four hours a day. I do it several different ways, but the best is when I try to sit quietly. Alcoholics Anonymous was a trigger. It says, seek through prayer and meditation. So I seek. Prayer is nothing more than talking. I ask a lot of questions. Meditation is when I sit and listen. Thought through prayer and meditation to improve my conscious contact. To me consciousness is our soul. If I connect, I know what God's will is for me. Without His strength and courage I could never do it on my own. Once I found the Source and asked the energy in, I've been able to keep the negative at bay and have been able to blossom into the sunlight, into the positive of my life.

I received full parole in July 1967. I met the woman who is my wife today, Lorna, while on parole. She didn't know I was on parole, that I was a gangster. She was 19 going on 20. We met at a bar one night and she came back to the house with me because she was drunk. When I woke up in the morning she was there. I didn't know who she was, how she got there. We got talking and she said, "Do you have anything to drink?" There were just empty bottles and glasses with cigarette butts. We strained it all and were drinking. Then she said, "I'm going, I'll be back." Cops were looking for me already because I had violated my parole. I was using drugs and committing robberies. Two or three hours later there was a knock on the door. Lorna was standing there with a bottle of gin and $70. She was a godsend.

But while she was gone, I went looking for my gun. When she came back I said, "Did you take a gun?"

She said "Yeah. I threw it away. I don't like guns."

"Where the fuck did you throw my gun?"

"I'm not telling you."

We got into an argument but right then I was so sick, never mind the gun, I wanted the booze. The next thing I remember we wake up in Niagara Falls. Then in New York. Then in California. I got arrested in

California for attempted murder. I tried to kill a highway patrolman with a stolen car. They deported me back to Canada. When I came back I had to do the year-and-a-half I had left. During the time I was in jail she was coming up to visit. She was pregnant with my son. I was making her promises the same way I had done to my first wife. I knew as soon as I got out I was gone.

My last sentence was for 52 armed robberies. It was easier to rob. We robbed partly for the money, partly for the power. Money brought you prestige. Even back then I wore $500 to $1,000 suits. I wore Italian silks, funny little fedoras, smoked cigars. I picked up the style from the streets. I dressed and acted according to what I wanted to portray.

My sister used to say my actual personalities would change in front of her. I even had facial and body changes where she'd look at me across the table and didn't know me. As I physically changed, so did my personality. I believe that was drug-induced and alcohol was my first drug. It had a very powerful and dramatic affect on me. Immediate. I had to have it as often as I could because it was the only thing that quieted my mind, quieted the nightmares that were going on. It was like a tiger was clawing inside my head trying to get out.

It started when I was 11 years old, close to my twelfth birthday. We had just started back to school. I recognized the change taking place in me and became immediately very withdrawn and fearful because I said, "My God, if someone finds out that this is what I'm thinking..." The minute I started to drink I instantly hated my father and wanted to kill him. I was always thinking of ways to torture him.

I was born in 1936. My dad worked for the railroad until 1939, then joined the army and remained in the armed forces right through till he retired in 1957. He stayed in the army so he was away. I didn't really know my father that much. We stayed in Montreal and my mother raised us: me, my three brothers and sister. I'm the second to last. My oldest brother was identical to me in behaviour. The other three were fine. My mother and father were fine.

I remember my father once asking the judge if he could legally change my name because he felt he could no longer live with the embarrassment of what his son had brought on the family. I stole some guns from an army base he was stationed at in Victoria, B.C. He could have gotten into some really big trouble. I didn't care when my father asked that from the judge. I hated him anyways.

In the last 30 years I've done some really good inventory-taking. To be absolutely honest, I felt my father was always there. He was away because of his job. Like an airline pilot. And it was OK for my father to have a choice in life. It was OK for him to choose the army where he would be away.

I had very few friends. Ever. I liked living in my mind. I liked playing cowboys and Indians in my mind. My family wasn't even my friends because I didn't believe they understood me. If I said something to one of them, especially to my mom or dad, I always felt that we were in a different conversation because they always gave me a different answer back to what I thought I had asked. It got to maybe not bother me all that much because it always happened, so rather than tell them I kept quiet.

The voices started almost right away. When I was 11. Who was going to be the power? Who was going to have control over what I did? Who was I going to listen to? They were definitely different personalities. Some stronger than others. Some more manipulative than others. Some were smooth and subtle. They tried every way to win my favour. But if there was a me, I didn't know about it. I just knew I had no identity with anyone else and these entities were trying to control this physical body. I used to think I was from a different planet. I really did think there were people from outer space and I got here by mistake, that's why I didn't feel, think or act like anyone else.

Back then if you had a mentally retarded or a physically handicapped child, they were always hidden in a closet or put in an institution. Well, I looked OK but I knew that I wasn't OK, so I did everything in my power not to be put in one of these institutions I used to hear them talk about. Mental hospitals were torture chambers. Fifty people slept in one room, you only ate porridge, they kept you medicated, took part of your brain away.

I thought a form of insanity was coming over me. My thoughts were mainly about means and ways to hurt people physically, emotionally and mentally. Especially in a combination of all three. How could I torture them to the point before actually killing them? How could I drive them to the brink of insanity? Then I would end it because I would finally give in and put them out of their misery. I laid awake at night thinking about how to mass murder. What I would do with them? Cook them and eat them. Dismember them. Maim them. I'd actually play a motion picture in my head of what I was going to do and how. That would give me great pleasure.

Is it only me who thinks this way? Acts this way? Am I the only guy who tortured the cat in the alley? The only guy who tied the cats' tails together and set them on fire? What's the thinking of the majority of society? Is it rational? What is rational? To me, my kind of thinking has always been rational because that's all I ever had.

When people talked about joy, I thought of stabbing someone. That was joy to me. Joy wasn't getting an ice cream cone. Joy was seeing someone squirm, seeing someone walk across a yard full of broken glass bottles. Joy was stripping somebody and painting them with shutter green or boxcar red paint which was full of lead and you just couldn't get it off. Ecstasy is what it was! A voice inside me said, there are bigger and better things. Once I painted you I didn't want to do it again. What's next? I didn't want the end to be too close to the beginning. I wanted the fear to be in people and to last a long time.

I believe once I violated the values given to me as a child by drinking the way I did, I broke a moral code. The first time I did it nothing happened to me, so it became easier and easier. In retrospect, I can say there were two doors and I opened the wrong one.

From the moment these thoughts started, control and power were the motivating force. I stopped caring what my parents thought. I didn't listen to them. I became violent and aggressive. I started to stay out all night. The police started to come to the door for minor things.

In school I would make all the kids be disobedient. One day, in the fourth grade, a young substitute teacher came in. The blackboard was up front and the door to leave was at the back of the room. I made everyone in the two back rows masturbate in front of her and she was captured. She couldn't get out except to run through them. I loved that kind of power. And if my friends didn't do what I told them to they were in big trouble. I might have been small but I was very violent. I would really beat them up or throw them in the canal if they couldn't swim. I would always make sure someone would jump in to get them but I would frighten them to death. I would threaten to throw them in front of streetcars.

The kind of friends I had were people I could control. Me and friends who obeyed me used to get the sulphur from the railroad barrels and the rags full of oil that kept the wheels of boxcars from burning out the brakes. We would mix the sulphur, oil and rags, throw them down sewers and throw in a match. We'd blow the sewers up.

I went to school with the son of a famous Mafia family. The father was a night watchman. One morning, when he came home from work, the son decided to take his father's gun and bring it to school to show off. This was in Grade 2 or 3. We lined everyone up in the schoolyard. We didn't do nothing or shoot anyone but we held everybody hostage. I was always taking people hostage.

I held my family hostage. My mother would get my father's pay cheque and say, "I'm going to take you kids to the store for ice cream."

I'd say, "I don't want ice cream. I want a chocolate bar."

My mother would say, "We're all getting ice cream."

"I want a chocolate bar." I would absolutely refuse to go for an ice cream and knew that within five minutes my brothers and sister would be fighting with each other and with me. They would want to go for a picnic to a beach and I wouldn't want to go, so my mother couldn't go and they couldn't go.

The only history of mental illness was my grandmother, my father's mother, and only when she drank, like me and my oldest brother. Then she was a raving maniac. When she was drunk she would hit you with a chair, break a bottle over your head, roll around the ground with you and pull your hair out. She was always fighting with my father and his brothers if she was visiting for Mother's Day and happened to get into some booze. She'd fist fight with them. They had to wrestle her to the ground and hold her down. It was quite a scene most of the time with Grandma.

While my father was growing up she was never there. There are five boys in my father's family and they brought themselves up on the street because their father died in the First World War. They were street kids. When their mother would come home and they were there, she used to beat them beyond description. Yet every one of those boys turned out perfect.

My brother was seven years older than me and a raving maniac far exceeding me at that time. I got to blame everything on him. I liked his lifestyle because nothing seemed to affect him. No matter what my mother said he never listened. He never came home on time, never did things. As I got to be about 10 or 11 years old I started to act that way and it worked. I was never there for supper when I was supposed to be.

My brothers and sister disliked me because my mother would have them out on the street looking for me, so that meant they didn't get their supper until I got home.

I liked hearing people talk about my brother. They'd say, "Don't fuck with Crazy Rad." My brother would hit you over the head with a crowbar. He would throw you through a plate glass window. All of us are small in stature yet are extremely violent. The biggest of men were frightened of me. I was king of my wing in San Quentin Penitentiary where 99.9 percent of inmates were black, twice my age, three times my size. Yet I was feared like Satan and knew how to push people's buttons.

From almost the first time I drank, I emotionally died. I was instantly thrown into a state of indifference and that's where the insanity came from. I couldn't understand why it was a joy to hurt my mother, not the reverse. I loved to torture her because I knew she loved me so. The more she loved me, the more I hurt her. I called her a slut and a pig. It had absolutely nothing to do with reality. My mother's reaction was to hide. Go into another room. Leave the house. Not deal with it. Say, "I'm going to pray for you."

I bummed a lot of school. I would hang around the poolroom and run messages for crooks and gangsters. I met this man. I knew he carried a gun because every once in a while, in the poolroom, he showed his weapon. Some people would leave or back away. He walked up to people and say, "I need $10," and they'd give it to him. I saw how much power that man had over people.

I was 11 and one day I said to him, "I want a gun."

He said, "Tonight we'll go rob the tavern." Before the robbery he gave me the gun.

He was teaching me the trade. This man was 72 and about 6-4, lanky. He had a very heavy English accent. Always dressed impeccably. He was a ladies' man. He still wasn't like my brother. My brother was my best idol because he had the insanity and this man didn't, but he had a coolness about him that I liked. I never had the coolness because I could lose it. He knew he could trust me with his back and that's what robbery is all about. If he went in and I was his backup, he knew that if someone would try to hurt him I would act. I would shoot. The thought of shooting back excited me.

One of the last taverns we robbed we came running out and there was a police car. I got arrested for the first time at the age of nearly 12 for five armed robberies. We were both sent to jail. He got five years and I got 18 months.

I was sent to Bordeaux. They put me in a cell that was four-foot wide, six-foot long, and had a solid steel door. They slammed that door shut. I thought I would die through absolute insanity. Instinctively I knew that life was over at that point. That's why the indifference came into my life. It was instantaneous. I couldn't even think about causing trouble, or holding my mother, talking to my sister. Life was over.

The day they slammed that solid steel door shut I lost all identity to the rest of the world and to my family. When I hear that slam my ears go up and I want to remember. I want to remember dying. I instantly knew that in order to survive I had to get the men that shut the door on me. Ten minutes later a guard opened the door to feed me for the first time and I attacked him. I ended up spending four or five months in the hole on bread and water. No lights. I felt absolutely alone. Absolutely deserted. I wanted to hurt any name that came into my mind because they had done it to me. My mother, father, brothers, sister. The guard. The judge. It was everyone else's fault that I was in this state. I kept trying to get out so I pounded my head against the wall. It was a relief compared to what was actually going on in my head.

But jail was a fantastic experience because my older brother was already in. I got to hang around with him on the wing. I got to beat people up. I got to hang around with the big boys. People said, "Don't fuck with him. That's Crazy Rad's brother." If I wanted a package of cigarettes I'd just snap my fingers. My brother taught me how to hit people over the head with crowbars. I learned to have fun in prison. I learned how to survive in that world.

My brother and I were in jail together twice. The first time and the third time. The only thing we ever talked about, when at least four other people were listening, was how we were going to be the best hit men in the world, how we were going to be the Irish Mafia, how people were going to seek us out. He died about 10 years ago, when he was 57, a chronic alcoholic, an addict, in a psychiatric hospital.

I tried to rape my mother just after I came out. I remember being ill, sick to my stomach, and she came and laid down beside me in bed, trying to comfort me. And I tried to rape her. She was very nice about it, I didn't penetrate, she just pushed me away and told me that she loved me and that was the wrong thing for me to do and I should try to get some sleep. I just rolled over and forgot about it. I ignored it like she ignored it. That was the first and only sexual thing that was part of my background, except my wife, but in those days I didn't think what I was doing to her was actual rape.

Soon after that I remember sitting in a restaurant with a really good friend of mine and his girlfriend. He had to go somewhere and asked me to walk her home. I walked her home and instantly fell in love. Once he turned her over to me she became mine and not his. I would not let anyone go near her including him. Several days later I stabbed him 15 times because she wanted to be with him and not me. I stalked her. I sat on her doorstep 24 hours a day. Her parents phoned the police on me. My friend ended up very seriously injured in the hospital. Thank God he didn't die. I hadn't tortured him enough. I stabbed him too quickly.

Then I went to New York because I started to hear about the glamour of places like New York, Chicago, the big cities. But I got arrested and deported for breaking and entering. Six months after I got back I married my first wife. We had grown up together, were childhood friends. I was 17 going on 18 and she was 15 going on 16. I got her pregnant. I married her because good Catholic boys marry the girls they get pregnant.

Shortly after I was married, my next sentence was five years for another armed robbery. In jail I started to take heroin and continued to take it every day for nine years. I used sleeping pills, downers, depressants. In jail you always pick up different attitudes, different behaviours. You heard of robberies that could have been done but never were. There were thoughts of maybe changing my MO, modus operandi, hanging around with guys that were big-time boosters. But I wasn't interested in breaking into people's houses and carrying out TVs or jewellery. I wanted to go in, get the money, and get out in two or three minutes. There was no power in the other.

I would go in and out of prison. Every time I would be coming out, I would promise her to get a normal job and do normal things. But I always went back to robberies because it was easy. Every time I went in I made promises so she would take me back and every time she took me back she got pregnant. So there were three children to that marriage. My oldest daughter is 42. One of my sons has definitely shown some signs. My youngest daughter has the exact same traits except physically, to my knowledge, hasn't hurt anyone. But emotionally and mentally she's really hurt a lot of people. She's 36 and has been on the street since she's 14. She's prostituted all over the world, nearly died several times from severe beatings by pimps. I didn't see her for 14 years. Recently she came in from Vancouver because she heard I had a heart attack. She said she came in to make amends but started right away with the torture. "It was your fault, you did this to me." She wouldn't shut up.

I said, "I've past the stage where you can harm me." And she kept trying to do it and it doesn't work anymore because I know the Source.

The reason she couldn't harm me was because I was much more powerful than her. I would concentrate on something to the point where…if I wanted to use the negative side of it, I could really focus in on you and make you squirm and dance right there on the sofa. You could be walking down the street and wonder why you were paranoid. I would torture people that way and would make subtle phone calls. I would plant little thoughts in your mind so you would be afraid to leave your house. I would set up a number of people to call you. And once I got into a rage I could hurt you really badly. Like my first wife. She ended up with water on the brain. When she appeared in court her head was three times the size. It was absolutely purple where I had beaten her. My oldest daughter, who loves me dearly today, I beat her within an inch of her life.

I would write a letter to my first wife saying, "Don't go to bed tonight because I'm coming." She had special permission to phone the prison every night. She would phone the chief guard on the midnight shift to make sure I was in my cell because I emotionally and mentally tortured her to the point where she never slept. Or she would always wake up thinking that I was going to be there. I was with my first wife about 10 years, in and out of prison, before we were actually divorced. The last encounter I had with her was in a bedroom where I kept her in bed with a gun in her mouth or ear for three days while I was stoned. She didn't move. She went to the bathroom right in the bed. If she slept, it was because she would pass out. Neither of us ate. I just sat there and took drugs, went into rages and raped her constantly.

Again I ended up in New York. It was still cops and robbers time. Mobs were different back in those days than they are now. They were mobsters. Now they're white-collar mobsters. I liked being chosen by some of the people I worked for. I did work for some pretty important Mafia types in cities all over Canada and the U.S. A few in Europe.

The mob gravitated toward me because of my insanity. I was known as the Iceman. I could be looking at you, kissing you and killing you at the same time. I was in a state of absolute indifference and nothing mattered except… It was difficult for me to work for them because they wanted it done fast and I liked to torture you. Killing someone fast was no good. It had to be emotional torture. To the extreme, really extreme. If the mob wanted someone iced or if they wanted someone really hurt very badly, I didn't like doing it right away. One time I remember breaking a guy's kneecaps with a baseball bat. I didn't enjoy it because I just went in and out of his house. I didn't get time to scare him. The torture gave me the greatest amount of pleasure. I've only killed three people in my life but I've killed 10,000 emotionally and mentally. They will never, ever recover from the scars.

I tortured people both inside and outside of prison. It used to be nicer in prison because they were locked in a cell and couldn't get out. I was not locked in the cell with them but it could be arranged. I would torture someone because he mightn't have passed the salt when I asked. Maybe he didn't pay my friend the debt of cigarettes. I remember in the old pen, in St. Vincent de Paul, they used to have a rock quarry. The railroad went inside. Two men picked up a third, who owed them a package of cigarettes, and put him between two knuckles of a car as someone was guiding the train back to hook up. I've seen young boys get their penises bitten right off. I've seen people get broomsticks up their rectum and have their spines broken. I was part of it all.

I worked in the bakery of a prison. We had a machine about the size of a room. I was making bread, thousands of loaves, because we supplied the other prisons in the area. I was sitting in a chair, watching the bread in the oven. Two men walked in, shut the machine off, threw a body in the dough machine and turned it back on. I didn't move off my chair. I continued to read my comic book. I couldn't even read but I looked at pictures. I was almost illiterate. Fifteen minutes later I called a guard over and said, "Somebody put some red food colouring in my machine. The dough is ruined, it's all red." He stopped the machine and the first thing he found was a finger.

Your identity is gone, so part of your madness is who am I, where am I, where do I belong, what's happening to me? You have no identity with any race, colour, creed, person, family, even institution. I'd be in prison with 5,000 men and feel alone. I didn't feel any connection. Why should I feel all alone at a baseball game with 10,000 people? While everyone is screaming and hollering, I feel empty, alone, detached. I use the word fear because it would make me strike out. My agitations were real fast and heavy and I always physically struck out. So many things triggered the rages. I was actually more violent when I was not using.

After I had started drinking as a child, after I felt that I lost my identity with the rest of the world and I became indifferent, nothing mattered to me. The torment of my mind drove me insane. I was afraid of it because I knew what would happen. I had no control. I couldn't stop it. I'd get in a fetus position on a cold cement floor, especially in prison, and say, I want to change, I want to change, I want to change, I need to change, I need to change, and I couldn't change because this power wouldn't let me. But I wanted to, needed to change, but couldn't. No matter what I did.

I've done time in five major penitentiaries. I spent a lot of time in the southern part of the U.S. Did five years in San Quentin for armed robbery, a bank job where a policeman got killed. I was driving the car and got five to 15.

Two murders happened during robberies where I pulled the trigger. One in Illinois in a big linen factory and another in Philadelphia in an abattoir. The third one was in a fight over drugs in a motel room. I was charged right away. All three were dropped to second-degree murder. I was sentenced to eight years and would probably do two-and-a-half to three years, so you just go in and out, in and out. I was never charged with first-degree murder because it was always reduced through plea bargaining.

If I was up on a charge, the lawyer would sometimes ask for a psychiatric evaluation and if they found you not sound psychiatrically, you either got a lesser sentence or they put you in a mental hospital. Instead of getting five or 10 years, it was an indefinite sentence. In six months time, if you played the game right, you were cured and they would let you out. I learned how to play the game. That's why I'm a therapist, the easiest people in the world for me to fool were the therapists, psychiatrists or psychologists. They were a piece of cake. The ones I couldn't fool were other cons because they knew my game. You can't con a con.

Doctors refuse to listen to the truth because they say it can't be that way. But it is that way. The more they tried to rearrange me the worse I got. The more they tried to fix me the worse I got.

First time I was put into a mental hospital I was about 19. But I escaped. I had two stays in the Douglas Psychiatric Hospital in Verdun, Quebec and three in U.S. prison mental hospitals. I also spent 60 days in evaluation at Bordeaux, on the wing for the criminally insane. I was totally disobedient. I would run around the ward and light all the waste-paper baskets. I was always causing trouble, always into fist fights with other inmates. Every time I acted out or did something that wasn't right, I got punished. Got a needle in the arse. Was put into the rubber room with no clothes and padded walls because I would ram my head into the wall.

Shock treatment was prevalent in those days, so I got shock treatment. When you come out of it, your energy is all gone. You're docile. You're weak. You know you're frightened but you don't know what you're frightened of. The mind and body didn't feel the way they normally did, even though they were crazy. As long as they were crazy, it was OK. Any time a sign of sanity came, it wasn't OK. There was something desperately wrong. But after the treatments I got back to my old self.

I kept looking in the mirror, looking for this insanity that I couldn't see. I would look at other inmates and could see the insanity. I could see the twisted minds and hear their slurred speeches. But I looked like I look now. I couldn't see my own insanity.

My sister described me well. I could change with a snap of a finger. I remember awakening in a chicken coop on a farm, I don't know how I got there, and I was having sex with a chicken. Still today that does awful things to me mentally because I'm afraid that if people ever find out they're going to lock me up in a crazy house and I know I don't belong there. I have no control over any of these things. I'm trying to give you the sense of powerlessness. I mean I tore that chicken into a million little pieces.

When people would talk about feelings, it was, "How would you feel if someone stabbed your mother?" Fine. And they would look at you. But it was fine because I had a point in my life where my mother deserved to have her heart cut out. Perfectly normal. To me. Did it upset me? No. It made me feel that I was different, that I wasn't understood.

Why wasn't it OK for me to feel that way? Why did you want me to feel some way that I didn't feel?

I remember actually watching an elderly woman when we were robbing a bank. We had her in an open area where other people could see her and she was peeing in her pants. She was very, very embarrassed and I pointed it out to everybody. That elated me. Not only did I have the power to make her pee in her pants, but I made everybody watch.

I was in a police station when they brought in a couple of transvestites. I made them strip, as if they were strippers, in front of all the boys and then I made them have oral sex with some of the guys. The police cheered us on. They thought it was fun. That was the kind of violence in me.

For the longest time in my life I couldn't feel physical pain. One of the last examples of that was when I had 11 teeth still in my head. I went to the dentist and asked him to extract them because they were all rotten. He said, "I'll either have to put you to sleep or give you freezing."

I said I didn't want either. "Just pull them."

I sat in the dentist's chair and had 11 teeth pulled without any emotion whatsoever. I didn't feel anything. Heard just the crunching. I didn't think the dentist would make it through the 11 teeth without passing out.

I got into many car accidents while drunk, running from the police, being chased. I broke my back three times. I broke my seventh, eighth, ninth and tenth vertebrae. I'm lucky to be walking. I have a plastic kneecap. I shattered my knee and there's a couple of pins in that. I don't actually have an elbow. The bone came through and they just cauterized it.

I thought there would come a day when I would be able to get someone to understand my pain through causing them pain. That's a paradox, I know. I was always in pain. The pain that I was in was indifference, absolutely no feeling, which is even worse than cutting my head off. When you can't feel anything, when nothing matters, it's the greatest pain that I think anybody can ever feel. I don't think I would have reacted if someone would have raped my daughter in front of me. There was total emptiness. Basically I was creating all this pain around me to stop the indifference. That's a word I learned from the doctors involved with me, state of indifference.

The only identity I had was with my thoughts. No identity with other criminals. I could identify with other real weirdos, like the ones that dared tell. If you look at the Bernardo case, he said very little. It was all present on tape but he never told anyone what his thoughts really were. But I know what his thoughts were.

What you're actually doing gives you an identity. We try to identify with things, people, places, and we can't. We don't even come close. We lie a lot. Life is meaningless. There is a total disassociation from the self, total, except from your thoughts. But your thoughts are always unstable, changing. The violence comes from the agitation the thoughts create.

There are several characters within me and they're all violent. It's almost like they describe schizophrenia or multiple personalities. I never actually heard voices but I heard a lot of thoughts. Charlie would say to me, "I want you to do this." Sam would say, "I want you to do that." John would say something different. Michael would say something else. I was always being talked to. I never put any names to the voices but they were distinctly separate. They just drove me crazy. They were all vicious. They always tried to get me into trouble, always had power over me. They took over my physical being. I actually went out and did most of the things my thoughts told me to do. The people I tortured emotionally and mentally would have been better off if I had killed them.

Because of my mother and because of being Catholic, I knew I had been possessed by Satan. At least that was an answer to why I was the way I was. My prayers were, "Please release me of this bondage because my thoughts are driving me crazy." All the times I tried to stay sober and clean I couldn't because the insanity would be so great that I would go right back to the drugs. That was the only thing which could quiet it.

My life was a state of indifference and insanity. Now I talk about my past without emotion. There are times when I do have a great deal of emotion and it throws me for days and days, so I don't allow it to come back. I don't need the pain.

Before I started praying there were moments of clarity and sanity in prison, but I would push it away, get rid of it. When I had a thought like, you're going to be OK, I thought, this is hopeless. It's not going to happen. So I'd get rid of it.

I was released from prison for the last time in 1967. I walked away from the past. I went into AA and that's where I found salvation. The insanity actually started to subside the longer I was away from drugs and alcohol. I was released about a year and started to help kids on the street.

I accept the fact that I'm very different, yet I've learned to play the worldly game. But now I know the Source and knowing the Source has been able to take away the power that controlled me so I absolutely have no fears.

Now I feel gratitude that I'm able to recognize the pain I caused. I'm truly regretful that I did hurt or damage anybody. I wouldn't harm anybody today. I know that. I truly believe that there is a power of positive and a power of negative. I believe in God and I believe in Satan. You could call Satan whatever you want. It's a force that drives some people to the brink of insanity. That's one of the reasons that I got into therapy. There are a lot of us out there but in different degrees. Some I have treated in the work I do today. The majority of people I've treated, the insanity has only stayed on an emotional and mental level. There's been very little or no action. Few of us have taken it beyond, like Bernardo. His wife, Homolka, was much better at it than he because she got the system to let her off. I understand those kinds of people. Once the thought is put into our mind, the action must take place. We are completely powerless. There are no deterrents against us.

I'm the first non-medical person to actually design medical treatment facilities for alcoholics and addicts. So I'm highly recognized for my work in behavioural therapy, behavioural modification. And I never use any other tool but the spiritual re-entry, having someone spiritually come back to life again. I believe it's spiritual death that causes the problem. Some of us go so far beyond the bottom that we die or go absolutely insane and never recover. Spirituality was the basis of my recovery. I have yet to see any other magic work.

In 1966 there was a young man in the cell next to me and he was taking a Bible study course. He asked me if I would help him with his test. I had to ask him questions that had to do with belief; "Whoever shall believe in me shall have everlasting life."

That night I prayed for the first time in my life. I think I might have said, because of my mother, "If there is a God, please help me." I had asked for forgiveness of all my thoughts and all the things I had done. About two o'clock that morning, when the guard made his round, he woke me with his flashlight. I was kneeling down beside my bed. I got up. Went to bed. After that I stopped all drugs but I was basically still a very troubled person, but I thought I knew the Source.

And I've been OK since. That was the other door that I opened and kept opening. I recognize that the thing that was controlling me, I could control by asking God into my life and by being willing to develop a spiritual way of life.

A lot of things really made sense to me in 1971. That's when I went to Germany on a visit. It was kind of a gift. A priest was taking a bunch of teenagers to look at what the Holocaust had done and they needed an extra adult as a supervisor. They had four or five adults but one of them had backed out the last minute. I knew this Catholic priest and he asked me if I would go. I was clean then and had been since 1967. One of the first places we went to was the Dachau concentration camp. As I was viewing Dachau I knew exactly who and what I was. I was one of those men that tortured the Jewish people. I had already had thoughts as a child, even before them, of maybe strapping someone to a rack and peeling their skin off. It was the first sign that I wasn't the only one on the face of the earth. Up until that time I thought maybe I was. Most of the time I could hide it from the rest of the world. But my insanity kept me awake. I never slept. I lived at night. I hated the light. I very rarely went out during the day.

I stayed in Dachau maybe 20 minutes. I viewed several of the photographs and then someone said, "Let's go see the ovens." That's when I had to get out. I ended up in a chapel on the grounds. A nun saw the state of mind I was in. She must have seen my insanity and sat down to talk to me. I spilled it out. It was the first time I had talked to anybody.

At the end she said, "It's OK, God loves you just like he would have loved Hitler had he asked for forgiveness." She then went to find Father Dermitt on the property. He had known about my criminal background but not the insanity. We spent several days together and he sent me home.

Today I communicate with thoughts that are positive, except for Sam and Charlie. Sam is the good guy and Charlie is the agitator. In the past they would really drive me crazy. It was like a board of directors up there and no one was agreeing. We call it the racing mind. Everyone is arguing with everyone else and nobody is getting anywhere. Charlie would plant a thought in my mind. I would harbour the thought for a while because I liked playing with it. Then I would get mad and chase him away. Sometimes he would try to come back quickly. Sometimes he would stay away for days. The longer I was sober, the longer I stayed away from drugs, the less he appeared. Even now when he has appeared it has always been very mild, a playful kind of provocation, up until I met Cathy.

Lorna, the lady I've been with for the last 30 years since I've come out of prison, is a wonderful person. I feel the need to embrace people, comfort them and all the rest of it. I thought that's what love was. Then I met Cathy about six months ago and fell in love. I never knew it existed. It's something totally brand new in my life. Never thought that two people could actually become one.

We met at McDonald's. We were just standing there and started talking. I have a bad habit of talking to a lot of people. I ate with her, her four children and her husband. She asked me what I did for a living and I gave her a business card. She's kept in touch with me.

I believe, again, a door. I keep talking about doors, a door opened in the restaurant and our souls actually met and touched. Our minds melted into one. Something happened to us. It was just a brand new emotion that I didn't think existed. I didn't think that someone could love another person that deeply.

I saw her after that first meeting and kept wanting to see her more and more and more and more. The first meetings were so complete. It didn't matter where we went, in the car or walking, I just wanted to be with her.

Nothing has happened to us in these six months except there's an overwhelming emotional desire to be near her, to share her life, to never be separated. She told me she shared my feelings.

I know I'm not going to take this any further and I won't allow her to. She hasn't asked for more and I haven't asked for more. She's 31 and I'm 60. That's one thing. Two, for the last three years, because of my severe diabetes, I'm sexually inactive. So there's nothing there except for the bond which is really beautiful. When I talk to her on the phone, when I share with her, I'm tremendously enjoying it. It's an experience I never thought possible. I don't need to act upon it. We just share thoughts. She says it's easier for her to share her bad day with her four kids with me than with her husband because he doesn't want to listen.

I think one of the reasons a lot of us don't speak out is either we're misunderstood or people are frightened of us. Or what I can say would harm me in many ways if I shared some of the control that these voices, these entities, have. In 1966, in the prison cell, I was able to stop it to the point where actions stopped. But since meeting Cathy, the actions haven't started yet but the thoughts are there and it's like they never stopped and it's like I've been growing the world's largest pumpkin. It's been amazing how it never really died in me. It was just arrested. I really think that this young lady...I'm going to say it...the angel that I saw standing in front of me is really a witch who has great powers over me and has triggered off these thoughts of violence, thoughts of things that I was before.

How do I get rid of the husband? The first thoughts are not, how do you kill him, but how do you set him up? Remember, killing some-one for me is unimportant. I want to torture him. I want him to be in a lot of pain. How do I plant the seed in his mind that his wife is the best cocksucker that ever was? When she was making love to me, yet I told you that I can't, she told me how much she hated you. The torture has already started in my mind. How do I plant seeds in the children's mind that would get them to turn against him? It's already happening. I want this woman. I want everyone away from her.

I haven't made love to her, yet making love to her would be ecstasy. In my mind, when I'm with her sexually, the climaxes are so great that she loses her ability to control her own body and I love it because the pleasure is gone. It's something she can't stop and she's telling me to stop and I won't.

When we meet I make the father mind the four kids. I threaten him. He has a motorcycle that he loves dearly. I told him he'll find it in a million pieces in his yard. Then I would start on him, one finger at a time. We spoke last night at two in the morning. Every time she says no to me, these personalities that I talked about come out and they be-come very pronounced and all four are starting to reactivate themselves. It's easy for someone to realize they're not safe if they resist the demands of that entity. But she calls me.

I know it's the first time in my life that I'm telling someone. No one has ever really shared what happens emotionally and mentally in-side because we're too afraid. I'm telling you things that are damaging. They could be damaging to me, to my family. So people don't tell you what's going on with them. I could walk along St. Catherine Street and pick out the walking dead. I'm a magnet for them. I wonder if I would ever allow a room full of psychiatrists or psychologists to pick my brain? I wonder if I would be honest with them? They would be looking for something that isn't there. Well, it's really not that way. But it is that way. That's the way it really is.

In the last couple of days I've had a tremendous struggle with myself not to just wander off somewhere and I don't know if it's because I'm now faced with all this stuff that's really inside of me, really never dealt with except on the surface. I never sat down with anybody before and talked about the real mental violence, the real mental anguish that I've suffered. Maybe I want to go away like my cat without anyone knowing about it. I have to get away from this relationship because it's killing me. I'm emotionally dead. I'm not completely there yet.

It hasn't been clear whether I would act on these thoughts. My mind hasn't gone that far. I meditated an hour this morning. Though these thoughts are not part of the centre, the Source, nevertheless they're trying to enter all the time. They're coming closer. I'm a little concerned that maybe this relationship has triggered off something...having fallen in love six months ago...might have triggered off something that's reversing...am I turning back to what I was when I was a child? I have never felt love in my life, never throughout my 60 years, and now I can't have it.

Me and my grandmother, my father's mother, were best of friends. She would let me stay at her place. She used to hide me from the police. I did everything I could with my grandma. I took her for joyrides in stolen cars. She was a chronic alcoholic and I guess I became an automatic partner. My father and his brothers were always trying to prevent her from drinking. I encouraged her to drink. I would rob places, then with a pocketful of money take my grandma to the bar to drink. She used to do up her hair, put on rouge. I'd buy her and her friends booze. We would get drunk together. There were certain bars where the alkies hung around, the older set. And this was her grandson. I was her knight in shining armour.

One night I remember stealing a brand new Buick convertible. I parked it in front of the bar. Around one o'clock in the morning we got in the car ready to go home. I got halfway through a red light and the damn thing stalled. Before I know it, a police car was behind me. The policeman gets out and, seeing my grandmother is tipsy and so am I, he asks what the problem is. I look down at the needle and say, "I'm driving my grandmother home and I just realized that my gas tank is empty." There was only one gas station open at that time and it was for taxis.

The cop says, "I'll go get you some gas." The cop got me five gallons of gas. And here I am sitting in a stolen car with my grandma. They didn't ask for a licence or anything. They were more interested in this nice guy driving his grandma home.

I loved my grandmother. Very much. She excited me. She was fun to be with. She would do things that I would do. She died in my arms of a heart attack on her way to the hospital in the ambulance. On Mother's Day. I was about 20 years old. I was in the ambulance that took her away. I don't know how I felt when she died. I never thought about it. I guess there are a lot of things I never thought about.

I need Cathy now. I want to hurt her.

Maybe I didn't have any emotions when she died. Maybe she was just a fun old lady. Maybe I disguised how I really felt. Maybe I really thought she was a dirty old slut, fucking around and not taking care of my father and his brothers. Maybe the things that I did with her was to hurt her, not to have fun with her, to make her worse.

I don't want to stop it, the voices. I do, but I don't. I have to honestly say to you I don't know why. All I know is that I don't. My spirit of darkness is always trying to win me. The light was clear until I met her, a few months ago. And then the waters got mucky again.

I'm just talking about going off. For many years I've thrived on solitude. Solitude was a great comforter. Lately I see myself slipping back into solitude. I want to be alone. I don't want people around me. When I think of being alone it brings up emotions that I don't want. It's really been very horrid for me for the last few days. Really, really horrid.

I want to do like my little cat. I want to get away from her but I also want to get away from everything else because I feel that's the only way I can survive mentally. Even if there are children involved. My youngest is almost 26. There is a marriage. But I'm saying for the first time in my life that I count and that's what I want to do in whatever time I have left. I want to live on a highway somewhere with a sack over my back and a bandanna around my head. They keep driving me and driving me in that direction.

I think that being alone is going to be my only salvation. Salvation from myself, my thoughts and eventually my actions. The only people I'll have to fight with are my board of directors, Sam and Charlie.

I came here to show you a real person, what I really am, which very few people have ever seen.

RICHARD

Richard (36) was recommended to me by his parole officer. At the initial phone contact he was immediately willing to participate in the hope that his story would help the families of his victims to understand where a murderer comes from. He wanted them to comprehend how such an act could have been committed. He hoped to explain his actions. He thought that when his story came to light some of their questions would be answered and their fears that a murderer could now be loose might be calmed.

He was very direct. He told his story in a clear chronological flow and acknowledged that recounting the drama he had lived through, yet again, still had an emotional impact on him. Once he said, "I want to stop here. I have to live through this week and what I've just told you has been heavy."

He was French Canadian from northern Quebec. He was medium height, compact, with a slim build, dark, curly hair with a clean-cut, upfront and attractive manner.

For the first three crimes I was never arrested and questioned. For the fourth I leave the bar. He leaves the bar and follows me. I agree to walk with him till the end of the street because he says he's going in the same direction. Then I say I'm going another block and he says he's also going another block. Then I turn and he says he also has to turn.

Then I say, "I'm going down there because I live just behind this street."

He says, "I also live in the area."

Shit! I didn't want him to know where I lived. He was about my age. We talk a bit.

It's summer. I say, "I have to pick something up from a friend here."

He said, "I'll wait for you."

I feel stuck. I can't go home, neither can I go to my friend's house and stay there. I notice from the hallway that he's sitting on the fence waiting for me. He was waiting for a good 25 minutes. I thought, shit, this guy isn't going to leave. If he thinks I've gone to my friend's house and I don't leave, then he's going to think I'm gay. I think he must be gay and he wants me. I hate homosexuals because they destroy family life. I'm going to fight him. I take a small, old knife that doesn't cut very well. I wasn't interested in the quality of the knife wound. I just wanted to hurt him. I didn't want to take a good knife. I thought about that as I chose the knife.

The inspector asked, "Why didn't you take a big knife.""

"No, my big knife is a good knife. I wanted to keep that one."

I leave the apartment building. He's still waiting. I have the knife in my hand. I want to do it fast. I go to the end of the street and jump him. He wanted to give me his wallet. He wanted to give me everything. I stabbed him all over. Early on my knife broke at the handle. I kept hitting him with the handle. I just saw a black ball. I didn't see a person. I kept on stabbing. Punching.

He cried out and all of a sudden I noticed a light go on at the end of the street. He left in one direction and I left running in the other direction. I went home. I kept looking at the light that had lit up. I knew that he wasn't going to talk because he was obviously provoking me. I took a shower and went to bed. I had problems sleeping that night. I was disturbed because there might have been witnesses.

At eight the next morning I left for work. I got out on the street and there were three or four police cars. One policemen came over to me, "You live here?"

"Yes."

"What's your name? You're going to work?"

"Yes."

"Will you come to the police station after your shift? There was a stabbing on your street last night and we'd like to ask some questions." They were asking everyone questions.

I worked that morning as usual. I thought, I'll go see them. Maybe they'll help me. I thought I could tell them that I was provoked. Surely they wouldn't punish me for that. I have nothing to be afraid of. It'll be cleared up.

After work I went to the police. They asked questions. I said, "If you help me then I will help you." That's how it started. I had police inspectors who were gentlemen. They didn't mistreat me, didn't beat me. They weren't even rude to me.

Then one officer said, "We have a case similar to this one."

I said, "Yes, that was me."

They made me go through the whole description. They brought me supper. I thought if the police asked me questions, then everything will be clear from my answers. I used to watch westerns. I loved westerns, still today. It's a fetish. How do the westerns deal with a problem? Exactly the way I had reacted in life and exactly the way my mother had reacted while I was growing up. My mother also liked watching westerns. If something is not working, you take out your gun and shoot. I had the same attitude as the westerns. It's logical.

My third crime happened three months after the second one. This was winter. I went to the bar, danced a bit, went home. While crossing the bridge there were four guys who tried to steal my watch and wallet. They didn't succeed. I escaped. I was afraid. I ran home. Once I got home, to my fourth-floor apartment, I looked outside in case they had followed me. I saw one on the other side of the street. He was walking up and down, from one end of the street to the other. And he spotted me. Imagine how you feel! I look out the window and see someone looking up at me. I turned off the light. I closed the curtains. But he had seen me. He knew where I lived. I started to get very scared. What's going to happen? Is he going to come up and beat me because he doesn't want me to tell anyone that he had tried to rob me? What does he want? Why was he there? I said to myself, he's going to get it. I got ready for a fight. He's at my house and he's spying on me. I take a small knife from the kitchen. Maybe seven inches long. I'm going to give him one stab. Then he's going to stop spying on me.

I went downstairs. He's at the corner of the street. I'm afraid but I'm going. As soon as he sees me he begins to walk away. I follow him. I walked faster to catch up. He turned a corner and I turned a corner. When he got near the school I went for him. I stabbed him in the back. He turned around and I stabbed him in the stomach. He sat down in the snow bank. He looked up at me and didn't say a word. Nothing. It seemed as if the stab wounds didn't even hurt him. I said, "Do you have what you want?" I felt I finally I had peace. The fear left. I did what I had to do. I left to go home. A truck was picking up snow from the streets and I put the knife into a snow bank. At home I took a shower, drank two Cognacs.

He had two knife wounds. He didn't die. I never heard about him again. I read nothing about it in the papers. Maybe he didn't want to talk about it. He knew he was asking for it. He was provoking me by spying in front of my house. He had been there for an hour-and-a-half. Maybe he thought that as soon as I was asleep he could come up and rob me. I didn't want to go to sleep while he was still there. If during the time of the westerns that way of life was accepted, why not today? For me it was a settling of accounts.

Two or three months before that my mother was calling my father a homosexual because in the mine there was a communal shower. The same old fight was starting all over again. I was caught between them. My mother used to say, "It's worse in other houses, in other families." So you're happy with what you've got.

Then I see that the inspectors are closing their dossier. It's solved. I panic. "No, it's not finished. There weren't just two, there were four." I said there was a crime New Year's Eve and then there was another crime at the bridge.

Three or four other investigators arrived. "Tell us." I finished the whole story in the small hours of the morning. They gave me coffee. I was well-treated. They said, "Let's take a break. We'll also give you a break. You'll go to sleep. We'll give you a cell."

"Can't I go home?"

"No."

I didn't realize how serious my crime was. I thought I could go home. I would have gone home to sleep and would have gone back to the police station the next day at two or three in the afternoon, after work.

They said, "We can't let you go. You're under arrest."

That's when I had a shock. I said, "Can I call my father?" I called my father who was with another woman for the past week. That bothered me. Here I was in jail.

My father came to see me. He said, "It's not possible, it wasn't you."

"Yes, it was."

"No."

"Yes, it was me!"

"It can't be. It's a mistake."

"Yes. Yes, it's me. Stop saying what you want to hear, this is what happened."

From that point on I became very harsh. If I say that's a green sweater I don't want them to tell me, no, no, it's blue. It's green! No, it couldn't have been you. They made a mistake. It was me! Stop saying what you want to hear. Stop!

A lawyer who I didn't even pay asked me for one thing. "Tell the truth or you'll be in for 25 years."

I said, "I want my sentence to be based on the truth. If they think I was crazy, I'll accept it. If they put me away for 25 years, that's fine." I wanted to get to the bottom of things. I wanted to know why I did what I did.

The terrible shock was to realize that I had allowed myself to live in such fear and the fear pushed me to act in extreme ways. Why do I right away think of the worse thing that can happen? He had lived in the same area as myself. Everything scared me. I was paranoid. My mother made me hate a lot of people. Just watching people walk on the sidewalk, she'd say so-and-so is a whore, so-and-so is disgusting, so-and-so is just passing the house to see if she can see in. If it's a man, he's a fag. But she didn't know any of these people. They were just walking on the street. We had a big window with a curtain. You could see outside but the people from the outside couldn't see in. She stood in front of the window constantly criticizing everyone who passed by. If someone walked into a hotel just to get warm in the winter, he's a drunkard. I say, "I'm going to take a beer and watch TV."

She'd say, "You're going to get drunk." You immediately amplify the situation to the maximum.

At one point I was told I had a visitor. I go out to the visiting area and there is my mother. She came to see me in prison three or four weeks after my arrest. I hadn't asked her to come. I hadn't called her from prison.

I said, "How are you?"

"I'm miserable. Things aren't going so well. It's hard to make ends meet."

I had had news about my mother from my father. He said she was always at the hotel drinking with a group of Indians. If she complains about not having money it's because she is drinking it away. She was getting money from welfare since she had gone to a battered women's shelter.

Then she said, "I don't have what you have here. You have a roof over your head, you're fed, you don't have to pay for your own phone, you have three meals a day, you're clothed," she could see I had prison clothes. "It's not like me."

I stood up and said, "I would deprive myself of two meals a day in order to be on the outside. This door and the walls are to protect me from you." I said to the guard, "Get her out of here. I don't want to see her."

In a certain sense she was right. I don't have a rent to pay at the end of the month. I have food. But, boy, I would prefer to pay my rent and eat what I choose. If you think I'm in such an enviable position, take my place. I thought that was totally cruel. Is she crazy?

My lawyer wanted a well-known psychiatrist to look at me. In Amos they didn't have any competent people. He wanted someone with expertise to write a report that would be acceptable to the judge and would not be argued. My lawyer asked that I be looked at in Montreal because the experts were there. From Abitibi I left for the Parthenais Detention Centre in Montreal to have a psychiatric evaluation at Pinel Institution, a psychiatric hospital. As soon as you arrive they put you on medication. The next day I missed breakfast and lunch because I didn't wake up. The medication was too strong. The second night I complained. I was told the doctor said I had to take the medication. I wanted the evaluation based on what I said of my own accord, without the medication.

I collected it. I figured it all out. One pill had the effect of about six beers. Six pills would be enough for an overdose. I opened a packet of sugar I had in my room, poured out the sugar and put the capsule powder in there. Then I put it back among the other sugar packets. There are regular searches in Parthenais. They never found anything.

I thought from Parthenais I would go to Pinel to see a psychiatrist but I didn't even leave Parthenais. For one month I collected my medication. When they told me I would return to Amos I felt really depressed because I felt I hadn't seen anyone during the time I was there. I saw one doctor for three days, that was it. I didn't think that was the psychiatrist who was supposed to evaluate me.

I took two large pieces of bread, put butter on them, put all the powder from the medications on, put the two breads together and, after the security check at night, I ate it. I then went to sleep. I had an internal hemorrhage and the next morning they found me lying in my own blood. I was taken to hospital where I was in a coma for three days. During those three days I entered one end of a tunnel and was in a state similar to a fetus in the mother's womb. You're floating. You don't know if you're upside down or right side up, it's always dark, always the same temperature. There was light at the other end of the tunnel but it was far from me. I heard a voice. "Return to earth to live what you must live and you will come back when the time is right. It's not your hour of death. We'll call you. It's not for you to kill yourself. Finish your journey."

The whole experience felt like I had gone up to the sky. Then I felt like I had fallen back to earth and screamed. But I heard everything around me. I screamed for 12 hours, I was in such pain. You have three internal skins in the stomach and two of the skins had burned. Big pieces of skin were coming out of my mouth. I was within inches of death.

When I returned to Parthenais and the nurse asked me what had happened, I fell into her arms crying. I told her I was here for an evaluation and nothing has happened. I didn't realize the doctor had already done the evaluation during those three days, I thought I was supposed to go elsewhere. The next day I saw the same doctor. He had to re-evaluate everything because I hadn't been under medication during the first evaluation. He had to mention in his conclusions that I had taken no sedatives, no barbiturates, nothing. That changed the conclusions of his report which helped me tremendously in court.

From there they asked another psychiatrist to look at the whole family. Everyone was called to Montreal. While the family inquest was taking place, we couldn't talk to each other. The psychiatrist saw us individually, me, my father and my brother. Then he stopped. He said, "I don't need to see anyone else. Your story is substantiated by two people and that's enough." The information connected.

When I first began to relate what had happened at home, it was like I had put a pin in a fully blown-up balloon inside my stomach. I exploded. My past began to seep out. It made me feel so much better to be able to talk about all those secrets, like the loaded gun in the house. I never had the right to tell anyone what was going on, what happened in our house. Now the silence was broken. I had the right to say what I've lived through.

I always felt I was adopted because in 1959 my father found my mother at the doctor's. She had gone to his office but not because she was sick. He saw them making love through the office window. My father took the doctor to court. My mother had said my father wasn't giving her enough sex so she went elsewhere.

The first week of their marriage my father had left for a week for Ontario to help drive logs downriver. She went in a taxi to a club in La Sarre to see men. When he came back, his sister told him what his wife had done. My father felt guilty that he had left for a week so soon after the marriage. He blamed himself. I think that's why he put up with a lot of things.

My father pardoned her after her affair with the doctor. He didn't want to leave her because of the children. After the court case they started again with a new baby, the third one. That was me. I was born in January of 1960. If I arrived in 1960 and she had an affair with the doctor in 1959, then I must be the doctor's child.

After I was born my father stopped having sex with her. You'll have one child but this will be your last one. I know she often said, "He doesn't touch me, he doesn't give me any affection." The resentment was intense and profound.

A few years ago I found out my mother wasn't the one he really wanted to marry. He wanted to marry one of her sisters. My mother was second choice. When it started to go badly between them, he told us, "We'll try to make a lady out of her and later we'll see." He said that over the years. He wanted to change her so she would become the kind of woman he preferred. My father didn't like her going out. He worked all week and wanted her to stay in the house. One always wanted to control the other. After that affair with the doctor my mother took control.

My father studied to be a mechanic. She never wanted him to work at his trade because there are too many calendars of naked women in a garage. And my father put up with it.

My mother was beautiful when she was young. I don't remember ever seeing her in a dress, but in photos up to the time I was five and before the marriage she was always in a pretty little summer dress. Before the marriage she had nice dresses. But since I can remember my mother always wore pyjamas and on top she wore another layer of clothes. She always had about two or three layers of clothing. She had her camisole, her pyjamas, then a flannel shirt with the red and black squares. Even in the summer. Today she wears only thin pyjamas. It's no longer always long sleeves.

She argued with Denise, my brother's wife, because she was wearing a shirt that came two inches below her neck. My mother called her a whore, a dog, because her shirt was low-cut. It wasn't all the way up to her neck. For my mother it's others who are sick, never her.

During my adolescence my mother always called me Alain. One in 50 times she called me Richard. Of course, I thought I was adopted. I was the doctor's son. But I certainly couldn't ask any questions about it at home. Even today she calls me Alain. Alain is my oldest brother. I think my mother, in having been forgiven, started her marriage anew by having another child. She had had Alain as a first child, when the marriage really started, so she had Alain still in her mind. She must have been as happy this time as right at the beginning with her first son.

I never played with my brother. When I was five he was 15 and I stayed at home to play alone. My mother never let me do things because of the experience she had with Alain. Alain played hockey. He had cut himself, his shirt was torn and my mother said, "You can't play hockey because you're going to come back like Alain." I was never allowed to experience things for myself.

I wasn't allowed to take gym in school because I dared to ask for a pair of shorts and we all changed together in a group. She said, "You're not going to show your behind in school." She took me out of gym. I had wanted to continue but I didn't dare ask because of the control she had over me.

I had problems with sports. I was always the last one to be chosen for a team. I didn't know how to play because my mother had taken me out of gym where you learned the games. Teams don't like it when you keep making mistakes. They didn't like me. So I never played.

I felt apart from the rest of the world. I couldn't go beyond the land that surrounded our house except to go to the store. Whenever I had friends over my mother would call from the porch, "Richard, bring me a carton of milk." My friends in the meantime left and went to play somewhere else. The store was about 12 minutes from the house. Just enough time to cut a contact. Each time I had a connection with someone my mother broke it. I was very much alone.

In Normétal, in Abitibi, we had land that was about 40 by 50 feet. It was a normal amount of land but we couldn't really see our neighbours. The only window which faced a neighbour was in my mother's room and the blinds were always down. We often played in front of the garage but we had a high hedge so no one could see us, but it was also so my father couldn't see the others.

After the first year of therapy, the psychiatrist said, "You never spoke to me about your father."

I said, "My father was never there."

He was there, but he never did anything. He went hunting, was in the garage, or at work. He didn't have a place in the family. I can't say I had a relationship with him. Sometimes my father took me out in the boat or he took me hunting. But often my mother came with us. She went to check up on him, to make sure he had spent his full time hunting before he got home. But she did like hunting. Or we worked together on the asphalt or in the garage. Then my mother always came to get me. I couldn't be alone with my father for a stretch of time. As soon as I was in the garage with him she immediately sent me to the store to buy butter or bread, anything. If I was alone with him she thought I was talking against her. I went to the store five or six times a day, every day.

My father and I sometimes went to the store together but never in good weather. We always had to go shopping when it was raining and my father had to concentrate on the white line in the middle of the road. If we went shopping when it was nice, my father could look at the women, at the broads, the cheesecakes. Those were my mother's words. He could look at women in short skirts, shorts, tight T-shirts. No, he wasn't going to see that! She always censored what we were allowed to see. For anatomy, in school, there was a man's body and a woman's body. She tore the picture out.

I was never able to watch one single movie in our house without my mother as a chaperone, sitting next to me. When a neckline was too low she unplugged the TV or turned the brightness control to black. I never saw Elvis Presley movies because of all the girls in bikinis. She broke three or four TVs, she cut the wire with a knife so I wouldn't watch when she wasn't there. A bedroom scene on TV meant immediate unplugging because she had her chair next to the TV extension cord. "You're not going to watch such filth." In my head I was always persecuted. She was always right and I didn't want to provoke her.

I said what she wanted me to say. I obeyed her, almost mechanically. She kept me at home to keep me from knowing what was happening elsewhere. She had a monopoly over me. If you don't know other things you can't rebel. I couldn't say the opposite of what she said. I could say nothing when she called my father a queer, a fag, a homosexual.

My father worked in the mine and usually came home by 3:05. If he arrived at 3:10 she accused him, "You stopped at the hotel, you've been with prostitutes, with cheesecakes." The control she had over everyone!

One time, when I was around 14, I went to my aunt's, my mother's sister. She lived at the other end of Normétal. I arrived and she asked, "What's happening?"

I said, "My mother is drunk again."

She said, "Stay here." She gave me a cookie and made me go to sleep on the couch. She said, "I'll speak to your mother tomorrow."

The next day I go to school from her house and from school I go home at four. When I get home my mother says, "Go and kneel in the corner!" My punishment was on my knees with my arms outstretched. And you can't lower your arms. She punished me because I gossiped about what was going on in our house. You don't talk to anyone about what goes on in the house. You don't talk about your problems. Sex was taboo.

My birthday was on the 8th of January and it was celebrated till I was four. After that I had my birthday during Christmas. The birthday gifts were part of the Christmas gifts to make them look bigger. I was about 14 when I started to bake my own birthday cakes. I made desserts for the weekend and made all sorts of little pastries. I consulted a cookbook my mother had. She never really encouraged my cooking but she ate it. When I was cooking she no longer needed to do anything. She was happy. She sat in her chair with her legs crossed and drank. On Sundays there was always a roast chicken with peeled potatoes and the rest of the week we ate out of cans or my father cooked.

Ever since I was small, I always liked playing with pots and pans. Today I'm a cook, a pastry chef. It's really my vocation. One day I wanted to make a cake but my sister, Jocelyn, who was four years older than me, had cleaned everything. It was always Jocelyn who cleaned house. She had waxed the kitchen floors so she didn't want me to bake a cake. It was the first and only time that I laid a hand on her. I pushed her in a corner. She said, "Stop it, you're hurting me."

I said, "You're not going to do the same thing as Ma. You're not going to stop me from doing things."

At one point my mother had me spying on my sister. Jocelyn went to the arena to watch the hockey games with friends. My mother asked me to follow her to see if she had a boyfriend. I was the detective. I liked that. I did something for my mother. I had peace. Also, I was allowed to go out of the house. While playing detective I got to go to the arena, the cinema. I benefitted from the situation. At one point my mother wanted to know if my sister smoked. I embarked upon that mission. I left three minutes after the others. They were going to mass. I arrived in church a good 15 minutes before them. How could I have passed them without seeing them and how could I have arrived before them when I left after them? The next time I left before them to see where they were going and where they were stopping. A real drama. It was like a film.

It was winter. There was a little garage near the church. They stopped there to smoke a cigarette. I reported back to my mother. She then asked Jocelyn, "Do you smoke? I don't care if you smoke but at least tell me." She had such fear of fire that she preferred to allow us to openly smoke instead of hiding cigarettes in the house or the garage. It always revolved around her.

My father would bring home a case of beer. He'd drink one bottle after work and before going to bed he'd say to my mother, "Don't touch any of the bottles that're still in the fridge."

When he went to bed my mother stayed up and finished the case. The next day she said, "Don't buy it anymore."

"You're not going to stop me from having a bottle of beer!"

"When you buy beer you don't just buy a bottle, you buy a dozen. If you take one glass, you have to take two. If you drink two, you have to drink six."

It was too much for my mother. She had no control over it. If she knew there was drink in the house she went crazy. Then she called my father a homosexual, a queer, and broke everything in the house.

After a while he stopped buying beer and only bought alcohol for Christmas. Every holiday she would put someone out of the house because she was drunk. She threw out her own mother, her sister, my brother and sister-in-law. Later she often went by herself to buy alcohol.

At first the drinking was every month. Once a month she got drunk but the next day she washed the walls, the ceilings. The house was kept clean, the washing was done. Meals were made. Next it was three or four times a week. She wanted to stop drinking but she kept falling back into it. Between her getting drunk there were nice periods, she was affectionate and we tried to forget about her drinking. She was a real mother, a good mother during that time.

My father or mother repaired things in the house. She fixed the wires. My mother was a tomboy. She worked with tar, with asphalt. She worked in the woods. She went hunting. She sometimes fixed the snowmobile. She checked the oil. She wasn't a feminine woman. She was the kind of woman who liked to work with male things. She liked to do a man's job. She would have liked to be a man to fight my father. She often said, "If I were a man!" My father closed himself off and sat there. "Goddamn you, you son of a bitch, you motherfucker." She strung a bunch of swear words together before she started talking. She had to be stronger than my father.

When she was drunk she always called my father a homosexual because at the time they were married he had a tumour in one breast. He had about two or three cysts and had to have an operation. My sister had the same problem. Also, at the mine everyone changed in a large, communal changing room. My father was nude with other men, therefore he must be a homosexual.

My mother had a brother who was a homosexual. He always lived with a colleague. They went hunting together and did everything together. I don't think it bothered my mother but it shouldn't be known. Exactly my dilemma. I would have liked a homosexual relationship but I wouldn't have wanted it to be known. Because I didn't want it to be known I resisted it. There was a battle within me. The fear of confronting the truth forced me to react in an extremely violent manner.

Just because my mother saw someone in shorts, she called them a faggot. She was in a rage against the whole world. She was suspicious of everyone, judged everyone. The rage that my mother had was transmitted to me and came out in my crimes. I said that to the psychologist. The rage and anger that she had against everyone, I also had. When my mother was hurt by anyone she took vengeance. Either she kicked them out of the house or she changed stores. She considered someone had hurt her when they had lied to her. If they said something she disagreed with, that meant they had lied.

I was never strong enough to defend myself, in school or anywhere else. So for me the way that man acted in my car was a tremendous form of aggression. It was either all or nothing. I was totally vulnerable. I couldn't make decisions without considering my mother's views or my father's views. Their opinions made up who I was. I couldn't do what I wanted. I was stuck in a mould of my mother's making. I do what someone else tells me. I breathe when someone allows me to breathe. If something happens to me I lose control because I don't know who I am, how to react.

I was never allowed to answer my mother or to argue with her. I could not have an opinion different from her. I could not say what I thought either in front of my mother or father. I said what my father wanted to hear and I said what my mother wanted to hear. I never did what I wanted to do, said what I thought. In front of my father I always had to put down my mother and in front of my mother I always had to put down my father. I was a model little boy. Very nice and polite. Always knew his place. And I cultivated this image.

To make my mother happy I had to think and do like she did. To do like her I also had to hate homosexuals and if I hated them even more than she did, or if I censored the TV movies myself, I surpassed her. I didn't want her fury so I tried to do it even better than her to make sure she didn't catch me watching anything I shouldn't. You're trained to be in a certain way even if you're alone. I started to censor the TV when I began to watch it alone. I turned the picture to black. I was allowed to listen to the volume as long as there weren't sexual sound effects, heavy breathing. She couldn't stand to hear a love scene. I cheated sometimes but often I got caught so I censored it even more often. My mother could come in any time. She could leave and suddenly return. When I knew she was on the second floor or outside I took risks. But she could always come back unexpectedly and go to black.

Any sexual curiosity was blocked. You can't have someone who is too big, who's a flirt, cheap, sloppy, a dog, a pig. There were so many criteria. I liked one girl. She lived one street over. She had long hair. I could see her moving in the house. I thought, if I could marry her I would spend the rest of my life with her. But I could say nothing. I was totally incapable of expressing my love. My mother was always behind me. All of a sudden she was not good enough. I could not act.

When my mother asked me to prepare her a drink, instead of putting a small amount of liquor to a large amount of water, or a small amount of liquor to a large amount of soft drink, I sometimes made it half and half. When she was drunk she went to sleep and there was peace. I wanted her to sleep to get rid of her. At that time I was going to school. I repeated my seventh and eleventh year. Those were the two big periods when my mother was hardly ever on her feet. I used to go to sleep at 1 a.m. and had school the next morning. Just before I went to sleep I would ask, "OK, are you all right because I'm going to sleep? I have to go to school in the morning."

I went into my room and sat on my bed. I wait 10 minutes and she doesn't say a word. As soon as I laid down, you'd think she had a camera, that dog, as soon as my head touched the pillow she'd holler, "Richard! Come and help me." In an irritating voice. "I need a cigarette."

I got up. I gave her the cigarette and lit it. "OK? I'm going to sleep." As soon as I got back into the room I immediately laid down so I would have at least 10 minutes of sleep. Again, as soon as I touched the pillow, "Richard," in that drunken voice with all the words slurring, "Get me a glass of water. I want you near me."

Each time I touched the pillow she was screaming at the other end of the house that she needed me. I couldn't go to sleep. I would sleep one or one-and-a-half hours during the night before I had to go to school. At that time my father worked at night. The next day she was all apologetic. Give me a kiss. Then it started all over again.

When I got home from school all the windows were closed and, if I didn't have my key, I would never be able to get in because she would be on the sofa, passed out. The curtains would be in shreds, torn. The biscuit jar was broken. When I came back from school I picked up all the pieces and cleaned up. It was all dark in the house. You weren't allowed to put the lights on. She said her eyes hurt.

When she was drunk she always fell all over the place and was full of black and blue marks. She would have black eyes and have to wear sunglasses. Sometimes I would trip her on purpose so she would fall.

For about two years, from the age of 15 to about 17, I was so upset by what was going on in the house that I went to bed like I was sleeping in a coffin. There wasn't a crease on the covers, everything was perfect. I lay on my back, two hands joined together on my chest. I didn't move. My nightly prayer was, "Come for me. I'm ready for You to come and get me." I didn't try to commit suicide, all I could do was ask God to come and get me. I did that every night. If she came in to see me after I went to bed I messed up the blankets a bit and turned on my side. When she left I turned on my back again and re-organized the sheets so they would be neat. Of course in the morning I woke up on my side and the sheets would be a mess.

I don't think death hurts, probably because my father has had two big accidents, one in the mine at Normétal where he was buried under 50 tons of rock. He broke his leg in two places at the bottom and three places at the top. When she heard about the accident she said, "That pig, he can die."

While my father was in hospital my mother got drunk at least three or four times. She said, "He did this on purpose to have the nurses spoil him at the hospital." My father was washed all over by the nurses. My mother felt like she had fallen to second place. She couldn't be at the hospital all the time. She didn't like that. He was in a cast for one month, his leg up with pulleys. When he came home he couldn't go to the toilet. His cast was up to his waist. Jocelyn changed the sheets. It was more Jocelyn than my mother who took care of him. My mother even tried to break his cast when she was drunk. They began to fight and when the fight escalated to a certain point, she attacked him. My sister took me out of the room and my brother and sister had helped my father because she was trying to break his leg. Because of that accident my father still limps today and one leg is shorter than the other.

Later my sister left to study in Ottawa and my brother left for a small town near James Bay in the north of Quebec. I was left alone.

Then we moved from Normétal which was a mining town. When the mine closed my parents sold the house. They bought a farm in St. Lambert. The closest neighbour was two kilometres away. At the time I was 17 years old and in the tenth grade at La Sarre.

I started the cooking school in the tenth grade. It was a big school with a work program. It gave you the basis of education and half your day was spent learning a trade. I went to my courses and worked in the cafeteria in the afternoon. When I had 15 minutes between classes I went to see Sister Louise, my religion teacher, in her class. I often went there because it was a place of peace. There were no questions about my family or friends. I didn't hang around with the other students. After school I couldn't play sports with the others, I had to go home.

I made a friend in my cooking course. He was exactly my age and we did the first and second year together. In the second year he committed suicide. I took most of the girls in the class to the funeral service in my car. Then I had a Pontiac Phoenix for which my father had signed the loan. They were the ones who consoled me. I was crying and crying. I think I was the one who was the most affected by his suicide. We had already made plans for the future.

Since it was so depressing at home during the last two years of my courses I worked full time outside. School was from eight to four. From four to 11 I worked at the Swiss Chalet, a steak house at the ski lodge. That gave me a good excuse to have an apartment in La Sarre because it would save me the one-hour commute.

I also worked on Saturday and Sunday. I just had Saturday and Sunday morning to do my washing. Monday and Sunday night I had off. I sometimes went out Sunday night to the discotheque but I was very shy. I was afraid to be rejected. The people taking the courses with me came from all over, so it was rare for me to meet anyone I knew in town.

I took the fourth-year master's course offered at the school. Canadian Pacific was interested in all the graduating students. We were guaranteed a job at Château Lac Louise in Alberta. I never waited for permission from my mother to go. I liked cooking too much. I liked working in a group. The job started on such and such a date and I was simply part of the group that was going.

My nicest three years were in Alberta. That's also where I had my first sexual experience at 20. I was far from my mother, far from the family situation, I was independent. There were 450 people working at Château Lac Louise, just in front of the ski trails where they had the Olympics. We all stayed in dormitories. I never said anything to my mother about it. I had several friends, as if what had happened at home didn't even exist. We often went to have a beer together at a nearby bar. We would go six at a time on a trip. We would visit waterfalls, had picnics, roasted marshmallows. There was always something to do. I went with a girl from Peterborough. At the end of the season she returned to her studies and I went to the Banff Springs Hotel for the winter. We were supposed to see each other the next season. I'm very faithful. If I have a girlfriend no one else exists for me. For me it's one at a time. But I usually had about two or three friends each season.

Then I had a promotion as an assistant chef at Château Montébello, between Montreal and Hull. It's the biggest hotel made of logs in Canada. There I was a loner. It was quite isolated and I lived there, worked a split shift, in the morning and at night, so that doesn't give much time for socializing.

A hotel guest made homosexual advances. I wanted to find out what it was like. With all the taboos I had from my mother I couldn't decide on my own without trying it first. We did it behind the swimming pool on the grass. While he was doing what he wanted I noticed his wallet beside me. I took it. When it was done I went in one direction, he went in the other.

I took his wallet as revenge. I didn't like what had happened. I couldn't be direct, I couldn't stand up for myself and say how I felt. So it became something twisted and nasty. The next day I tried to use one of his credit cards in the village. By then he had already reported the missing wallet and had put a stop to his cards. I was arrested, taken to the police station for a couple of hours.

That was the first time I did something that obviously went counter to my mother's ideas. I did it but I was punished. Each time I did something on my own, I was forced to go back to the same old pattern because what I tried didn't work. I couldn't escape my mother's world, her judgements.

The man didn't press charges. He said he had lost his wallet. I said I found it. He probably didn't want the affair to come to light. Maybe he was with his wife and family or with someone else. But because he was a guest of the hotel and I was an employee, they asked me to leave. I left Montébello after a year of working there.

The next day I had to call my father because I had to leave immediately. My father called Alain, who was in Montreal, to tell him to pick me up and take me to Abitibi to take care of him because my father had slipped on the ice and broken his leg. I didn't tell my brother or father that I had had a homosexual affair. I simply told them that I had found a guest's wallet and had tried to use his credit card.

My brother drove me home. During the eight-hour drive we spoke maybe one hour and he did all the talking. I didn't want to listen to his disbelief, his outrage. I didn't reply. I felt even more embarrassed. I simply swallowed the bitter pill. Once more I ended up home, in the family. I didn't like it but felt I had no other choice. I felt too diminished to know what else to do. I was too humiliated.

I found work almost the same day that I returned. The Coq d'Or was looking for a chef in the evenings. I went to see them and was hired because I had worked at the Swiss Chalet and was known in the area. I worked there eight or nine months before the owner of Brasserie 111 offered me a better salary. My clients from the Coq d'Or followed me. I enjoyed working at the Brasserie. There were three of us and I was the boss. When there was a lobster festival we'd sell at least 1,000 lobsters. The owner did everything I asked for in terms of presentation and service. They made money with me. I raised the Brasserie's profile.

Instead of constantly travelling back and forth from home, I got an apartment in La Sarre. I went home on weekends to help out in the house. I sometimes had Monday and Tuesday off and again I'd go back home like a good little boy.

I had been back in Abitibi about a year-and-a-half before my parents were officially separated. The separation happened from one day to the next. I found out about it through my sister in Ottawa. During this period I went home less often.

My parents had gone to another farmer's house who had some tools to sell. My father and the farmer went to look at the farm instruments and left the two women alone. My mother was forced to stay with the other woman. I'm sure she didn't like that. Probably she would have liked to go and see the instruments and to keep an eye on Pa. Who knows what can happen if you leave two men alone? But she couldn't go. She didn't want the others to know she was suspicious of her husband.

When the men came back my father had a drink and fell asleep. According to him someone had put something in his glass. My mother claimed he had fallen asleep under the table, drunk. He woke up four or five hours later and wanted to leave.

On the way home my mother accused him of all sorts of wrongdoings while he was drunk. She told him that he had slept with both the farmer and his wife.

My father said, "I couldn't have done that. It's not possible."

He accused her of having committed all sorts of sins, like sleeping with the other woman. They had a terrible fight which lasted all the way home.

The next day she was very nice and said, "I'm sorry, I won't do that again."

He said, "That's it. We're not going out again."

A tension remained. Each had called the other a liar. Put the other down.

Six months afterwards, the divorce began. My mother always threatened to leave and my father said, "Fine, go." But my mother never left. When she finally left, he reacted. He loved her. When she left she took half of the chemicals they had used for taxidermy. My father and mother had taken a course in taxidermy and stuffed animals they had hunted. There were ducks, owls, a baby beaver, all kinds of animals. They stuffed the animals together. They did things together which is why there were also good times. When they were stuffing an animal you might have two months of peace. Later he said she took the chemicals because she wanted to poison him.

She went to a shelter for battered women. But she wasn't a battered wife. At the shelter they counselled her to get a divorce. She got a divorce because she wanted to be on welfare. She wasn't even in court when the decision was passed. Jocelyn said to my father, "Keep quiet, don't say she wasn't a battered wife. You'll be better off without her."

He said, "But I didn't beat her." Finally, he agreed that he had battered his wife in order to have the divorce.

My mother got a basement apartment in Amos after she left the battered women's shelter. She wanted me to go and see her but my father didn't want me to. I was there once, one or two months before my arrest. I felt obliged to see her out of pity. It was her birthday, she was my mother, you had to go. She had made a chicken. My father had told me not to eat there. He said, "She's capable of anything. It's dangerous to eat at her place." He told me to take her to a restaurant. So I took her to a restaurant. I acted according to what my father wanted, according to what my mother wanted. I felt like a marionette, a puppet being manipulated. Today I have no strings.

After they were separated she continued to call my father and say, "You're staying with some sort of slut. You're still my man and I'm holding on to you." There were at least 100 miles between them but she still called him. "You're my man. I'm keeping you." My mother had him followed by friends and knew where he went, and what he did. He did the same thing. He asked someone in Amos about her. She's in a bar with those Indians and she's drunk.

They were separated eight months to a year before I was arrested. It was during that time that I had a reaction, that I did the crimes. A little before the separation and a little after.

My first crime. I still have that bad experience from Montébello. It's a Saturday night. Summer. He was in shirtsleeves. I'm coming back from the farm to the city. As I'm driving home I see a hitchhiker. I stopped to pick him up. We drove no more than one mile and he put his hand on my knees. That was like an electric shock. We were coming to a small bridge at La Sarre and I said, "I'm going to stop by the side of this bridge and you can get out." I parked. He didn't want to get out of the car. We had a big fight. A very big fight. The argument took at least five or six minutes. He said I had to take him home. I certainly didn't want to take him home because who knows what he would do to me? I felt torn between having to do what he wanted and what he wanted I didn't want to do. I had stopped only to help him out. I was around 21. He was at least 40. Double my age. Older means more frightening for me.

I got out, walked around the car and tried to pull him out. He didn't want to get out. He was holding onto the steering wheel. Then I walked around to behind the driver's seat where my box of knives was. Because I worked in a restaurant, you need your own tools of the trade. I was taking my knives back to the house because I did the cooking there. I went to get a knife.

He said, "What are you doing there?"

I said, "I want you to get out of the car."

I took a knife and walked back around to his side. I said, "Get out of the car."

He didn't want to get out. He wanted me to take him home. I showed him the knife in my hand as a threat. When he saw the knife he wasn't even afraid. He didn't react. Maybe because I was never believed in my life I went to such an extreme. When I said something it was always, that's not true. You're not afraid? Nothing was ever true. He didn't believe me when I was threatening him. He never believed that I would actually do something with the knife. And in my family I was also never believed. What I said either wasn't true or it wasn't important.

I forced him to get out of the car and said, "I'm not taking you home." I threatened him with the knife. He refused to get out. I pulled him by the arm till I finally got him out.

I returned to the car quickly to leave but he had stood right behind the car, blocking me. I couldn't back out from the little road beside the bridge or I would have killed him. I got out of the car again, pushed him aside, got back into the car. He had stood behind the car a second time. He said, "You have to take me home!" He tried to force me to take him home.

"No!"

He opened the car door and got back into the car. The car door was open. I hadn't locked it. So I had to get him out of the car a second time.

I went around to the passenger side of the car and pulled him out again. I pushed him aside and gave him a stab with the knife as punishment. Take this. I want no trouble from you. I gave him only one stab. One. That was it. When I left him on the road he was still standing. I said, "Thumb another ride." Then I hurried to get back into the car and left. I felt trapped. I was furious and afraid. I had wanted to help him and ended up getting trapped.

When I arrived home I threw out the knife. I threw it in the huge furnace in the basement. Then I went to sleep. It was late. I wasn't troubled. He got what he deserved. The next night I went to work. The waiter said there was a fight on the bridge, there was a stabbing. I said, "It must have been a settling of accounts, must have been a disagreement."

He said, "One guy is dead."

For me it was just a little stab to try to push him out of the way. How could it have turned into such a tragedy? At first I felt terrible but then I told myself, he had asked for it. That's how I rationalized it to myself. He got what he deserved.

The next one happened six months later. There was about six to five months separating each one. It became a regular pattern. But each time I committed a crime, two or three months before something had always happened at home. Usually a horrendous, drunken fight between my parents. Then it would be quiet. My mother would just sit at the table and she couldn't care about anything. My father worked in the garage in order not to see her. A frightful tension. Then it would start again.

By talking to psychologists I was able to see the connection between my actions and the family situation. I struck out to erase the possibility that I might have said yes.

I felt sorry for them. I went back home on weekends to make sure my mother hadn't killed my father or my father hadn't killed my mother. I went to have news. By phone they said nothing. You have to be there to see what's happening. Each weekend I had to go home to see. One was at one end of the house, the other at the other end of the house. It was obvious that one or the other was going to leave. My father wouldn't because he was too weak. Or they beat each other and one of them was black and blue. Or my mother had walked into the door again and had a black eye. Or she fell on the table. So I had to go home to see. There were animals on the farm and I liked the animals. I liked the farm. I loved my parents. I was raised to love my family. If you leave your family and try to make a life for yourself without any family connections, it's not going to work. That was my education. My focus was my parents. I didn't have a life.

Six months after the first crime I am kicked out of the house at Christmas. My mother was drunk. If I say it's white, my mother says it's black. It's white. No, it's black. Because I said what I thought and not what she wanted to hear, she kicked me out. A few times in the past I disagreed with my mother and never won. This time, for the first time, I wanted to win. I held my ground. In the argument we had I felt I was right. I wanted her to acknowledge it. And I was totally rejected. Told to get out. I always felt rejected, not accepted as I was, but this time I felt completely cut off. Thrown out. My father said, "She'll calm down after she has some sleep. I'll try to get her to see reason."

I was very upset. I felt like a cat thrown out. I couldn't go back. I went into town and had a drink. For me it was the end of the world. It was like I no longer had any parents. I was all alone in the world. I had lost everything. I was shaking. I was angry at both my mother and my father because he hadn't done anything. He allowed my mother to win. It was a real crisis.

Usually I spent New Year's Eve with my family. This time I went to the hotel in La Sarre. When I was ready to leave my car wouldn't start. It was frozen. It was very cold that night. I had my box of knives in the car because the next day I was due to work. I took one knife out and put it in my cowboy boots because I had to walk home and near where

I lived there was a motorcycle club which always scared me. I took the knife just in case. I was becoming exactly like my mother who always had a loaded gun in one corner and a .22 in another, just in case. To protect herself. She had passed on the fear to me. To be afraid even before anything happened. To be afraid of what could happen. Security. As I was going home, just as I was leaving the hotel, I passed someone who was going in the same direction as me. When I passed him he started to walk at the same speed as me. We talked a bit. Then he put his hand on my thigh. That was like a switch. I already have enough problems. My car doesn't start. I was thrown out of the house. I couldn't dance with the girl I wanted. I had asked her but she said no. Rejection after rejection after rejection. Failure after failure after failure. This was too much.

I took out my knife and just as he turned around, probably ready to run when he saw my knife, I stabbed him in the back. I had the knife in my hand and ran. As I crossed the bridge I dropped it onto the ice. I went home. I was afraid because he might have followed me. I looked outside. I didn't see anyone. I took a long shower and was shaking. I took a drink to sleep better.

Two days later I heard people talking about a crime that had happened on New Year's. I stayed out of any talk. I never thought that I had killed him but he was dead. Why did he die? He must have been weak. I didn't hit him hard. Again I thought, I was right. I just gave him one stab. That's it. Too bad for him. He lost.

It took my mother four weeks to call me. Since she called, I felt I had won. Otherwise I would have had to call her and I didn't want to do that. My father had not called me during those four weeks either because he doesn't want to step in the middle. He doesn't implicate himself. She said, "Forgive me. I won't do that again. I promise." She was sorry and regretted what she had done. She felt she had made a big mistake throwing me out of the house. I forgave her. But for her having thrown me out wasn't such a grave offence. She throws people out of the house regularly. She thought if I had not called her it was because I was too busy. After that things calmed down. Everything was fine for a while, as if nothing had happened

When I told my story to the psychologist, the psychiatrist and all the others I felt so much better. Once my story came out my uncles and aunts started to see my father. At last they understood why he had been so unhappy. They also came to see me. They understood why I acted the way I did. I have an uncle who sent me $20 for Christmas and he's never done anything like that before. It did everyone a lot of good that I spoke out.

The trial took place nine months after my arrest. It took a half-a-day. Everything was agreed on before. I pleaded guilty so they didn't need to call witnesses, they didn't need to call me to the stand, they didn't need to call the family of the victims to the bar. My father was always in the courtroom. My brother came once. When it was all over, the judge, just before pronouncing the sentence, made a speech. He said, "What we see here is a family drama. It should really be your mother who is in your shoes today. But considering you have pleaded guilty I must now pronounce your sentence."

If I wouldn't have committed those crimes, I would have turned against my mother and would have killed her. After a while I saw her everywhere whenever I had problems. Even before committing those crimes I felt she stopped me from living. You will not tell me who I am. You're not going to make me do what you want. You're not going to make me do something I don't want to do. If I don't say what my mother wants to hear, that means I'm against her. I don't love her. I would have attacked her to finally put a stop to her aggression.

For me prison merely took away another one. I was freer in prison than at home. I wasn't put into maximum when I was 23 where the majority are much older than me and where I could have had problems. I was in a much tamer place. It was more like a medium. Still, there were lots of fights, a lot of tension, and from there I began to understand what I had lived. It helped me to look at what was inside of me.

I wanted to look at the past, really examine it. Each situation was exposed to numerous questions till it satisfied me, till I could finally own it. If I did not have the answers to all the questions about a given event, I put it aside until it was ready to be looked at again. Then I went on to the next episode. Once I had the full picture, I went over it with the psychologist to reconstruct it.

The first year I realized I had no right to act the way I did. I didn't have the right to be so afraid. It wasn't normal. Gradually I realized I had gone too far. That disturbed me. It ate away at me. Gnawed at me. I had actually hurt much more than one person. My crime had touched my family as well as their family.

When I entered prison I stayed to myself because everyone scared me. That wasn't a milieu I was familiar with. I didn't know my way around. During my first year of arrest I was quite solitary. I first started opening up to people I worked with. I became friends with some of the guys also working in the kitchen. I started walking around the yard with them. Little by little I found my own place.

I didn't talk about the crime I was in for. I only mentioned one part of my crime, one part of the truth. I said they tried to rob me and we fought. The homosexual part was never divulged. Just in case. I didn't want a prisoner to say, "He didn't get you but I'm going to have you." I cannot do the same thing in prison as I did outside. That caused a certain insecurity. I remained silent.

I never had any sexual relations in prison. I looked but I didn't find anyone who attracted me. One attracted me but he wasn't homosexual. He was a good friend. I would have liked to sleep with him. I never asked him. He didn't notice anything. In prison if you're marked as a homosexual, then everyone runs after you. There were some who had been homosexuals on the outside and there was a line to their door. That's not my style. If I'm going to experiment, it's going to be outside, not in prison.

Guys made passes at me. Hands on my behind. We had communal showers. Some guys said, "You have a nice little ass" or "I wouldn't mind doing it with you." Very direct.

I was also very direct. "When I want to I'll let you know before anyone else." Or I'd say, "You're not my taste." Since my arrest I had a right to state my opinion. "No, I'm not attracted to you." And it's fine. I no longer need to be afraid, I no longer need to defend myself, I no longer have to have fear.

I did three years alone. Alone in my little corner, alone with my work, my visits, a few friends, my little room, peace. I always called my cell my room. I never called it my cell, my hole. It bothered the others. They didn't like it when I said, "I'm going back to my room." I didn't use prison slang to live in prison. I didn't use prison vocabulary. Also, I was always clean and neat. When I left my room to go to work or to watch TV in the TV room, I combed my hair and wore a clean shirt. Just because you're in prison, you don't have to walk around in a torn T-shirt. Just because you're in prison doesn't mean you're worthless. You have to believe in yourself, do things for yourself. They called me sir.

Not Richard. They called me chef. I wasn't a chef.

There were drugs. I tried in secret to see what it was like. Prison gave me the opportunity to experiment. I wanted to know who I was and what I liked. Once I tried acid. I stayed up the whole night in front of the TV. It wasn't much fun. From time to time I liked hash. It relaxed me, put me to sleep. I tried cocaine but it keeps you up. To stay up all night and play cards wasn't much fun.

I tried not to find myself in a situation where you say yes to one person when you mean to say no and say no to another when you mean to say yes. I no longer wanted to be sandwiched between two people who each had their own idea. I no longer wanted to be controlled by someone else. I learned to assert myself. I learned to say no. At first I went through a period where I said no too often. I went to an extreme. I said no to everyone because before I had said yes all the time. It was always yes, yes, yes. I don't count. I had to relearn to say yes. Sometimes you have to say yes to something that you don't like because it might bring you something else. I was seeing a psychologist all this time. But when you're learning to say no, you're afraid to say yes even though you'd like to say yes.

I didn't want to just fall into a group. I wanted to choose. I chose carefully. I even chose the volunteers I wanted. I watched them and finally went over and introduced myself. I had contact with my case management officer, with the guards, the economist in the kitchen, normal contacts, straight, but the other prisoners didn't like that. If you're close to the personnel you're dangerous. But over the years they saw that I was honest. I didn't stool on anyone. I had credibility inside and was never afraid of anyone.

There was someone who was a little crazy in our section. He put his fingers in all the trays to see if the food was hot. I got angry. No one else did anything, so I acted. I took him by his T-shirt and pushed him down on the floor near the gate, near where the guard was sitting. The guard stood up and looked at me.

I said to the guy, "You're not going to move. You're going to get the last tray. In the future the last tray will be yours. You're not going to touch the food on all the trays. We're not going to eat what you've touched. You take what's left."

I was there only two months when I did that. No one said anything to me. No one asked, "Why did you tear his T-shirt?" Nothing.

He was crying. He wanted a new T-shirt. "Ask for a new T-shirt. They'll give you one."

From that point on he never put his finger into the trays. He didn't act crazy. He acted properly. He no longer touched the milk that we all kept near the windows. This taught me that even in prison I was allowed a certain aggressivity which I had never before allowed myself. And I was capable of controlling it. You stay there and don't move. You're going to listen to me. Never before in my life could I tell anyone, you're going to listen to me. I listened to others. I always listened and it was so oppressive that I lost myself. Today nothing scares me because I have the capacity to act in a variety of different ways without it being illegal. It was in jail where I understood that.

We could buy materials for our hobbies. I did painting. I won the Prison Heart Foundation contest. It was a contest across Canada for all the prisons. I did an acrylic painting of a man on a wharf. I was very pleased with it. It took me a month-and-a-half to do.

I looked at video cassettes on how to work with leather. I bought a huge piece of leather and started engraving on it. It has woods and a lake, a few animals. The whole thing is embossed. I sold it to my father in exchange for a new TV. It meant a lot to him because he loves hunting.

The other prisoners saw me doing different things. They came over to talk, ask questions, advice. I always had someone in my room. That's how I began to get to know people. They came to me. They broke through the silence I had created around myself. They came and told me about themselves. They came to tell me about their father, their mother. Listening to them encouraged me to continue with my own search. We helped each other. I was also learning. I realized I needed people around me. My mother had deprived me of social contact.

The guys are very tough. They watch to see if you talk to the guards, if you're plotting against someone, if you're cheating on something. But if they see you're clean, then they approach you and ask you to head certain activities. The others urged me to put my name forward as head of the sports committee because they didn't like the person who was doing it. Then all the prisoners voted. I was elected. I don't do sports, I'm not athletic, but I was a sports representative for two years. The guys knew I wasn't a sports person, yet they still voted for me. They trusted me.

As a sports representative I dared to implicate myself in problems to see how I would react. A fight breaks out and I have to deal with it. I took a stand. I had fun watching myself. I had to set up sports tournaments. I said whoever wants to participate has to contribute one packet of cigarettes and six drinks. Other people who did this before stole the cigarettes and drinks. I didn't even smoke, so the guys were safe. I had a book and each time someone signed up for a tournament I marked their name, what they gave and I made them sign it. Next to the signature was the total to date. When everyone signed up I divided the total amount of cigarettes and drinks by the number of tournaments. One-third went to the loser and the rest to the winner. We had semi-finals and finals. There were six tournaments a week. Everything was written down and posted. The guys never even lost a drink with me.

I became more active in the prison community. I wrote out the names of the volunteers for the security people in front for three or four years. I took advantage of what prison had to offer. I took three computer courses by mail. I transferred from the kitchen to the chapel where I worked full-time. I was tired of working in the kitchen and there were too many fights. Because I went to mass every Saturday night I was asked to be the verger by the priest. I was a verger for three years as well as the priest's secretary, so I had a lot of time to talk to him. I had peace there. I still go to retreats in St. Jerome. It's a way of keeping in touch with what's important, with the present.

I also took four cooking courses. One in pastry, one in grilling, one as a butcher and one in sauces. I didn't waste time. They gave me time and I used it. These were courses that lasted about eight or nine months with tests at the end. The courses were given by an outside college and had nothing to do with the prison. I got five diplomas in cooking.

When the cooking course finished I was asked to take charge of the gala supper. At a cooking school, at the end of the year, there's always a competition where you have to show what you've learned. I said, "We'll do it like at the end of the school year. We'll do a piece of pork, a piece of beef, a decorated salmon and that will give us a buffet." We had a warm and cold buffet, just like in a hotel. People put in their names to work on the salmon, the pork, the beef. It gave the guys who make hamburgers for a thousand people something different to do, something more creative. I got everyone involved. I collected prizes. I had a TV for first prize, a stereo for second prize and lot of cookbooks for third and fourth prizes.

Also, I never stopped working on the psychological front. I joined Alcoholics Anonymous which came into prison once a week. I liked the honesty. I didn't feel alone with my problems and it gave me contacts with the outside. I was even the secretary for a while. I'm still friends with some of the people in AA and they know I'm not an alcoholic but, because I had such a strong family dependence issue and my mother was an alcoholic, we share the same basic dilemma. Alcoholism is a problem that hides another. Take away the underlying situation and alcoholism will fall away by itself.

There were emotional disorders that might have taken me toward alcoholism if I hadn't gone to prison. That's what I talked about at a provincial conference of Alcoholics Anonymous. The co-ordinator of AA at prison asked me to speak. Each year they ask two or three guys from prison to speak at the conference. My basic problem is the same as people who turned toward alcohol. I was simply protected by prison from not falling into alcoholism like the others. Today I don't need to lose myself in alcohol in order to live, not like my mother.

Through Alain I told my mother we'll talk once I leave prison. She said, "Fine." My father came to see me regularly. He travelled 500 miles every two or three months to visit me in prison. He gave me money. We became good friends and were able to talk about everything. I'm very lucky that my father helped me but I blame him for having put up with my mother. At least he did what he could by coming to visit me and answering my questions. When I had a question I was no longer afraid to ask. It was like I had three million questions that I didn't want to answer myself. Even if I felt I knew what the answer might be, I still had to ask. I needed to hear it from the other. I didn't want to answer my own questions. That would be a monologue. Now I've also asked my mother questions and I'm putting their answers together like a puzzle. Their answers are a complement.

My sister, because I said what had happened in our house at the trial, broke contact with me for three or four years. I wasn't allowed to call her or write to her. She didn't write to me. Jocelyn needed to analyze the whole situation and ask herself, did I tell a bunch of lies in order not to have a long sentence? Did I tell those stories to get as little time as possible? Before she left for Ottawa my mother had been drinking only once or twice a month. There weren't as many fights. The worse part happened when she was gone and I was alone at the house. It was always degrading. Then she reconnected again as if nothing had happened.

I said, "Jocelyn, you can ask me whatever you like and maybe you can tell me things that would help me better understand."

She reacted very well. She said, "How could this have happened? How was it that we never talked about this?"

When I went before the parole board they asked me, "When you go outside and see your mother, how are you going to react? Are you going to kill her?" When the judge said, "It's not all your fault, she must shoulder the greater part of the blame," they thought I might kill her. That scared me. I said to myself, I have to write to her.

In the letter I sent her I wrote: "I should have noticed and accepted the love you were capable of giving me instead of wanting much more. I should have noticed that I couldn't have a truckload of love that I kept expecting and been happy with the little you could give. Maybe if I had accepted the small amount of love, I could have gotten more than I expected."

I should have recognized her limits instead of pushing for more. I did everything so she would love me. I kept wanting more and that destroyed me. She did give me love. When I was sick she was always there. And I loved her. We had some good times. I wrote: "Maybe I should have gone to speak to someone to ask for help." I felt a little guilty because I didn't do anything for her. I even pushed her toward the alcohol to make her go to sleep. So I contributed to her alcoholism. I asked her forgiveness.

That was the first gesture I made toward her. To try to change someone, to want a mother we always had hoped for, is wrong. I had a mother who was sometimes affectionate, sometimes fun and who knows my past.

I was proud of my letter. I said to myself, everyone is going to know what I wrote. I made photocopies and sent one to my brother, my sister, my father and I kept one in order to protect myself. With this letter I said stop saying what you want to hear and stop interpreting what I wrote according to what suits you. What I write is what I mean. I'm not writing two lines so you can read between the lines. There are no words between the lines. Stop saying it's not possible that he wrote to his mother that he loves her. That's what I wrote. Yes, I love her. I respect her. I can't erase those feelings. She disappointed me but that's all I had. My father always said, "Tough. You'll have to try to change her." No. This is the mother I have.

My brother said, "Richard, you're sick. That letter is way too nice for her. Do you actually believe what you wrote?"

"Yes, Alain. That's exactly how I feel and how I think."

Alain's wife got a phone call from my mother saying that I was crazy, I was sick, I understood nothing. She gave me a truckload of love. I just couldn't see it.

Jocelyn said, "You've done a lot of work and that was a nice letter."

My father said, "You shouldn't have written to her. You should have left her stewing in her own hole. She already gave you enough misery."

In spite of everything my mother has done I still love her, that's why I'm in touch with her today. She's my mother. I see her once in a while out of respect.

I spent nine-and-a-half years in prison. It didn't feel long. I got involved with a lot of cultural activities, with St. Valentine's and Christmas celebrations, community visits. I had a social life. I always worked. I worked before I went to prison and in prison I worked on myself. There hasn't been dead time. In prison I woke up. I was constantly asking myself questions and watching myself react. Who are you to have done what you did? What do you like to do? Who are you to think you can do what you want?

We create as we demolish by the daily decisions we make. I had cut out my mother. Then I brought her back. My father didn't like that because I discovered more pieces of the puzzle. I questioned what he had said. I wanted to have the whole story, both versions. From there I can make my own decisions and move forward. It bothers my father because he knows I'm finding things out that put him in the wrong. Like saying, "Let her be, leave her to herself." Why let her be? You have to resolve it. I had to search to find out that my father was to blame as much as my mother. I realized that she wasn't all wrong. My father also shared some of the blame.

I don't think the whole past needs to be thrown out. If you've burnt the vegetables, you haven't spoiled the whole meal, only the vegetables. Your life isn't ruined because of one situation. You have to clean up, throw out clothes you no longer wear, otherwise you have no room for the new. There is only one answer. You can try to find a million answers but there is only one answer for you. In the past my answers didn't satisfy me but they should have. My confidence had been totally destroyed. I need to rebuild it.

My father doesn't want me to see my mother. He says she takes my money. He has these ideas and thinks he knows the answers. The two of them are still against each other. After 12 years of separation they're still fighting. My father wants to hear bad things about my mother. I say nothing. It doesn't exactly please him because he hasn't come to see me in a year-and-a-half. It bothers him that I don't talk about her.

I will only have peace, real peace, when I'll be able to put a rose on my father's grave and a rose on my mother's grave. Then I'll be able to say, now you can no longer fight. The story is finished. The only connection will be one of love and compassion.

I learned things from my mother. I can sew, shorten my own slacks. She showed me how to do it very early on because she didn't want to do it. For a long time I hated her for that. You can't say to a friend, I didn't go to play hockey because I was hemming my slacks. I would be even more rejected. I had to iron my own clothes. I did my own washing. She showed me how to economize when you do the shopping. That's why today I can take care of myself. I know people who can't do any of this. I can cook anything for myself. I know people who can't make themselves toast. The confines and the strict parameters my mother gave me in my youth today have served me. I understand how one needs to focus and stay with one's dreams. I'm stubborn.

I had two jobs when I left prison. I arrived in the halfway house on a Tuesday. Friday I began at the Patisserie Valoise. I got that job through my parole officer. One of his friends had a pastry shop. He thought I was good and recommended me. It's very rare for a parole officer to recommend an ex-prisoner to a friend. It turned out to be a little family pastry shop. They were very happy with me. From there I got a job in Laval College. That was a recommendation from the priest at the church I went to. I go to mass from time to time but church can be anywhere, on a sidewalk. That's my conception of church today.

I worked at Laval College every weekend and for the rest of the week I worked at Valoise. Later I started full-time at Laval College. Then they cut my job and I had to look for another one. I took one at $6.50 an hour. While I had that job I looked around for another one which would pay me the same salary I had at the college. I found a job baking

215

cakes in Lachine.

I would like to make money and invest it in a pastry shop. It's my dream since I've been very small. I have hope. I prefer being a pastry chef but, if I can't find a position in that, I will work in the kitchen of a restaurant, but without losing sight of the fact that my preference and my forte is as a pastry chef.

Four months after leaving prison I rented an apartment while I was still at the halfway house. I returned to the halfway house to sleep during the week between 11 in the evening and four in the morning. The weekend and the rest of the time I was at home. After the halfway house I moved full-time into my apartment.

I gave myself one year as the first phase of my re-entry. I decided that first year I wasn't going to form any relationships. I went to restaurants alone. I spoiled myself, took care of myself and made up for what I had missed. I bought myself things. I thought of only myself. I took no one else into consideration. On my first birthday I bought a stereo. On my second birthday I bought a TV.

The first year I really took to create myself, to create a life on the outside. I went to straight discotheques and into the gay village. I did both sides. It was a time of discovery. Adventure. I was testing myself to see how I would react. I used to go to a straight bar one weekend and a gay bar the next. After a while I went only to the gay bars. I felt safe in the gay village. My parents didn't know where I was. I could do what I wanted. There were no fears. The worse part of those crimes was that I was afraid my mother would find out I had been approached by a homosexual. If she would have known a homosexual had his eye on me, she would have gone after him to kill him, to protect her little boy.

You can't just tell anyone about your past. You can't just casually talk about it. You have to wait for the right moment to present itself. I can't say, as soon as I meet someone, I have to tell you something. Circumstances either provide a chance for you to tell or not.

Six months after I got out I went looking to buy a second-hand car. Stephen was a car salesman and I asked him questions about cars and prices. I ended up buying a car from him. He was about my age. We became friends. We played pool or the slot machines. We went out together on weekends. For a year-and-a-half no situation came up where I could talk about my past, where I could say I was in prison. It took a year-and-a-half for such a circumstance to present itself.

One night he was at my house and he was very depressed. His girlfriend had just left him. He felt everything was going badly. Life was passing him by. He had bought a pipe and was going to lock himself in his car and commit suicide. He saw a huge mountain before him.

Finally, I said, "Listen, you're really disappointing. You're upsetting me. If you need to commit suicide because a girl has left you, you can't be worth very much."

He said, "Yes, but I've already been on probation because the police caught me with drugs in a bar."

I said, "That's nothing."

He told me other things which for him were enormous obstacles.

I said, "Well, I can tell you that I've committed two murders, two assaults and have just come out of nine-and-a-half years in prison."

He looked at me and said, "That's impossible!"

I then told him about my family problems and what caused the crimes. He couldn't believe it. All of a sudden his problems didn't seem so serious in comparison. When he finally left I said, "Don't do anything stupid. There are things much worse in life. You have to be able to got over this one." He got over it. And my telling him about my past only reinforced our friendship.

Robert was the second person I told about my past. I met him in a gay bar a little more than three years after I was out. I saw him and thought, he looks interesting. I'd like to talk to him. I was lonely that night but wasn't looking for anyone. I just wanted to have people around me. I thought, I'm not going to approach him unless he makes a move to indicate he is interested in talking to me. He stepped toward me and I invited him for a beer. We talked. He listened to me and I listened to him. We talked for about four or five hours. I was living in Lachine at the time and slept at Robert's that night because he had an apartment in Montreal. The next day we exchanged phone numbers and agreed to meet the following week.

I spent the next weekend at his house. From then on he came to my house for the weekend and the next weekend I went to his house. We were becoming intimate very fast. After three weeks we began to miss each other in between. A relationship was developing quite quickly. I felt I had to tell him about myself. There is always a fear that the other person will not accept your truth. But if we tell the truth, either it's accepted or it breaks everything. After the third week I said to him, "I

217

have something serious to tell you."

He said, "I have something even more important to tell you."

"Tell me. For me there is nothing worse than what I've lived through."

He said, "I'm HIV."

I said, "So? We just have to take the proper precautions." We had courses inside on AIDS. I was informed.

He said, "I was careless. Doesn't that scare you?"

"No. We just have to be careful."

"But I'm going to get sick one day."

"One day we're all going to die." We talked and talked.

Then he said, "What about you?"

I said I'd committed two manslaughters and two assaults. I did nine years in jail and came out three years ago. He said, "You've done your time so you paid for it. You're fine."

I said, "Yes, but…" I thought he accepted that a little too fast. I said, "Doesn't that scare you?"

"If they let you out it means you're fine."

Just as he didn't understand why his HIV didn't bother me, I didn't understand why what I had done didn't bother him. He told me he had worked for the justice department in Ottawa and his work involved him in the prison system. He had come across cases like mine.

Later I told him about my mother and father, the whole family. He understood. He's intelligent. From there a strong friendship developed. So when he ran into a problem with his landlord, I said, "Come to my place."

Each time I told my story I had a deeper understanding. The understanding I have today is not the same that I had even three years ago. I constantly evolve and find new things. It doesn't stop.

You have to know what you want in life. Before I was always too preoccupied with what other people wanted. I had no centre, no frame of reference. Now I do what I want. I make my own decisions.

Since the interview he and Robert have married. Richard's mother has died. She knew about Robert and accepted the relationship. She and Richard had a number of good conversations before her death. Everything was resolved. His father is not in contact with him because Claire, the woman he lives with, does not approve of his son's relationship with Robert. His sister no longer sees him because she thinks Richard will be a bad influence on her children. He speaks to his brother once or twice a year.

SHARON

When I first made phone contact with Sharon (45) I asked why she was willing to be interviewed. She said Helen, a friend and a woman who ran a program for ex-prisoners, thought it would be good for her to see her life on paper, to get a grasp of its totality.

The interviews took place at her house, in the mornings. She had burnished skin and black curly hair. She was quite striking, even without makeup, which was the only way I saw her. Casual yet alert. She was clearly comfortable in her own body and easy with herself. There was a relaxed calmness about her, a strong sense of herself and a no-nonsense attitude. As she told her story she laughed at herself with humour and ease.

At the end of each interview I realized my questions were stirring up a very difficult and dramatic past. After two interviews I asked how she felt talking about all this. She said that after each session, after I left, she went for a long walk and thought about what I had asked and what she had said.

During the whole trial they just saw me as a street person who killed this fine outstanding citizen, an archaeologist at McGill University. Right from the start I knew they weren't going to show me any mercy. I was going to get the book thrown at me. It didn't matter that he had a sword to my throat, that I was pregnant.

We got sentenced in the judge's chamber, not in a courtroom, because there was so much publicity around the case. They said for 1969 that was the worst murder across Canada.

I got such a long sentence because of who he was. His colleagues from McGill University came to court every day. They wanted to see justice done, revenge. I knew when Claude went out to steal all those furs to pay the Crown $100,000, even that wasn't going to help. His colleagues were not letting the judge or the lawyers forget that he was somebody. I was nobody. And I had stabbed him 17 times.

I definitely was an accident waiting for a place to happen.

First of all my father was 14 when he made me. My mother was double his age. I was nine months old when my mother died. She was black and there is some French and Scottish in there. My father was Indian. I have white relatives, black relatives, native relatives. It doesn't matter what part of the family I'm talking to, they're always running down the other side and I come to the rescue. I never felt I belonged anywhere.

After my mother died, my father went from Nova Scotia to Sudbury and later married a white woman. Aunt Dora, my father's sister, had me for the first four years of my life. I was like her first child. Then my father took me to Sudbury.

I taught myself how to read by the time I was four. I just lose myself in books. As a kid it was a form of escape. If I'm reading, I'm quiet. I can't be accused of doing anything.

For me, Sudbury and my stepmother was nightmare city. She just hated me from the word go, I think because I reminded her of my mother. Apparently my dad really loved my mother. My Aunt Dora had told me that I really looked like her. When my father wasn't home, she used to threaten me and give me beatings. I would have welts all over me. She said if you tell your father, when he goes, you're going to get it twice as bad. I remember once she beat me for eight hours to make me call her Mom. Beatings, physical pain, mental abuse were a part of my life.

From the time I was very young I had to do the dishes. I'd stand on a chair to reach the sink. If she found a fork that wasn't washed properly she'd throw all the dishes back. I'd have to do them all over again. I was five years old and I'm thinking of putting arsenic in her tea.

I would never tell my father about the beatings but when I couldn't sit down, he'd say, "What's wrong?" And I'd just start crying. Then he'd lift up my shirt, see my back and he just went crazy. He'd beat up my stepmother. Sometimes he'd throw the electric frying pan with what-ever was in there right at her. Then he'd take me out and buy me a bunch of new clothes.

I was always boarded out to some other place for a month or two till things cooled down back home. My dad used to say, "One day I'm going to come home and find you dead."

My stepmother had one child with my father. I hated him because he always got everything. He was four years younger than me and always used to hit me. If he hit me, I was to tell her and she would deal with it. "Oh, it's nothing, he's just a baby. He can't really hurt you." After a while, when he hit me, I beat him right back. One time he hit me so hard with a rock to the back of my head that my head felt numb. There was a broken light bulb on the ground so I just cut him. He got a scar down his face. Of course, he went bleeding into the house to his mother. She was screaming, "Now you're going to get it!"

Because my father used to drink all the time, he'd play rough. He was a maniac. He'd drive the car around the corner on two wheels at 100 miles per hour and say, "Are you scared?" I'd say no. He used to throw knives at me in the dark when he was drinking. "Are you scared?" Of course I was scared but I said no. He'd stop.

My father would try to play rough with my half-brother. He'd always cry. My stepmother would come running to his rescue, yelling, "Leave him alone."

Of course, she would get beat. My father would say, "You're turning him into a little sissy."

I had seen my father put a shotgun to my stepmother's head and beat her severely sometimes. I remember I used to jump in the middle because I didn't want him to go to jail, because then I was stuck with her.

My father brought me back to Nova Scotia when I was eight. I was supposed to go for a summer vacation but ended up staying for two years. They kept my half-brother. They just sent me back.

I stayed with Aunt Polly, my father's sister. She was getting paid to look after me. Soon I was the one who got up at 5:30 a.m. to make a fire in the stove so everyone could be warm when they get out of bed. We had no electricity down there, no hot and cold water. The toilet was outside. At night there was a bucket in the house which was my chore to dump every day. I learned how to make bread, cut off the chickens' heads, pluck the feathers for the Sunday meal. I had to chop wood for the stove. I got to do all the housework. Plus go to school.

There was violence everywhere, both Sudbury and Nova Scotia. Aunt Polly was beating me all the time, either for something stupid or because one of her kids said that I did something. She didn't beat her own three kids.

Everyone knew what was going on but no one said anything. My sister, who was 10 years older than me and had a different father, said they were working me from dawn to dusk.

The store was two miles away, country miles. I was always the one to get sent to the store, sometimes two or three times a day. It was scary to go there in the dark. During the day I didn't mind. Actually it was a form of escape because I was assured, at least for a little while, I wasn't going to be asked to do some major work or I wasn't getting beat.

On the way to the store there was one man who used to live up at the top of the hill by himself in this big house. A couple of times he would motion me to come in. I thought, I'm not going in there by myself. But after a while I did go in. He would give me peppermints and have his hand on my leg.

The next thing you know he was offering me 25 cents if I laid on the bed. But I didn't have too much choice. He had a firm grip on me. He put me on the bed and had his fingers down there. I told him he was hurting me. He stopped only after I started to really cry and carry on. I never told anyone but I wouldn't go back there again.

Then there were my father's younger brothers. During the summer vacation when I was home all day watching the other kids and my aunt was working at the clam factory, my uncles would be down regularly because they just lived in the next house. They'd send the boys outside in the woods to play and throw me on the bed. They'd take my pants down and take their pants down. They never penetrated but it was very close. Then they'd slap me and say I better not tell anyone.

My father came down the following year and I thought I was going home. They stayed at my Aunt Mary's place on my mother's side, where my sister stayed. They had electricity. I told him I didn't like it here, I wanted to go back. I get beat. But I got left again and it was back to the same old routine.

When I was finally back in Sudbury the beatings from my step-mother were more frequent. Every day this woman hit me. At least in Sudbury I wasn't living in hillbilly days. On the coldest days when there were snowstorms I wasn't out there chopping wood.

My father was a womanizer. And women found him very, very attractive. When he took me to the store or wherever, women were always looking at him. And he was a big flirt everywhere he went. I thought, oh, that's the way of the world. My father's friends all messed around with other woman.

There was a time when my stepmother messed around, too. That was a time she was very nice to me. I can remember my Uncle Charles coming to visit us by himself, without Aunt June. There were sexual overtones in their conversation. Then my stepmother says, "Here's 50 cents, go to the store and play for a while at the playground." This was just before my bedtime on a school night. My Uncle Charles also gave me some money. I thought, they're up to no good. I came back around 9:30 on a school night. Uncle Charles would be with his clothes all done not right. He was sweating. My stepmother's hair was glued to her head.

This carried on for a couple of weeks. Now I had something over her head. One night my father came home really angry at my step-mother. Uncle Charles had said to my father, "I can tell you something about your wife that would make your hair curl."

My father was beating my stepmother all around the room saying, "What the hell does he mean by that?" This carried on for the next two days. Once my father has a bee in his bonnet, he ain't letting up till he has a resolution.

One day my stepmother beat me. When my father was home, that subject came up again while I'm sitting at the table doing my home-work. I said, "I know what Uncle Charles means."

My stepmother's eyes grew huge. My father turned around and looked at me. "What did you say?"

"I know what Uncle Charles means when he says he could tell you something about your wife that would make your hair curl."

"What?"

"When you were working at the nickel mines from 4 to 12 o'clock, Uncle Charles used to come here every day after you left. They'd give me money and tell me I could go outside to play when I'm supposed to be in bed for 8 o'clock. A few times I saw Uncle Charles come out of the bedroom and they're all sweaty."

My father hit the roof. He gave me $1 and said, "Go."

By the time I was 10 years old I was running the household. At that time both my parents were working. I'd come home from school and make supper. On weekends it wasn't time to play, it was to do housecleaning.

I started to do a lot of babysitting. Everyone wanted me to babysit because when I babysat I cleaned your whole house as well. It was something to do. I used to do the dishes, wash and wax their floors, vacuum the rugs, clean their bedrooms. They loved it.

My stepmother converted me to Catholicism. From 10 to 12 I was raised a Catholic girl. Convent, nuns. That was a big culture shock. In Nova Scotia I was brought up a Baptist. In a Baptist church we say our prayers and there's a lot of singing with guitars. In a Catholic Church you're on your knees all the time.

I went down the tubes in the Catholic school. In English school I was very good. Here, if you didn't pass religion, you didn't pass period. Also I was the only black person there. When I was a junior, the seniors nicknamed me Snowball.

My sister at this time had moved to Montreal. She sent me a ticket to come and visit her. What a difference! In Montreal I met all kinds of friends. We were out every day. There was the Negro Community Centre. We used to go to dances. I started smoking cigarettes. I even met a little boyfriend.

Back in Sudbury it was so dull. That's when I decided I'm not going to church and my stepmother was flipping right out. My father said, "If she doesn't want to go to church she doesn't have to."

I started talking back to my stepmother and standing up for myself. She would say, "Wait till your father comes home, you're going to get it." My father would come home and I would deny whatever she'd accused me of. In the past she had lied about me so many times and my father found out. Now, when I began to lie, she couldn't believe it.

I came home after school one day and my stepmother was there with a letter. My boyfriend from Montreal wrote me and she opened up my mail. He had put a cigarette inside the envelope. She wanted me to write him a letter telling him not to write anymore. I stood my ground and refused. She was hitting me and hitting me. I wouldn't cry. Before I would always cower in fear and cry. This time I just looked at her. As I went to my room, she hit me over the head with an iron frying pan. I saw stars and I said to myself, Sharon, you're not going to pass out. I turned around and I don't even remember what I did, but I left her on the kitchen floor in blood.

Before this incident I had run away a few times to Clark's, one of the few black families in Sudbury and one of the families I stayed with when my stepmother was sick of me. So now when I went to his house he said, "You can't stay here because the police will come here straight away."

Clark took me to the bikers' clubhouse, Satan's Choice. He asked if I could stay overnight. Then he put me on the bus for Montreal. The bus stopped right in Little Burgundy, in front of the Negro Community Centre. And I found out that my sister had moved.

My only other relative here was my Aunt Edna. I just stopped a person on the street and asked, "Do you know where Edna Packer lives?"

They said, "Yep," and brought me right to the house.

I stayed with my aunt for a few days. But her kids were running around all over the place, the house was all torn apart. I came from a middle-class family in Sudbury. I said to myself, I can't stay here. I just wasn't used to having to hide my things from the other kids.

Eventually I found my sister. I went to live with her and went to school. But I lost all interest in school. My sister would leave for work and my friend, who lived around the corner from me, came over to my house, plus a few other kids. We would just listen to music and smoke cigarettes all day.

My sister was saying, "You're going to have to straighten out."

I said, "I'm going to live with my aunt."

After I left my stepmother on the floor, my father looked for me. My aunt talked him into leaving me down there. My stepmother was fine. She just had a broken nose. I was so afraid of my stepmother that when I escaped there I vowed that I would never allow myself to be afraid of anyone like that again. I feared her so much. I was scared all the time. After I left I thought, no one is going to touch me again, no one is going to hurt me. After her I was afraid of nobody.

My aunt was an alcoholic. She was on her own with 10 kids. Money went fast. She collected welfare and also used to go to bars to con men. One of the games was that I would come to the bar about 45 minutes after she got there and say, "Mom, do you have any money, I'm hungry."

"Well, babe, I have no money right now."

But whoever she was drinking with would say, "Here, here."

And everyone at the table would give money. My aunt was very pretty. Men liked her. Some of these guys were her drinking buddies and they would have drunk at her home. They knew her home situation and would just give me money. I would go to the Chinese restaurant, order all kinds of food and bring it back home for the kids.

I started to drink. I used to drink from the time I opened my eyes till the time I went to bed. Emotionally I was numb. Then I started to go downtown. The men were trying to get me to turn tricks. It was like, "I'll be your manager and I'll keep your money."

I said, "I don't need any manager to keep my money."

Men used to give me $200 just to sit at their table. They thought I was 18. I used to get real disgusted with them and say, "You know, I'm only 12 years old."

Then they said, "I'll give you more money."

I thought, you disgusting, fucking pigs. I'll take your money and you can keep looking at my tits. I used to wear these low dresses. And there were the wigs, the false eyelashes, make-up. I looked like Diana Ross.

I got away with blue bloody murder because I was cute and had big tits. They didn't care how old I was. When men talked to me, they literally looked right at my boobs. I thought, I'll take them for whatever they want to give me. I would be outrageous. The more outrageous I was, the more I got. I used to have lots of sugar daddies. You used to go out to have dinner with them. I'd say I want $500. They'd give it to me.

I had an argument with my aunt and left the house. I was walking along St. Catherine Street and Ann, this black girl I knew who worked downtown, said, "What are you doing?"

I said, "What does it look like I'm doing? I'm walking."

She said, "Girl, get over here and stop your nonsense. What are you doing?"

I said, "I ran away."

"Where are you staying tonight?"

"No place."

"You're staying at my place." She took me under her wing and brought me home.

For almost two years she kept a firm hand on me. I could go downtown but she was always there. Then she said, "Do you really want a job?" By now I was about 14 and getting more attractive to the guys. She said, "Do you like to dance?" She was a dancer and used to go out of town on contract. She hooked me up with her manager. This was go-

go dancing, little bikini with the fringes, the white boots, mesh stockings. I was in and out of town.

I went to Valleyfield to dance in a club and there was a guy I knew. I was talking to him and drinking at his table. Then I said, "Excuse me, I have to change because I'm up next." I went into my room. He came in right behind me. Didn't say a word, threw me down on the bed and I felt this really sharp pain. He got up and left the room. I cleaned myself, went out there and danced.

I thought, if this is sex you can keep it. I knew I had lost my virginity. There was blood. After that happened I was more or less blaming myself. OK, you dressed up like you're 18, shaking your boobies all the time. I thought I deserved it.

A few weeks later I came back to Montreal and saw him. He came up to me and said, "I want to apologize. I'm so sorry, I didn't know how old you were."

When he told his friend that he had me, his friend beat him up. "Don't you realize this girl is only 14." But if I was 18, that would make it OK?

Once, when I was out of town, Ann got two years in the penitentiary. She had beaten up this man, someone important. Here I am on my own. I enjoyed dancing but Ann wasn't there. I was lonely. Where do I go? Back downtown to all the familiar places, familiar people.

I used to see these girls go with men for a short period of time and make $50. I thought, this is easy money. I'm going to try it. I was curious.

I went to the room with this man. I thought I was really slick and knew everything. The deed was done and the man said to me, "You're new at this, aren't you?"

"No, I've been doing this for a long time."

"Really? Let me tell you something, sweetie, you should always get the money first."

I had forgotten all about the money. I was so embarrassed.

I started going out with this one guy. He was a pimp and just gorgeous. He wanted to take my money. I said, "No thank you, I can manage my money quite well." But he was very, very jealous. Any guy talking to me, he would want to kill. One time he hit me with his open hand. My face and my eye came out about two inches. He was 250 pounds and 6-4. I was 90 pounds soaking wet and 5-3. I said, "No, no, no. I'm not putting up with this." It just reminded me of home.

I was living with him at this time. I waited till he was sleeping, broke a Scotch bottle and said, "Wake up!" I had the jagged edge of the bottle right at his throat. I said, "I'm too small to be hit. You make your living by your face, pretty boy. I'll cut it and you won't make anything. And if you think about hitting me after I let you up you better kill me because I'm going to cut you all up."

After that he never touched me. If he got out of hand I used to say, "Don't get too cute, pretty boy." He knew exactly what that meant. And he knew that I was quite capable of cutting him up with no problem. He had seen me fighting with other men.

I just had so much anger in me. I used to fight in the bars. Men who wanted to go out with me, and I never wanted to, would get on my nerves. I'm drinking and the next thing you know they're wearing a chair upside down on their head. The drinking made me nastier. I threw tables, chairs, whatever was around if you got in my face.

A pimp sat down at my table and said, "Man, if you were my woman I would beat you for two weeks."

I said, "Just get away from my table. I don't want to hear this."

The next thing you know the tables and chairs are upset. He said, "What's the matter? What did I do?"

"Get the fuck out of my face!"

I was the antithesis of what a whore should have been. I worked when I wanted to work. I made the money, I'm keeping it. I disrupted a lot of rules pimps had back then. It boiled down to no one could control me.

Prostitution was a tool, a means to an end. I never looked at sex as fun. I knew that I was different, that I didn't feel all these things that people were feeling. When I was going out with men, you can always fake an orgasm. If you never had one, all you had to do was breathe heavy and they thought you did. I saw movies. I heard the other girls talking.

Once when I turned a trick I did have an orgasm and felt so friggin' mad and guilty. This was not supposed to happen. It happened twice. I was shocked. What's going on here? Other than that, it was just a job.

The tricks would say, "Are you coming, do you feel it?"

"Oh yes, baby, oh, oh."

And he comes. They need to hear they are good.

I had my youth going for me and that's what the men wanted. For some of them it was like fucking their daughter. I used to say, "Is this what you would like your daughter to feel?" And they would come. I thought, you pig. I became outrageous, demanding more money, thinking that would send them away, but they just kept returning. I was drinking 20 hours a day. I just drank and drank till I used to blank out and not remember the things I did.

I was having fun but I wasn't having fun. How the fuck do I get out of this? Then at 15 I discovered I was pregnant by the guy I was living with. I was going to have this baby. The Roman Catholic was embedded in me. It was wrong to get an abortion.

The guy said, "Are you going to get rid of it?"

"No way. And you don't have to be with me either."

I would still go out. At that time they had those sack dresses with the psychedelic colours, so you never knew I was pregnant, up to the day the baby was born. I carried small. At that time I didn't really have to turn tricks. I had sugar daddies. Some were 70 years old. They just liked to have someone listen to their ramblings.

After eight months Ann got out of prison. At this point I'm living by myself. When she saw me, she just cried. She heard I was turning tricks.

"I knew this would happen if I wasn't around."

"It's OK, I'm fine. I'll survive."

I had this really good friend who was involved with bikers. He's dead now, of an overdose. He was there when I had the baby, Gordon, which was my father's first name. We stayed at his mother's and somehow my father heard that I had a baby. He wanted me to come home.

I said, "I'm not staying."

He said, "No, no, I just want to see the baby."

I went. It was the first time I ever saw my father cry.

He said, "You're just a baby having a baby. Leave him here."

"No."

My father had money. He was quite capable of looking after another child. After two weeks I decided, OK.

By this time my stepmother was gone. He blamed her for my running away. At the time I went with the baby, my father had two girls pregnant at the same time. He had both of them living in the same house together. I used to go to school with them. I kept in contact for about six months and after that I didn't call or keep in touch. I just thought, he's my dad, he's going to look after my son.

After I came back from my father, I got involved with this Frenchman, Claude. I had known him from before. He was a gangster. Back then the Irish, the Italians, the blacks, the French, all had their own gangs. They were heavy into drugs, anything illegal. He wined and dined me. I was waiting for the axe to fall. You're giving me diamonds and fur coats. What do you want from me? But it was just a very fast life. Basically I was an asset, I always looked pretty on anyone's arm. It was almost like a contest. Who could get me? I was very elusive. I was there but I wasn't there. I belonged to nobody.

The bars used to cut me off when I was too drunk. When I was cut off I jumped behind the bar and smashed all the bottles. They didn't touch me because of who I was with. They wouldn't dare. I had no limits, no boundaries of what I could or couldn't do.

Then I was 16 and pregnant again. This time I did try. I've seen a lot of things that I shouldn't have seen. With Claude I went from hooking and drinking to a whole new dimension in my life. I've seen vast amounts of money, lots of drugs, people's arms and legs being broken, people being beaten to near death. I've seen people die, two people got blown away in front of me.

I just took diamond rings and flushed them down the toilet. I'd tear up my fur coats. Look, this is what all this means to me. I think this is what Claude liked about me. He knew these things could not keep me. They meant absolutely nothing to him either. They were so easy to get.

I got my own place. I didn't really want to have this baby but I was having it. All I was doing was drinking and drinking, wanting to get out of this rat race. I'd be taking sleeping pills while drinking and blacking out all over. I'd be in fights, come to and there was blood all over the bar and it wasn't mine. Ambulances were coming and they just put me out the back door into a taxi because they knew who I was with.

Then one night Ann and I went to a bar. We were taking pills and the next thing we knew we came to 30 miles outside of Montreal. We are on a dirt road with nothing but miles and miles of grass all around. How the hell did we get here? We start walking. A car comes. A guy is drinking and he picks us up. He was from Pakistan or Egypt. He asks us where we're from.

I say, "New York. Can you give us a ride back to town?"

"Sure."

He took us to the damn mountain.

I said, "Well, that's very nice but could you take us downtown."

Then he drove us back to where he had picked us up. I'm still feeling the effect of the pills and the booze. He says he had to go to a friend's house nearby. They're on vacation and he promised to look after their plants.

Once in the house, the guy said he wanted me. I said, "Well, it's going to cost you." Ann is watching TV. He's pouring us a drink. Gin. I hate gin. There are all kinds of big plants around and I threw it in a plant.

He went downstairs and when he came back up he said, "Oh, you finished your drink." He gave me another. While he was downstairs I poured it down the kitchen sink.

In the kitchen I had looked around and saw these knives on the wall, on a board. As I'm rinsing the glass, he comes up from another way and he has a curved ceremonial sword in his hand. He comes in, puts the curve of the sword right to my neck and says, "I'm taking what I want and I'm not paying."

I can't believe this is happening to me. My back is against the cupboard and the knives are right near me. I take a knife and thrust it at him. But the blade bends back around. It was a very flexible breadknife. I look down. He looks down. I guess what went through his mind is that she would have stabbed me had she picked the right knife. He raises his ceremonial sword. I reach up for another knife and stab him. This time the knife goes in and I just keep stabbing him. He is lying on the ground and I am still stabbing him. I don't want to be hurt again.

Ann came into the kitchen and I didn't recognize her. I thought it was someone coming to hurt me and I stuck the knife right into her forehead. She yelled, "Sharon!"

I saw the knife in her head and yanked it out. She started bleeding all over the place. I said, "Let's burn the place down."

"No."

At that point she was scared of me. She was holding a cloth to her head and backing away from me. She said, "Let's go."

It was about three or four in the morning. We got out in the middle of the road and half-a-mile down there was a house. We knocked on the door and asked them to call us a cab. I had on gold shoes, a black sweater and black slacks. I kept looking down at the shoes and there were bloodstains on them. I thought to myself, I'll never wear gold shoes again.

I went to my aunt's. She was in bed, drunk.

I said, "Wake up. I killed someone."

She said, "Sharon, stop your joking."

"I killed somebody."

She realized I was serious and woke right up.

A couple of days later Ann's sister, Linda, came to my aunt's house to say Ann got charged for the murder. I found out the police had picked up Ann for robbing another guy. She was famous for going with tricks and not doing anything, just taking their money. But when there's a murder, automatically when someone gets picked up, their fingerprints are compared to the fingerprints at the scene of the crime. Hers had matched. Her fingerprints were in the house. She was charged. I said, "I can't let her go, she didn't do it. I'm turning myself in."

They asked me what happened. But Ann already had a record of violence and she was big. They assumed I came in to cover for her. I was 90 pounds and three months pregnant. The guy who was murdered was very large. Ann was built like a brick shithouse. So it had to be her and not me. Finally I convinced them because of some details only the person who was there, in the kitchen, could have known.

I was with Ann during the robbery for which she had been picked up. She had asked me to go along with her and the trick. We all went to the tourist room in a cab. She started to undress and told me to undress. We just went through the motions. Then she grabbed his wallet. He was screaming at the top of his lungs, "Give me my money back!" His screams brought the owner of the place in. We were already dressed. The owner had seen us often enough. He knew what we were doing. We got our coats and left.

The man put a complaint in to the police. They put Ann in a line-up with all white girls and they put me, who was 5-3, in a lineup with girls who were 5-8 and 5-10. He identified us.

I was sentenced to two years less a day. That's provincial. Two years is federal. Ann got two years because she had a history of robbery and violence. I said, "I'll take the day," so I could go with my friend to Kingston. The judge is always ready to accommodate you when you're asking for more time.

It was raining hard the day we arrived in Kingston. I'm looking at this dank, dismal, limestone building, thinking this is something out of a horror book I read. We went in through a regular door, then through a sliding door that the guards control. When you pass through, it slides back and the noise I heard when the door closed, this big clunk, really loud and sharp, sounded so final. I remember looking back and thinking, this door is the difference between being free and not being free.

Inside, Ann knew all the girls. She was talking to them and I was standing back, looking on. These girls all looked like guys. They have on dresses but their hair is all slicked back and cut short. They have on dresses and the hairiest legs you ever did see with ankle socks and men's shoes on. I'm thinking, what's wrong with this picture?

Before we went in, everyone was always telling me Ann was gay. Ann and I would take off drinking. Claude would say to me, "You were gone with your lesbian friend doing lesbian acts."

"What the hell are you talking about? She's not gay."

She never made any passes at me. One day in the bar I asked Ann, "Are you gay?"

Her eyes got big and she said, "Yeah. Why?"

"I just want to know because people are telling me you're a lesbian and I'm denying up a storm that you're not."

Then things fell into place about the girlfriends she brought home. But it never changed anything, how I felt about her, our friendship, or anything else.

So now I'm in jail and it's all around me, hitting me full in the face. Some of them are even pregnant. That really confused me. Looking like men and pregnant. For a long time I didn't speak to anyone except Ann.

We were travelling back and forth for the murder trial from Kingston. Claude paid the lawyers. They waited till I had the child because the Crown didn't want the court to show me any mercy or feel sorry for me because I was pregnant. Then there was this big court hearing. That's when we found out the person I murdered was an archaeologist at McGill University. All his colleagues came and they wanted justice. They didn't care that I was pregnant. They didn't care what he did. It was who he was. He had the clout. They didn't consider that he was a pervert or that he had a sword to my throat. No one could believe that Professor so-and-so would do that. It was just unthinkable. They used my background against me. And I stabbed him 17 times.

I had the baby in the hospital. When he was born, the father came and brought the baby back to his aunt. His aunt was 47 and they had no kids. So they were quite happy when this baby boy came into their lives. A year later she had a heart attack and then Children's Aid took the baby because she wasn't able to look after a child. I didn't know anything of this till Children's Aid got in touch with me and I'm thinking, where is this man? I'm going out of my mind. Claude was doing his business and he didn't know till after the baby was at Children's Aid and then he couldn't get him back.

The murder happened the beginning of April and my birthday is May 1. They waited until my eighteenth birthday to charge me in adult court. I got sentenced in the judge's chambers. Fifteen years. Ann also got 15 years. Altogether, it turned out to be a 17-year sentence, two years for the robbery and 15 for the murder.

After I was sentenced I heard from Children's Aid in Sudbury. The girls had taken my son, Gordon, and put him with Children's Aid saying they couldn't look after him. I went from Kingston to Sudbury, accompanied by someone. I went up there twice. The last time I stayed overnight in the Sudbury jail. They had me on Valium, I was shaking so badly. I didn't know which way it was going to go. My father came to court and said the girls had put Gordon there while he was away. He went all over the world to do construction. He worked in really high places like skyscrapers that no one else would do. He said he was willing to pay support for Gordon as long as I was in jail. Ann's sister, Linda, had moved to New Brunswick and was going to look after him. My father took Gordon down there after the court case. He was three or four at the time.

I continued to do my time in the penitentiary. You were assigned a number when you got there. My number was 622. That's the way they wanted to treat you. I said, "I'm not a number. I'm a person."

The guards were used to giving orders for something to be done right away. But it was how they asked me to do something that really bothered me. Had they come out and said, "Sharon, would you mind doing this?"

"Hey, no problem."

But it was "622 go there" or "YOU do this."

And I'd say, "Go fuck yourself!"

Right away, boom, I was in trouble. I said to myself, damn, I'm here doing my time but I want some respect.

For the first two years I was there, I was more in the hole than outside. I fought. I hit them. There was an incident where a screw used to call me Sunshine all the time. "OK, Sunshine, wake up." You might as well call me nigger. You're not calling anyone else Sunshine. It was the same thing when at school they called me Snowball.

I said to her, "If you can't call me Sharon, don't call me anything. If you come to my cell tomorrow morning and call me Sunshine, I'm punching you out."

The next morning she comes around, "Good morning, Sunshine." I punched her out. I lost something like 90 days.

Later, when I was mad, instead of smashing one of the guards, I'd smash the windows. I had seen other girls do it, that's how I got the idea. I must have smashed about 100 of them. My hand was all bleeding. After smashing the window I'd bring my hand back and catch my arm on the broken glass. I still have the marks. I stood on top of the table to smash the windows I couldn't reach. I used a broom for the ones even higher. The guards weren't going anywhere near me. They restrained some girls but not me because they had been hit too many times. They would wait for the male guards to come from across the street, from the men's pen.

Even if you weren't crazy, you had to act crazier than everyone else so they would leave you alone. If another prisoner, known as a fighter, came on to you, most girls would just give in. I said, "I will die going down but I will not let anyone bully me in here." I always knew if I lost I would come back with a big stick the next time. I got into a fight with a girl there three times my size but the next day I just waited with a baseball bat. I had snuck it up to my room from the gym. When I saw her, I whacked her. I ended up going to the hole. When I came back out, the girl never bothered me again.

Once I had wanted to hang myself. I had stripped these horse blankets, grey old blankets that they give you in there, lengthwise. I tied the pieces altogether to make a long rope. When we were locked up, if someone needed something, we used to use them to swing things from one cell to the other. I had tied all the strips together and was winding it around my neck. I was going to hang myself from the bars. I ended up having this rope around my neck that was a foot out. I thought I was doing it loose and all of a sudden I was paralyzed. I couldn't move. I could feel my ears popping. I broke the blood vessels in my eyes. The screws would not come in my cell. They're telling me, "Come close enough to the bars so we could cut it." But I was paralyzed. I couldn't move. This was not my plan. My plan was to hang from the bars. Other girls had tried to hang themselves and they would go in and cut them down. Not me. They thought I was playing a trick. Finally I managed to fall over in their direction and they started cutting all this rope around my neck.

At that point all the fight was gone out of me. I was quiet for the rest of the night. For about a week-and-a-half my throat was sore. It was just like someone had strangled me. After that I started acting up again.

The last time they put me in the hole, I was in there for six months. What happened was a girl had epileptic seizures all the time. She was on medication but her medication didn't always work. She came out of the nurse's office and suddenly she's flopping around on the floor. We're yelling to the screws that we need some help. They're just sitting there. I said, "Get off your fucking asses and get the fucking nurse." The nurse finally comes and they take her to the hospital.

Toward the end of the evening, just as we were locking ourselves in, they said to me, "You're charged under Penitentiary Standard Regulation 230, for the good order of the institution."

"What the fuck is that?"

"A riot. Just go to your cell."

I said, "Fuck you, I'm not going to my cell."

"Go to bed."

"I'm not going to bed. What are you talking about, for the good order of the institution? All I did was scream and holler for a girl who was having seizures. What does that have anything to do with a fucking riot?"

They wouldn't explain anything to me. Then the warden came in. The warden was afraid of me because I had threatened his life. I always called him Sherlock because he reminded me of Sherlock Holmes with his pipe, the tweed herringbone jacket with patches on the elbows.

He said, "We'll talk in the morning."

I said, "You're not going to talk in the morning."

It was Ann who finally talked me into my cell. She said, "They're going to talk to us in the morning."

Ann was really tough. No one messed with her in jail. She was saying, "Go to bed." But 90 percent of me was sure there was going to be no talk in the morning.

I went to my cell and, sure enough, the next day I hear everyone walking around and I'm in my cell.

I say to the girl next to me, "They forgot to open my door."

She says, "You and the nine others are all locked in."

I was screaming and hollering then. I said to Ann, "You see, big talk in the morning?" Ann was feeling like shit.

Then along comes the warden. "Are you going to go to the hole willingly or do you need help?"

I said, "Get out of my sight you fucking wimp."

Suddenly I smell all this stuff. I see these guards who look like they come from another planet with their masks and shields. Everyone else was off the ranges.

I said, "What's going on?"

Someone said, "They tear-gassed us."

I can't believe it. All this is way out of proportion to what happened.

They came around trying to get us out of our cells. Some girls went. But some were afraid to go and break the clique. I said, "Those who want to go into the hole, go. It won't strain our friendship." I knew some of them were really scared. So that left about four of us.

There are about six guards in a little two-by-four cell. I have a pair of scissors. They were trying to get it out of my hand but there was no way in hell. They punched me, they did everything to make me release the scissors.

They said, "We'll break your arm."

"You fucking break it then because I'm not letting go!"

By then everyone is sweating. There are about 10 bodies in the cell. I'm this little 90-pound terror. I am spitting out teeth and am just bloody. The guards had worked me over, boots and everything. I was never so sore in all my life as after that experience. They backed out saying, "This isn't working."

They went out and regrouped. They had tear gas in a little canister and sprayed it directly on my body, on my skin. It was burning all over. I couldn't see. My eyes were swollen shut. The SWAT team came in with masks and their shields. A part of me was laughing. I said, "OK, OK, I'm going to walk."

They let me go. I jumped over the top of the balcony. We did that often, jump from upstairs to downstairs. I started smashing windows.

They said, "You little bitch."

Finally they grabbed me by my feet and dragged me down, banging my head on every step. They got me into the cell. They had a big horse needle and they put it right through my fucking jeans. When I came to, they knocked me out again. They had me knocked out for about three days. By this time I was in the hole. When I came to, they charged me with everything under the sun.

A month later some of the girls who were involved got out. Then some others got out. Pretty soon it was down to me, Ann and another girl. They said if we behave ourselves, we would get out. So everyone started behaving and the others got out. Every month they would come to my cell and say, "Your case will be reviewed next month." Next month. I thought, I'm never getting out of here. I'd break windows when I'd go have my bath. They could have kept me under that section code, PRS 230, for the good of the institution, till the end of time.

After the sixth month I came to the decision that I wasn't ever going to get out of there. So I bent the tobacco tin top in half till it broke and pulled it up my arm and across. There was blood spurting everywhere. I was so mad I ended up hurting myself. Feeling helpless, not in control. The screws and the nurse came in wanting to fix it but I said, "No, you're not touching me."

The nurse said, "Sharon, please, I'm going to try and help you get out of here."

"You just want to put a bandage on me so you can say you gave me medical help if I should die."

"No, I promise, this isn't right."

She said to the screws, "If you're going to treat her like an animal, she's going to act like an animal."

The nurse was the one who got me out of the hole. She left over that incident. After I got out I followed the rules.

Two years after the uprising, they gave me passes to let me go outside job-hunting. I found a job immediately. But I had to pay rent for my room and board. That was part of life skills. I worked outside and reported back to jail at night. At that time you could do that. I found a job as a waitress in a restaurant downtown. On Sundays I was the only one working and had the whole place covered.

I left for work at 8 a.m. and was allowed out till 2 a.m. I finished at midnight and they allowed me a period to unwind before coming back. They should have seen how I was unwinding. Shooting speed. I used to carry it in for the other girls.

I was serving this guy who used to come in every night. I got to know him.

He says, "Do you want to come over after work to relax? I live just around the corner."

I thought, well, that would be a good place to unwind. So I'm hanging out there and little did I know he was a drug dealer.

Then they came up with the urine tests. I got in and was presented with a bottle to piss in. When I analyzed speed, they were really shocked because I didn't have a drug record. They stopped the passes. I could no longer go out.

Two years after the restaurant, I got a job working in the Kingston Psychiatric Hospital as a volunteer. I was so good they hired me. Little by little they showed me how things worked and I got to go to their meetings and understand their jargon.

I went and asked the director if I could change wards.

He said, "What ward do you want?"

"Ward 5."

"You don't want to go there. They make messes, shit themselves and smear it all over."

I still wanted to go to Ward 5 because the most interesting ones were locked up.

The first time I entered the locked ward was when I went in to report for work. I had the keys to the office, opened the door and no one was there. When I went out and closed the door, I found myself next to this guy who was 6-5. He looked like Frankenstein's monster.

He said, "You see that line? You step over that line and I'll break your neck."

And there's no one in the office. All the people on this ward were not only retarded or mentally ill, they were also violent.

I said, "You see that line over there? You step over that and I'll break your fucking neck."

I was improvising. He backed off. "OK, OK." That was my introduction to the ward. His name was Frank. He spoke very slowly but he could play the piano like no one's business.

241

I started working half-a-day on the locked ward and half-a-day in the workshop where people worked as therapy. Judy was the head of that department. The next thing you know, she's offering to take me out to supper. Then down the line told me she was gay. I was going with her for a while. If I had a couple of hours after work, or three-day passes, or the weekend, I spent it with her.

The first time I went for parole they just ran me to the ground. They called me a mass killer. The second time I went up I had a different parole officer. One month before I was due to go to the parole meeting, he called me into his office. He put me through the questions they were likely to ask me. He said, "You can't show any emotion, Sharon, like clenching your fists, the chair, doing anything noticeable they usually look for." I went before the board, had all the recommendations, had a job, and they still said no.

Later they moved me to the house across the street. It was really nice inside. Everyone had their own rooms and schedules to follow. I could have company in. Judy could come and have supper with us. I was moved because they didn't think it was good for me to work on a psychiatric ward every day, come back to prison and be shoved back into the same violent environment.

When I was at the house for a while they said, "You made parole."

"I didn't write for no parole."

"No, but we wrote for you."

"Why?"

They said I was a volunteer and was good enough to be hired. Now all my connections are on the outside. If I were to stay in jail, they were afraid I would regress.

I moved to Judy's house when I got the parole. I was still working at the hospital. Hardly any of them made any sense. But when you're around them long enough you know what they're talking about. I had a few who were very special to me.

I had worked at the mental institution for a couple of years, then they started the cutbacks. The last to be hired was the first to go. It was hard separating from them. Even after I left I used to go there, pick them up and take them somewhere for a couple of hours. Then take them back.

By then I had moved into my own place and I was only friends with Judy. The bottom line was that I wasn't really gay. When I had my own place I was ready to pick up my son and bring him back to live with me. I had to pay $500 to get him back from Linda. Judy gave me the money. We drove down to New Brunswick, paid Linda and drove all the way back with him. I didn't find out till later that it was hell for Gordie. Linda had a son around his age and it was Gordie who had to do all the work, always go to the store. It was me all over again.

When I brought him back Gordie was nine and really acting out. He was missing school. Stealing. Fighting with other kids. I couldn't handle him. I went with him to meetings with the therapist at Children's Aid. The therapist thought my son should really be in care because I was just starting out. Children's Aid took him. But this was supposed to be just till I got back on my feet. Then Children's Aid wouldn't let me see Gordie anymore because they said I wasn't psychologically well and felt he could only have a firm standing if I didn't see him for a while. I agreed to it in part because I thought he needed grounding. But they just put him up for adoption. I wasn't told anything about him.

I had met a guy in Kingston and we had a relationship. When I was three months pregnant he went off to jail for doing B and E's.

Then I got the call from Montreal on Friday to say one of my close friends, a big criminal, was killed and his funeral was going to be on Monday. I come down to Montreal for the funeral and the RCMP are there taking pictures.

I got back to Kingston. I had a baby girl, Rykia. Five months later my parole officer comes with the RCMP and says, "You broke your parole." They showed pictures of me being at the funeral. They said because I had left the area without permission I had to go back to prison. I was really mad. I called Ann who was living in Kingston and left the baby with her.

When I was on day parole I started to go to Hamilton. I didn't know anyone there and it was a fresh start. In 1979 I made full parole and went to the Elizabeth Fry Halfway House in Hamilton. I was looking for any kind of work but just couldn't find anything.

There were a lot of group homes for youth offenders in the Hamilton area. Sonny, this extraordinary lady who worked at the halfway house and was my parole officer, said, "Why don't you approach them."

I had to tell them where I was from. I said, "I'd like to do volunteer work."

243

They said, "No problem."

I ended up going there every day. Then people were quitting and they said they might need me for part time on weekends. It worked up to a full-time job.

Sonny saw the good in me. She made me see that I wasn't this rotten person that was on paper. That kind of turned me around. I keep fucking up and this person just keeps telling me I'm good. She persevered with me. She started to make me believe in myself.

In the meantime I left the halfway house, got my own place and Rykia was back with me. She was around three or four at the time. I even started to work weekends with the Elizabeth Fry. I used to bring Rykia with me.

At work they were pushing me to go to college. People at the group home said, "It's time for you to get the education behind the work."

I said, "No, I'm going to be stupid."

They said, "Start out by taking a couple of courses and see if you can handle it."

So I took English Lit., Psych. 101. Just to get to school I was going through all this anxiety. I'm too stupid, I'll fail and I'll feel like a fool. I persevered.

I took the prerequisites for the child care program. Then there were about 300 people applying for 15 openings to the college program and I got in. The first two years I took night classes and the third year I went full-time. I was doing cocaine while going to school to stay awake. A line here and a line there. I did that for about five years. Sniffing away. At this time I also had two part-time jobs.

In the group home the kids I was working with had all been placed there by Children's Aid. At work I was looking at me all the time. That's how I related to the kids.

They used to tell me, "You don't understand how I feel."

"Oh yes, I know exactly how you feel." And I would explain it to them.

They would say, "How do you know? You can't possibly know this."

I basically told them, "I was the same as you at that age."

They gave me a lot of respect. I was happy with that.

I was also working with emotionally disturbed kids and teenagers. Everything was either yes or no, black or white. I thought, just like me.

I learned right along with the kids how to compromise so both sides are happy. I learned something about myself.

At this same time I was having a relationship with a guy I had met in a bar. Here was this red-headed guy and he just caught my eye. We clicked. We started to see each other but it was only on the weekend. After about a year I'm wondering what is this mysterious thing that I only see him on the weekend. I told this to Sonny who said I should confront him. So I did. He said it was because he was going to school. I said, "How fucking old are you?" He was 17 and going to Grade 13. During the week he was studying. But he was built. He didn't remind me of a kid.

When I told Sonny I said, "I have to break off with him." I was 28 years old.

She said, "Well, how do you feel about each other?"

I said, "We love each other."

She said, "Go for it. Age is just a number."

We really did get along. Rykia just loved him. He was helping her with her homework. We used to go to a really nice restaurant once a week and take her. We did a lot of fun things together. This was probably the first time I was in love with a man.

From the time I went to Elizabeth Fry I also started to hunt around for a good psychiatrist. That was one of my conditions, the parole board wanted me to see a psychiatrist to get control of my anger. In the beginning I said, "Don't give me any pills." After three sessions I asked for nerve medication and they gave me Valium. I said, "You're no good for me."

I told the third psychiatrist the same story, "Don't give me any pills." After a few sessions I tried a similar game, give me some pills. He said no. I said, "What do you mean, no?" I tried my damnedest for a couple of months to get pills from him and there was no way on earth he was giving me any. So I went to him and we started dealing with my feelings for my mother and father. I did a lot of crying. That was the weepiest year of my life.

Dave went to university to take engineering but dropped out because it was too hard for him. He starts selling weed. Then this wonderful lady, Sonny, she was just everything to me, told me she was moving out west. I thought, oh, no. How am I going to survive?

My work with the psychiatrist helped. Things progressed. We started dealing with my anger. He said, "Before you get to the point where you want to hurt someone, you have to do something else. There are ways of diffusing anger. Leave the room and calm down. Then you could go back and discuss it. Tell them how you're feeling."

I was talking to myself a lot, Sharon, you can do this. Just walk away. Don't say anything. That was the hardest thing in my life.

Then I did the complete opposite. I was letting people run all over me, shit on me. I wasn't doing or saying anything. I thought, at least I'm not using my fists. Even though I didn't hit them, I still had the anger inside. The therapist said, "You can't be a doormat. You gotta start saying no." But I feel so guilty if I say no.

In Kingston I never felt anything about the murder. Now I realized I had killed someone and I didn't have any right to do that. I could have taken a lamp, smashed him over the head and left. In dealing with the murder I started crying. He said, "Welcome to the real world. You can cry, you have feelings."

I just stopped having feelings, because if I had feelings then I could get hurt. Everything I remembered and had no feelings about just came flooding in. It turned out I had really felt bad and wished that I could change things but couldn't. It was really, really rough.

My therapist helped me a lot but he wasn't aware of all the work I was doing, all the hours I was putting in, plus going to college. I worked for seven years and never took a day off. At one time I had three jobs. Two of them were part-time and one was full-time.

Meanwhile, I had graduated in 1984 or 1985. To see me with my graduating cap and being called up there, my name, that was a big accomplishment in my life.

In college we had to get a placement in child care. I had done a placement working with teenagers. There was an opening where I was working and it was almost a sure thing I would get it after graduation. The girls I worked with even said, "It's just a matter of formality."

I said to my parole officer at the time, "Should I disclose or not that I have a record."

She said, "You don't have to because your school already knows."

We just assumed the school had told them. A person who was working there ended up divulging that I had a record for murder. I get a call saying, "Your services are no longer required here."

"Why?"

"Because you have a record."

The person who told them I had a record ended up getting the job. That just blew me away. After three years of going to college and working my ass off, not taking any days off, and then for that to happen. People always say to me, "Just forget about your past and go on." It's not me; it's other people who never allow me to forget the past.

When we had graduated we were told to send our resumes everywhere. I sent one to Children's Aid as a joke. They called me in for an interview. I told them right away that I had a record. I went to three or four interviews and they hired me.

I was seeing the therapist quite regularly and we were making headway, plus I was with Dave. I was working in the all-boys' group home from Sunday night to Wednesday morning. I slept over there. On weekends I went to another group home from Friday till Sunday morning. Plus I'm working for Children's Aid. Then one day I get a phone call at Children's Aid from the mother of one of Rykia's schoolmates. She tells me Rykia was molested. Rykia had described to the little girl what she had been doing for the babysitter's father-in-law. The girl told her mother.

I freaked out. I called my family doctor and he says, "Sharon, come to my office right now." My doctors knew me really well. I was so honest and open about my life. He said, "Don't go there, you cannot kill that man. I know what you're thinking."

By this time I had already moved to a high-rise and had changed babysitters because we were living too far away. The new babysitter was the janitor of the building and she was living by herself.

When I got to the doctor's office, the first thing he did was give me a shot. But I was so hyped up there was no drug on this earth that could keep me knocked out. We called the babysitter and said, "You have to keep Rykia home because I have to bring her to the doctor's." I took her to the doctor's and everything was intact. The doctor said she was not penetrated. But Rykia, who was six or seven at the time, was so ashamed for having to go through all of that. Then the police came.

The police took her into Children's Aid. They had these dolls and did the whole play-acting thing. She showed them what he did to her but it was very embarrassing for her. After they put her through all this, they said they couldn't do anything because it was his word against hers.

The molestation happened over a two-year period. The babysitter used to live in the house with her husband's father and mother. The molestation would happen when the father-in-law would take Rykia out by herself. If you could see this man. He looks fucking gorgeous, distinguished. He could have any woman he wanted. He, of course, said to Rykia, "No one will believe you if you tell. People will think you're lying."

I am feeling so bad because I'm supposed to be looking out for these signs. I do with other kids. Why not my own? How come I didn't know my own child was molested? I'm out there with other kids and I see the signs.

The psychologist at Children's Aid said Rykia was fine but she wasn't. I had this totally different girl. She didn't trust me because I allowed this to happen to her. I had always told her I would protect her. Mummy will always be there for you. Finally, she had to see a therapist by herself.

When I got out of jail one of my restrictions was no drinking. After finding out about Rykia I started drinking. But not at work. I was trying to forget, trying to get it out of my head because it was in my head every second that I was awake. Finally, after a year-and-a-half at Children's Aid, I had to leave. I wanted to spend more time with Rykia. They said, "Anytime you're ready to come back, you're welcome."

Then close to a year later I get a phone call from the police saying they were reopening this guy's case. I said, "You're not putting my daughter through all this again." The way she looked at it was that she told on him and nothing happened to him. And she was scared all the time that he would come and get her. She was seeing purple men at her window. The police said they were really charging him this time because they caught him doing it to his own granddaughter.

He had taken pictures. They had an attic in the house and that's where he used to take her. They went up there and they found pictures of Rykia nude and some other kids too, both boys and girls. He had some of his own daughters. Once his daughter came with her daughter, then all the girls came forward.

I was in a real funk. The whole setting was there for me to have a nervous breakdown. I got agoraphobic and couldn't go anywhere. All I could do was cry. I couldn't eat. I couldn't swallow. I only felt safe within my house.

Rykia at that time stayed at the babysitter's, downstairs. I had to be left alone. They told her I was sick. She would come up once in a while but not for very long. Of course, kids that age are very inquisitive and ask all kinds of questions. It took all of me even to answer.

A nervous breakdown is another form of nothingness. It's terrible. I became anorexic. I couldn't swallow for the longest time. Someone was trying to feed me lobster and all I could do was cry. I couldn't deal with the thoughts in my head because they were flitting by so fast. It was like being in a whirlpool, a vortex. I was down here looking up. I was at the bottom and there are people at the top, all around me, going about their lives. If I can get to the top, I'll be OK. But how? I would put up my hands and they would just disappear inside this vortex. There was nothing to hang onto, to get up there.

I used to talk to my psychiatrist by phone. Then he said, "I want you to come here by bus." I had panic anxiety. I got off that bus about 10 times because there were people. Everything was just taking my breath away.

I had a parole officer who was bugging me up my ass all the time. Plus she was gay. "Talk to me, you can talk to me about anything."

"Leave me alone!" I grabbed her. I said, "Get the fuck out of my face. I'm going to kill you. Get out."

I was lying in my bed. The next thing I know I'm looking out my bedroom door and there are all these guys dressed in black with shotguns. I thought I was hallucinating. I just looked at them and then looked back, like I'm seeing things. Then they started talking. My parole officer had called the SWAT team because she thought I would harm myself. Plus I was a very violent person, make no mistake about that. I was very volatile.

They took me to the nuthouse. I called my psychiatrist and he was friggin' mad at my parole officer. He came to see me at the hospital. He said, "Stay here for just a couple of weeks so you can rest."

I came out of the hospital and everyone thought I was cured. I wasn't. My parole officer was still on my case. I'm standing in the middle of the street with two drinks, one in each hand, staring at her, drinking them and throwing the empty glasses in the middle of the street. "See, see, I'm drinking, what are you going to do about it?" I blamed myself for Rykia's molestation and basically I self-destructed again.

She pulled my parole. The police said I had a choice, I either go to a psychiatric institution for treatment or go back to jail. I had been out for seven years and I was so good. They thought I would pick the hospital. I said, "I'll go back to jail." I'm not going to a psychiatric hospital where they're going to put me on all kinds of medication and I'm going to be drooling at the mouth. That is not treatment. That is control.

I had thought getting up every day, going to a job, school, coming back, this is it, my stepping stone to being normal. And everything just blew up in my face. There was a lot of putting my feelings back inside again, back to not trusting people, back to not fucking caring, keeping everyone at arm's-length distance from me.

When I went back to Kingston in 1986, I had money because I had ripped off this insurance company. I wrecked my own house with the help of a neighbour and collected about $17,000. Rykia wanted to be near me so Ann, who was living in Kingston, went to get her. The money was basically used for her care.

When I went back to prison I was still unsteady. I went in there for six months. The screws said, "Sharon, we thought you were the baddest thing that walked on two legs when you came here. But you were an angel compared to what we have now." These girls were a whole new breed. They were younger and a lot of them were in for violent crimes. They just didn't give a shit about anybody. They had no respect for themselves, so how could they respect anybody else?

First they put me on the range. Then they moved me down to the wing where there were doors and the girls there were better.

When I left, I went to stay with Ann and her girlfriend in Kingston. Then I thought, Kingston is not really for me. I'm going back to Montreal. I literally had a fist-fight with them because they didn't want me to move. They got attached to having Rykia around. They had it in their minds that this is going to be a little family here. Needless to say, I lost the fight because they are both big girls. They put me out and wouldn't give me Rykia. I called my parole officer. She said, "Leave Rykia there for the night." In the morning Rykia was at school and in the afternoon we went to get her.

When I came to Montreal in 1988 I was 37. From 37 to 43 it was all downhill. I came here because I knew my aunt was here. She would be my stepping stone. Rykia was 10 at this time. My aunt was really happy to see us. For Rykia this was culture shock. There were all those kids. The whole family speaks loud and there was drinking. In the bedroom my cousins were basing, smoking rocks. It was a wild house. There were cockroaches all over the place and my daughter was flipping right out.

I ended up getting my own place because my aunt wanted to hit my daughter. I jumped in her face and said, "No. If I don't hit her, nobody on this earth is." There was a big argument and she told me to get out.

I was on welfare and my cousins were trying to find ways of getting money from me for these so-called rocks, cocaine. For the longest time I said no. After a few months I got curious. We would put it on a pipe, light it and smoke it.

I met this guy Chuck on Walkley Street. One day he appeared at my door with roses in his hand and being super nice. He would take me to shows. Wine and dine me. He was a pimp but he wasn't pimping me. He had sidelines. Then we were both into this stuff.

With Rykia, I always tried to piece her off with money. I would be in the room smoking. She had her little friends and when it was time for food I would give her money. I did the same thing my father did. To make it better, here is money, when in actuality she needed me. But the drug had gotten a hold on me.

Chuck was basing too and all the money was going into cocaine. Then I started working out of town. I'd fly down to New Brunswick to work in a massage parlour, for an escort service. While I was away my aunt took care of Rykia. I said to her, "Don't hit." I used to call home just about every second night to check. My aunt never hit her.

I'd come back with $3,000 to $4,000. All of it went up in smoke. Then I'd fly to Newfoundland to work for an escort service there. I did that for a couple of years.

Working out of town, the hours were wicked, 24 hours a day. Because of the lack of sleep, I'd do more cocaine to stay awake. It was a vicious circle. I stopped working out of town and started working in town. Rykia was still with my aunt but I lived just across the street from her. I was supplying two people's habit, Chuck's and mine. I said, "I'm not supplying anybody's habit," and broke off with him.

Then I met this other crazy guy, Terry. He used to rip off all the dealers. Then we had to go to Halifax because he ripped off the Italians and they were after him. Rykia came with us. In Halifax he got arrested and I was stuck there. I go to work downtown on the stroll. I do prostitution and the money is great. In a couple of hours I could make $400 to $500 easy.

Rykia was staying with this other woman and I got really bad. I went down to about 80 pounds. I got to know the dealers. Then I said to a friend, "Do me a favour, give me airfare back home. One way. If I don't leave I'm going to die or someone else is going to die." My friend gave me some money, a bunch of rocks and I got on the plane. Rykia stayed in Halifax.

Back in Montreal I started working downtown and selling drugs for the bikers. I'm still doing rocks and acting crazy. I got a little place and Rykia came back to live with me.

One night I was drinking with my cousin and she picked up a client. She wanted me to come with her. Halfway there he changed his mind. He and Teresa were arguing in the front of the car. I'm getting out of the back. The guy gets out at the same time and he has this knife. I took the knife from him. He says, "I'm calling the police. You stole something." The police came and he said to them, "This girl hit me."

"I didn't hit him, I just pushed him and took away the knife."

He was carrying on saying, "They robbed me." I hit him right in front of the police.

"Now you can say I fucking hit you!"

There was a female and a male police officer. She said, "Don't push him!"

And she pushed me. I wasn't expecting it and fell right on my ass. I just got right up without even thinking and hit her. The next thing I know he's on the phone yelling, "Officer down, officer down!" Police cars come from all over. There must have been 20 cars. The next thing I know, they're handcuffing me and putting me in the car.

On the way to Station 15 I was still mouthing off. They stopped the car and beat me. Then they grabbed me in between the handcuffs and shook my hands. And they had the handcuffs on me so tight it went right into my skin. I had the marks for a year-and-a-half.

They took me to the station. An officer comes in and says, "You're charged with armed robbery."

"What are you talking about?"

The policewoman I hit, her arm was broken. In one punch. I went to court and got a year. In four months I got out and went to a halfway house.

Here we're starting to deal with my drug and alcohol problem. While I was at the house, doing the drug and alcohol program and seeing the psychiatrist, I didn't do drugs. The first time I didn't do it for two months. Then I had a relapse. Then I didn't do it for four months. A relapse. Then six months.

But I was still associating with my family and they all did drugs. At the program they said, "What does it take for you not to do drugs?"

I said, "My weakest ties are around my family. In order not to do drugs I can't be around my family."

They said I had to make a choice, seeing my family and doing drugs, or not seeing my family and being straight. I stopped seeing my family and started doing drugs by myself. I was lonely. Then I just stopped doing it. I didn't know what else to do.

They said I could leave the house when I found an apartment. I found one. The bombshell between all this was that Rykia told me she was pregnant. She was 16. Rykia wanted to have the baby. The only thing I could do was be there for her. But the trigger for me to take drugs was stress. The stress came from Rykia being pregnant. I wasn't ready for a baby. I was ready for typical teenage behaviour. She said, "I'm not letting my child stay with you if you're doing these drugs." I knew if I didn't stop I wouldn't be able to see my grandson.

I started to work at STAR [Self-awareness Training Against Recidivism] as a receptionist and doing the books. It was a place for English-speaking people who were in conflict with the law. It was against recidivism. We had self-awareness groups, relaxation classes, yoga. I was involved in the discussion groups on drugs and alcohol. Helen was the director.

Helen was another person just like Sonny. When I started working at STAR, my self-esteem came back. Helen built it up. She persevered with me. That's probably the key. It didn't matter what I did; she was not turned off. She saw something in me. It stunned and amazed me that someone really cared.

For the longest time I would have these yearnings. I wanted to do it, didn't matter what the consequences. But Helen would talk to me. I would go over to her place and be around her.

Then STAR closed. Now both Sonny and Helen have gone out west. When Helen left I was really sad. After she left I was marking the calendar just to see how long it would take me to fuck up. How many days will it be after she's gone that I end up back in jail?

One month went by, two months, three months. Every day is a battle because sometimes I think, why don't I just do it this time? Then I remember that after I do my first blast, it's not fun. Not doing drugs is already an accomplishment.

Now I look at one day at a time. I didn't do drugs today. I'd just like to try for a couple of years being normal, drug-free. What is a normal life? Doing what the majority of people do every day. Just making your supper, running your shower, watching a little TV, lights out by 11 o'clock. I've never done anything normal my whole life. My whole life has been a reaction. Now I'm fighting for my life. I'm isolated but I've isolated myself. I don't really like to be around a lot of people. I get anxiety attacks.

I made some rules. No drugs are to pass my door. If you have drugs, you can't come in and if you are drinking, you can't come in. One thing always leads to the other. Now I'm able to say no and not feel guilty.

As far as work, there's not any, not that I'm qualified for. I have advanced arthritis in both my hips, my knee and spine. For years I didn't see a doctor because who cares about a doctor. When you do cocaine it takes your pain away. When I was off drugs the pain started. The doctor said my bones are like a person who is 70 years old. For most of my life I've been dealing with physical, mental or psychological pain. I've always been in pain of one sort or another. It's almost a norm for me.

I understand my own limits, which before I never could. I hadn't put limits on myself, I just kept going and going, ploughing through things. I now know how to deal with stress and a bad situation so that it will not happen again. I always learn something, even from a bad experience. You can't be bitter.

I miss my sons terribly. Every year, I've tried to find them a few times but it came to a dead end. But I'm not ready to really look for them. I don't know if I'm strong enough to stand a possible rejection. Maybe another year or two I'll be ready for it.

Right now something very quiet is in store for me. And reading is quiet. I like my own company. I had always liked my own company. I hardly ever feel lonely. Basically I have to get back in touch with myself before I do anything else. I have to heal me first. It's a healing process for my whole life.

Before I was never alone with myself. Now it's getting to know me, spending time with me. I think about the things I've done in the past. This I've done. It doesn't work. Just close that door. Never go there anymore. I sit here and it looks like I'm not doing anything but I'm putting closure on all the negative things. Am I still angry or sad about this? I deal with it, remember, and just close that door. It's no longer hanging around in my thoughts. I can go onto something else. The past is still there as a reference point. It's like a library in the back of my head. Eventually, when I put closure on everything, you will see a different person. It's just like being reborn. Exactly.

I'm gathering my energies but I don't know what I'm going to do yet. I think there is another phase coming on soon. I'm getting close to something but I don't exactly know what it is. Now I'm getting kind of bored. My eyes can only read so much. There's something there. I can just feel it in my body. Whatever it is, it's going to be positive.

To come out into the world. A rebirth of Sharon. I'm feeling pretty good about myself. Anything I do from here is going to be new for me.

MORRIS

Morris (33) was short, powerfully built, with long, straight black hair tied in the back. There was a strong sense of presence about him. He commanded attention even in silence.

As soon as I turned on the tape recorder he started talking without waiting for a question. He immediately placed his story within a political context before launching into it. It was obvious he had carefully thought about what he was going to relate. And he had a clear sense of chronology which fuelled his story. There was a passionate urgency yet no sentimentality in his description of events. It was important to him to present the facts without bias. His story was heart-breaking and the intelligence and sheer clarity with which he spoke made it even more so.

Right up to the mid-1970s there was a war to assimilate native people; take the children away from their parents, their language, their culture, everything that was theirs. Because we were living in shacks and tents on the outskirts of towns, the government felt these people weren't capable of rearing their children properly or giving them the basic essentials of life. So the child welfare people would come in on foot, because we had no roads, and take the child away. First they would come in alone. If they couldn't get the child, then they'd come in with the police to take the children by force and put them in foster homes.

Before the age of five, before I was taken away, my backyard was an entire forest. My siblings and parents were there. We had wild meat, which my mom and dad would trap. We had fish. We had meat drying, fish that had been smoked outside and hung up.

Our shack was four walls and the floor built with scraps of wood found here and there. Our roof was two layers of canvas so you always had constant light. We had a wood stove, an old barrel that someone had picked up and assembled to make a stove, so that kept us warm and helped us cook our food. We had a porch area in the front where we had the wood, pots and pans. There was also a camping stove on which we could boil water for laundry and washing. My mother would do some of her cooking there as well.

The shack was like a big room with two beds and a table. We had our clothes in drawers and in boxes on the bed. My mother had a bed. Opposite my sisters slept on their bed. Once in a while my sister would sleep with my mother when my dad was not there. When he did come home she would jump back to her bed. My brother and I slept under the bed. It was an adventure to be under there.

I had clean clothes on my back, food to eat and shelter. Life was good. No worries. I just had to walk through a trail, come to another encampment and there were my relatives. Many times we slept at relatives' tents when my parents were gone. It was great.

I had two older sisters and one older brother. My dad was a lumberjack in northern Quebec. He was away for stretches of time. My mother worked extremely hard. There was no electricity, no running water. We had to get water to drink, to wash. She was always busy running, washing our clothes. We lived in the woods and you tend to get dirty climbing trees, playing in the mud, jumping into rivers.

My mom got up early in the morning to put up snares to catch rabbits. She ran to check them, bring back the catch, clean them, feed us. My mom was a person who was constantly busy. Occasionally I would go out to put up snares with her and then pick them up. At night, to get us to sleep, she would tell us, "If you guys fool around tonight and you don't get up early, the crows will eat your rabbits." And that was actually a fact. If you didn't wake up early enough, the crows would be on your rabbits in the snares.

We spent most of our time in the woods or in the fields or walking around on the train tracks. We used to like going to the dump which was a half-hour walk from where we lived. We would scrummage, pick up toys, anything we could play with, or we'd find comic books even though we didn't know how to read. The pictures were interesting. We always thought non-native people threw away a lot of good stuff.

When I was about five I had a younger sister. She was on a bed swing that we made. I used to pull the string and she used to rock back and forth. I enjoyed pulling the string when she cried. She moved back and forth, then she was fine. It was fascinating to see a little baby. And one day she was gone and no one really told me anything. The baby was gone.

When I was around 12 I found out there was another family, a good friend of my dad's, who could not have any children, so he kind of gave them a child.

When she was gone there was something definitely missing in the house. There was no baby crying, no swing. There were just the strings hanging as opposed to the string with the blankets folded and the baby. A little later I was taken from my family and placed in a foster home.

I don't know how that occurred. One moment I was there and the next moment it seemed like I was somewhere else. When I was taken away I spoke only Cree. Cree was the language that was spoken in the house, with my friends, everybody around me.

In the family where I found myself I was the only child. There was an older woman with a daughter in her teens and an older son. Her two children had their own rooms and I shared a room with the lady. There was her bed and a bunk bed. Occasionally I'd sleep on her bed; it depended how cold it was at night. I think they took me because they were getting paid by some agency to keep me. They fed me but I didn't get any new clothes while I was there.

I wasn't going to school at the time so I was home all day. She had a washer and one day she was pointing, saying something. I was looking at her and didn't understand. She kept pointing at something. I just moved in the direction she was pointing and just stood there. She kept giving me the finger and I just stood there really confused. Then she walked over, slapped me across the head and I fell down. She picked up a box of soap and took it to the washer. That was the first time I got hit. After that it was a regular occurrence because I didn't really know what they wanted or what was going on. If the guy wanted something from the table and I didn't understand it, I'd get hit.

Even when I started picking up English I never really understood. Get this! Get that! They didn't always define what this and that was. This! I'd look at a shelf and there would be a bunch of things. Which one is "this"?

The woman would clean and cook and I'd have to help her out. The guy was gone most of the time but he was not working and the girl was in school. I didn't really like her or her friends. They would make fun of me. I'd be treated like a doll. Put rollers on this guy! I didn't feel comfortable.

In the summer we used to go to a chalet they had in the bush. When they went to buy something in town they left me locked up inside. Once they were painting the chalet and they had rollers. I looked at the rollers and they were all full of paint. I figured I'll just take a knife and scrub all the paint off. I was trying to be helpful. What happened was that I scrubbed all the fuzzy things off. When they came back I was all proud of myself. Of course I got a beating because I had destroyed the rollers.

When they went into town they didn't take me because I was a burden to them. But I was no longer locked inside the cabin because I could do damage, so they would tie a long string to a tree, make a little ball at the back of my shirt and tie the other part of the string to it. I just took off my shirt. When they came back and saw me running around with no shirt, I got hit. After that they would tie together my shirt and my pants. If you tried to pull off your shirt, your pants would come up. If you tried to pull off your pants, your shirt would pull down. When they left me tied to the tree I'd just sit there. Movement was really limited. One moment I had a whole forest to roam around in with my cousins, another moment I'm alone, tied to a tree with 10 feet of movement.

In the city, if she was gone for a few hours, she just locked me in the house or tied me to a tree. Sometimes they left me outside in the winter when it was snowing and cold and they'd go somewhere. I'd just go around in circles. At other times I'd be outside playing and the guy would grab a fistful of snow and just rub it in my face. It was cold and it would melt and I couldn't go anywhere. You don't want to follow him into the house so you're kind of locked out. I'd be really cold and my face would be wet.

The guy had the worst impact on my life. When I was locked up in the house alone, he'd come in and beat me. At first being alone was peace and quiet, no hitting, no yelling, no screaming. And then being alone was frightening. I was scared that this guy would come back while the lady was gone. So while I was alone I'd spend a lot of time hiding underneath the bed, waiting and waiting. The door would open and it was like, who is it? If I didn't hear a voice I just sat there. If it was the lady, she'd yell out, "Morris," and I'd be happy. OK, I'm going to get hit but I don't mind that. So I'd just crawl out.

If the son came home I would hear him walking around, going through room by room. I'd hear doors opening and closing. I'd be underneath the bed and I'd put pillows in front of me to shield me. Then he would pull the pillow, look under the bed and there I'd be. And he'd drag me out. He'd beat me up and I'd be crying and then he'd make me perform sexual acts on him. Mentally speaking, I sometimes wouldn't be there. Sometimes I would be brushing my teeth and all of a sudden I would just gag and feel like throwing up. Used to happen a lot when I was a teenager. I'd brush my teeth and I'd just gag.

At this point my English was better, I could understand. When everything was done and finished with, he'd look at me and say, "Look what you made me do!" So I felt totally responsible for all these things that were happening to me, the beatings, the sexual abuse. Somehow I was to blame. It seemed everything was my fault and I couldn't say anything because I was warned not to, otherwise things would get worse.

My parents came to visit me twice. Both times the people I was staying with gave me a dollar bill. I didn't know what it was for, so I gave it to my mother. Once they came for a day in the summer. I was really happy. I remember crying a lot. They said, "We can't take you back. You have to wait." When they left I cried even more. The second time they came was Christmas. They had brought me a toy train. Once again I thought, OK, now I'm going home. But I didn't. I was so enraged when they left, so mad that they didn't take me with them, that I just threw the train away.

One day I was playing outside and saw this little kid in front of his house. He was gesturing for me to come over. I crossed the street, pushed him down and he started crying. I just ran home. That was my first release of anger.

After nearly two years I was taken away from there. I was happy to be out but I didn't know where I was going. It turned out to be home, which was great, but I was still a little mad at my parents for not having taken me. I was scared to get close to them because I was scared to be taken away again. My mother didn't ask me anything. No one asked me anything. I began to play alone.

We had all been separated. My brother was somewhere else and my sisters were taken together to live with a family. First my brother moved back, then me, and eight months later my sisters arrived. No one talked about what happened.

By the time I went back home to my family we had moved to a small town called Val d'Or. My father moved for a job, something a little more stable than what he had previously. Now he was doing mining exploration. Or he had a job as a surveyor. And we had a house now.

But the transition of moving back meant uncertainty again. I lived in fear even in my own family. I was happy to be there but I wasn't secure. A car would drive up and that's it, I'm going back. Every moment of my life was nothing but fear. I was a very, very scared person, hence I pushed people away. There was no human contact. None with my parents or with my brother and sisters.

My younger brother was born in Val d'Or a few years after I got back. When he was six he moved to the reserve to go to school. People would often send their children to the reserve to a family who will watch the child. When I was a kid we didn't have a reserve, we didn't have a school and now we did.

He's 10 years younger than I am. The first time I saw him was four years ago, when I got out for Christmas and went home on a four-day pass. I was still in prison at the time. He was living with his girlfriend and had a little place on the reserve. We all had Christmas supper at my mother's, who has moved there. It was strange seeing him. One minute you see a six-year-old child and then you see a 19-year-old adult. He basically grew up on the reserve, so during the day he would show me around and tell me where this person or that person lived. We played street hockey in front of the house. It was my bridge back to the community.

I started school in Val d'Or when I was seven years old. My English wasn't too good and I was a little older than anybody else. Other than my brother, who was two years older than me, I was the only native person there. He spoke better English than I did. He had made friends and he was always off with them. I was usually by myself. I learned how to be pretty good at individual sports. I was very athletic, had speed, endurance. And I had a good sense of observation. The early part of my childhood was spent running around, climbing trees, so I learned to be agile. The first time I got into a social context with people was through sports. At the beginning I got picked last, then as time wore on, I got picked first. I was kind of happy about that.

Another thing I became good at doing was fighting. I faced a lot of discrimination. After school I didn't want to go home because I didn't feel comfortable there. Someone could always come and take me away. School ground was a place for me to play but I'd always get into fights. People would start taunting me. A group of them got together to push me around and a fight would break out. When I was beaten up I tried to fight back, but as soon as I'd get the upper hand, somebody else would jump in. They'd never let me have the upper hand.

Sometimes going home was like walking a gauntlet, having guys follow you in a circle, taunting you, pushing you all the time. Someone would hit you and they'd keep hitting you and you'd fall down. It wasn't much fun.

I spent Grade 1 to 3 getting beaten up on a regular basis. As time went by I got better at fighting. By the time I reached Grade 4 I learned how to fight.

I made a friend, Marcel. He was white. He was a good friend from Grade 3 on. When I used to get into fights in Grade 4 Marcel was the other guy beside me. I was no longer alone. If I had the upper hand, no one would jump in because Marcel was there. But during the summer he'd be gone and once again I found myself alone.

The only other person I knew in town was my uncle. My mother's brother, Uncle Walter, had moved into town and his daughter had a child named Adamee. Adamee was maybe two years old. I was nine or 10. During the summer months I used to go over and the only friend I had was Adamee. I'd take him for a walk, play ball with him, hide-and-seek. I used to spend hours with Adamee. He barely spoke which was great. He could be trusted. Adamee was someone I knew wouldn't hit me or beat me or hurt me because he was smaller than me. He was the only other native person I knew in the area, beside my family. Things weren't going so well at home, so it was nice to go to another family, a more stable environment where people actually talked to each other.

My uncle was the only person I knew and it got me out of the house where I didn't want to be. He lived a half-hour away. I'd walk the distance and sometimes spend the entire day there. I didn't only play with Adamee; I'd talk with my uncle, who taught me how to play card games and attempted to teach me guitar. But when he had things to do, I would play with Adamee.

Today Adamee lives in Wasawanipi. I saw him often this summer. Today he's 6-2 and 250 pounds. I'd tease him about when he was small. I'd tell him I used to play ball with him and when I left he cried. He'd be really offended by that: "No, I never cry."

Then I met a new friend, Donald. One day I just happened to be in the field in front of his house where people played sports. I was just tossing my football around. Some people were playing soccer and they asked me to join them. I said, "Sure."

At the end they said, "We're playing again tomorrow, come on over." Donald was the only one who came up and talked to me. He was the rich kid and all the balls were his. He would pick me for his team because I was the best player out there. So I developed a friendship with him.

Going to his place was fun. That was about the only fun I had. He lived not far from me. During the time I was friends with him, I didn't get into fights. I'd run out of school, go home, eat and go over to Donald's. He had like a toy store in the basement. He had everything. I noticed I never won, ever. He'd always win. "It's my house, my rules. I get first choice." I spent about eight months with him on a regular basis, eight months of losing every day. I didn't know half the games we played. "No, you can't do that." Fine. I'd never win. And I was the guy who'd run and do things for him.

One day we were playing football with his friends. He threw the ball and it hit my thumb. The ball flopped it back and my thumb became swollen. He looked at me and asked, "What's the matter, you can't catch a ball?" He just laid into me and I was in pain. I just punched him and left. I never saw him after that.

My father would be there for a while and then he'd be gone for a month or two, sometimes even longer. So he'd be in and out. Initially when we came back together, neither of my parents drank. A few years after I was with them, they started drinking. My dad would work in the bush, he'd come back and spend a lot of his money drinking. It wasn't ideal to be home because there were lots of arguments. My mother would drink too and during school she'd wake up and have to cook me breakfast. I used to get hit when she would have a hangover. I'd be making too much noise while eating and that would annoy her.

My mother went from one extreme to another. Drinking heavily or going to church. There was no middle ground. So either I spent time alone or I was forced to go to church. And for two weeks in the summer she sent me to Bible camp. I went to Bible camp from the time I moved back with them to the time I was 12. I had some relatives there and made some friends that I would see every summer for four or five years. What I didn't like was the amount of time spent on church. You'd have four hours of church a day. Plus the time they put you in your tents and explain the sermons. At nights we'd have to give an offering and most of us were extremely poor.

When I was 11 I started to let my hair grow to look different. I think I was screaming for help and if you're the same as everyone else, no one is going to notice you. Everyone had crewcuts except for me. In that setting I became someone who stuck out. If something would happen, it's that long-haired kid. Anything would go wrong, blame Morris, the oddball, the weird guy. That was the kind of attention I was getting as opposed to any kind of help. Nevertheless it was attention, no matter how negative.

Or people would ask me, "Do you know who stole cookies from the pantry?"

"Yeah, I did it." I began to accept responsibility for other people's actions.

Because people in my tent knew I would take responsibility for whatever happened our tent became the troublemakers. They'd sneak out and raid the pantry. They would toss worms, frogs or bugs into the girls' dorm and run out. We became the "in" tent.

It was my first real taste of friends, people wanting to be with me. I didn't want to lose them, so it became easier to assume responsibility. If they broke a window, I said, "Tell them it was me." Just to maintain the friendship. Just to have somebody around. People would break things, steal things. Just blame it on me. I felt taking responsibility would cement the friendship. It never occurred to me they would like me for who I was.

After a while you get tired and lonely from isolating yourself. You want to be part of something. You're afraid to be abandoned, afraid to be hurt and you do whatever it takes to be part of a group. All these little sacrifices I was making were trivial. The way I saw, it was that I was helping somebody and they will appreciate me for it.

There was also some positive attention. During the day we had to memorize Bible verses and at night, in church, we had to recite them. If you did, you won a prize. I always won prizes. I would bring home to my mom praying hands that you stuck on the wall, bookmarks with some religious thing on it.

Assuming responsibility carried to home. One day my mom said, "OK, someone stole $2 from my purse. Who did it?" I didn't do it, but I said I did. After a while it was a natural part of my life to assume responsibility. I did it to be part of a crowd. All I was doing was protecting myself from being alone. I isolated myself for a long time and now I was afraid to be alone.

When I was getting beaten up on school grounds by other students, there was always a group of them. When Marcel was with me and I had the upper hand, no one would jump in. Having someone beside me saved me from being beaten up. That's why I wanted to surround myself with people. I wanted these people beside me for protection.

By the time I got into high school I was a good fighter. And I wasn't very big. Up until I was 22 I weighed 135 pounds. My nickname was Tiny Tot because I was always very small. But I was athletic. I was fast with my hands. I was fast on my feet. I was able to foresee things and react. Reacting instead of thinking carried over to outside of sports. Students would walk towards me and I felt I was being menaced. I didn't wait to see what was going to happen. I just made things happen. Just defend yourself. Violence became a part of my life.

When I got into fights it always seemed like I was fighting for my life, my existence. I used everything and anything I could to get the upper hand. I wanted to be the guy on top doing the hurting. I couldn't see myself losing because I might die. When I was young survival meant you just submit. In school, getting beaten up, I was no longer submitting. I was getting hurt and that's when I started developing this sense of fighting for my life. I was fighting for survival but I felt really guilty after the fight was over. I'd be fighting for my life and at the same time feeling guilty about what I had done.

I grew up in Chapais and we were living in Val d'Or. Chapais was four-and-a-half hours away. When I went back, it was really strange because people had begun shoplifting and these were my relatives. So one night, around Christmas, they said, "Come on, Morris, let's go to the store and pick up some things we need."

I'd follow them. They shoplifted. Nothing happened. They said, "Try it, Morris, it's easy."

I said, "OK, I'll give it a try sometime."

I was in a store and there were these really nice walkie-talkies. I stole them. Then we stole batteries and we were playing with them. I went back to Val d'Or and took the walkie-talkies with me. Two days later the police were at my house. They went upstairs, took the walkie-talkies and left.

What happened is someone got caught shoplifting and said I taught them how to do it. After that the rumour was that I had taught everyone how to shoplift. My family abandoned me when I was young and now my family was accusing me of stealing. At that point in my life I actually gave up on everything and I became everything people were saying about me. Morris is a crazy guy. He steals. At this point I was 13. I stopped caring about myself and actually began to steal. I was so mad at everyone and everything. Do you think I'm a thief? Then I'll become a thief. Then my parents separated. Before that they would get into arguments. I thought their arguing and separation was because of me. It seemed if I wasn't here, they wouldn't have argued. My father would go out to a bar and my mother would complain that he was spending too much time and money in the bar. To try to bridge that a bit, I would steal. I used to steal food and bring it home. If our toaster broke down, there'd be an argument about when we were going to get another toaster, so I would get the toaster. When people asked me where I got it, I just said I found it in the garbage. That didn't sound so strange because when I was younger we went to the dump to pick up things we needed for our shack.

I had several motivations for becoming a thief: one, to prove people right; and two, to try bring the situation at home under control. When that didn't work, it became a habit to appease people. I just stole, stole, stole. Somebody would want something, I'd steal it. I never robbed someone's house. But I'd rob businesses. I'd break in through windows and take their money. I would take whatever people wanted, just to make them happy.

When I was 14 the town became more populated with native people so I would hang out with them. They were two or three years older than me and they had non-native friends who were their age. They accepted me because I stole and gave them things they wanted. I never bought myself anything with this money. I mostly gave it away. Both my sisters had children, so I'd give them money. Friends would say, "We need money to buy beer." I would buy them beer or give them money to buy beer. And I'd just be hanging out. Drink a pop. For me it was a really wonderful time because I was surrounded by all these people, people who wanted to have me around, appreciated me. So I'd just keep on stealing, doing break and entries.

At this point I was staying at my mom's only on occasion. She was drinking most of the time. Sometimes I stayed at my sisters'. I had a friend who was older and with the money I was giving him he had enough to get an apartment. So I used to stay with him once in a while. I really wasn't based anywhere.

I still had a lot of anger and fear in me, but with all this money I was surrounded by people. I felt safe. I just kept stealing. As time progressed, they said, "Morris, drink." Eventually I started to drink. At first I would get sick. After a while I would get drunk and feel nothing. It numbed everything. There was no anger. No pain. Absolutely nothing. It was wonderful. I started stealing more so I could drink more and still have all these people around me.

Then I started getting introduced to drugs. You have any money, let's buy some hash. The same thing as with the alcohol, where I would passively sit back and then I'd try it. I wanted to be like everyone else.

Smoking and drinking is all I really did and fight, fight, fight. In the meantime school was taking a back seat to everything. I was barely passing. From elementary to high school I was a very good student, plus I was at odds with the system, the monarchy, everything around me. I was aware of injustices and how it affected people.

Just after I turned 15, I had my first girlfriend. It was the thing to do, so I just went with it. She was two years older than I was. A really nice person. Ukrainian. Pretty intelligent. One day I woke up, saw her and said, "I don't want to be with you anymore." I didn't want to fall in love with someone and have this person go away on me. So I detached myself from her.

When I started to drink it became harder to wake up and get to school. Sometimes in the morning I would meet up with friends and hang out at the pool hall, go to the arena. More stealing. More money for more drugs, more alcohol. I quit school when I was 16.

All my relatives and acquaintances would come from northern

Quebec and ask me where to get drugs. I'd always bring them to some-body. I figured if I could eliminate the guy they buy drugs from then, I could make some money. One day I decided to buy two, three ounces of hash because I had robbed some place and got $1,500. I'd pay $200 for an ounce, send it up north and the people would send me back $1,000. I was 16 years old and making $2,000 to $3,000 a week.

I used to drink a lot and have blackouts. I'd be in a park and next morning I'd wake up at someone's place. Violence grew. I felt threat-ened by people when I was drinking. It wasn't about evaluating the situation, it was looking back and remembering. I was living in the past. It wasn't going to happen again. To ensure that it wouldn't happen again, I couldn't just sit around passively. When I felt threatened I would just react and attack people. I didn't like people looking at me a certain way. I don't want to be touched or pushed. I was always extremely defensive and aggressive at the same time.

There were a lot of parties with a lot of women around. Women approached me but it was the last thing on my mind. But people around me were all homophobic, putting gays down. In the back of my mind I was saying, am I gay because of what I did when I was young? I was confused. Then sex became an outlet for me, to somehow disprove that I was homosexual because of my childhood experiences. To be sure I'm not, I will have sex with as many girls as possible and as often as I can. That was easily achieved because I always had money. We always had parties. So I'd drink a little less. Do more drugs and be more awake and pursue this. Once I proved to myself that I wasn't gay, girls weren't a priority any more.

At first I would follow the crowd and then the crowd started to follow me. Let's follow the bank. I could actually send someone to the store or the restaurant to pick up things. When you start to discover this power over people, you begin to use it. People would be more than happy to do things for me. But I was still following them first. They'd dictate what we should do, where we should do it, who we should invite to the party and you just go along and say, fine.

After a while I began to consume and spend more than I was mak-ing with my little project up north. Eventually it all fell on its face and I was broke. I didn't steal that much anymore because I relied on what I was making from northern Quebec. People started disappearing. Once again I found myself alone.

Then I meet Nicole and fell in love. It was a time where I straightened myself out to a certain degree. I drank less. The money situation allowed me to take things a little easy. From then on I was with Nicole and I'd do other things beside drinking. I would actually go to a movie, which was totally new for me.

Nicole was like a security blanket. I was being held and hugged by her and that was the first time in a long time that there was any real tenderness in my life. I was extremely comfortable being with her, talking to her and the sex was OK, too. We had a relationship, on and off. The separations were motivated by my occasional binges. I would start drinking and go haywire, get into more fights, get into trouble. One night I was at a party. Nicole was there. I was really drunk when I went to bed with her. The next morning I woke up in another bed with another woman. Things would break apart. The security blanket was gone. Back to the drinking. Fights.

Back and forth. Somewhere in that relationship I learned to stop assuming responsibility. For most of my life I thought everything that happened was my fault. After a while I started looking at other people and blaming them for everything that happened in my life. It was no longer my fault, it was someone else's. I'd point people out and use them as scapegoats. I'd beat them to a pulp. Most of the fights I got into were with people taller and heavier than I was. But they didn't have to fight for their lives. When I'd get into a fight, this person was responsible for the abuse I suffered. There was a lot of anger, a lot of hate from my childhood, all surfacing and being unleashed at some poor individual who just happened to be at the wrong place at the wrong time.

When Nicole would leave, it was the same feeling I had when I was young, of being tossed aside and left on my own. In that state of fear I was extremely depressive. The way of dealing with it was to go out and be aggressive, hurt people before they hurt me.

Then she told me she needed time to think. One morning I woke up at my sister's house and got a letter from her saying it was over. She asked me to write back. I started to write two lines and this rage filled me. I went to some friends in the middle of the afternoon and started drinking and drinking. I did that into the evening. I was drowning myself in alcohol and whatever pills I could get. I was so full of rage. I didn't want to assume responsibility. And I couldn't see it as being Nicole's fault so I just pushed the burden on her family. In my mind it was her damn family who talked her into this.

I had seen Nicole earlier that day. She was walking across the street with her cousin. Her cousin lived a half a block from my sister. I walked home that night, full of rage. At 5 a.m. I rang her cousin's door. I figured she might be there. No one opened. I just busted the door down. Nicole wasn't there. Her cousin got up and confronted me. There was a scuffle. A fight ensued. We were in the kitchen, I picked up a knife from the counter and kept stabbing her over and over. Once again I was fighting for my survival. These people were hindering it. These people were responsible for everything that happened and they had to pay. I stabbed her cousin 45 times.

I left the house, went to a nearby park and went to sleep. It wasn't till I woke up that I realized what had happened. Police were all over the neighbourhood. I just stayed where I was. Later that night I went to my sister's and was arrested. I was 20 at this time.

When I got arrested I felt shocked and sad by what I did. In jail I came to the realization that I might be in here for the rest of my life and I turned myself off to everything and everyone, including myself. I just became a walking zombie with no emotions. I felt no remorse, no pity, no apathy, no sympathy. I was indifferent to the guilt, the pain, the suffering. Turning myself off was a form of survival.

I stayed at a detention centre for roughly eight months before going to court. My sisters came to the trial once in a while. My mother never came. My dad came once. The victim's family was all there. Nicole came on a few occasions. All I felt was shame and I just turned myself off till I had the strength to deal with it. I was convicted of second-degree murder. The difference between first and second degree is premeditation. I was given a minimum of 10 years up to life.

When I went to maximum security I was 135 pounds and 20 years old but looked 16. Here I am in jail, I don't know anybody, and these big guys are telling me, "You're going to be my woman."

I just said, "No thank you, please. No thank you, please."

Some people didn't take that as well as I thought they would. I made a few enemies but didn't get into any fights. For self-preservation I just stayed in my cell. I didn't go out for a year. Normally I would have said it was my fault, I should have accepted and then none of this would have happened. But I just said, I want no part of this. They have a problem, not me. They can't take rejection. It was the first time I actually directed responsibility to the proper people.

From the moment I entered prison my situation started to shift. I couldn't just react anymore because of the dangers that existed. In prison people hang out in gangs. When you have a problem with one person, you have a problem with 10 or 20 people, depending on the size of their gang. Talking back could cost you your life. I couldn't lash out. You have to learn to walk away.

You wake up in the morning, open your door and found your breakfast. You go back, close your door and eat. You go to work during the day. For meals you go down, pick them up and go back in your cell to eat. Everything is done by buttons and there are guards everywhere. At night I stayed in my cell. I did my push-ups and sit-ups. I did my reading and watching TV. I turned really white because I was getting no sun. I ignored everybody and kept to myself. I had no choice but to go off alcohol and drugs.

A year-and-a-half later I said, I'd rather die than spend the rest of my life in this little room. I went out. To my surprise I was not harassed as much as before. People left me alone. I started training again. Weights. Exercising. I played sports. Rather than try to cope with what I did, I was trying to cope with living right now.

I started to be a part of the prison mainstream and I started buying drugs. I knew where to get them now. I started going to the common room, talking to a few people, playing cards. The people I played cards with started talking about making a still, to make alcohol.

They were drinking a sort of brew which is tomato paste, water and sugar. You let it ferment and it turns into a bit of alcohol. They proposed that if we make a still where you process all this, copper pipes, heat up the stuff, alcohol evaporates faster than water. The alcohol goes in this tube, put it in your toilet with a block of ice and a copper top. It cools back, becomes liquid again and you get alcohol. Of course, you can die or go blind from this stuff but it doesn't matter. I said, "Sure, I can do that."

I'd be in my cell with this thing plugged in. The guard comes by every night to look in through the little window, to count you. I had it hidden on the side so you couldn't see it. Now I was getting high from the drugs and getting really drunk. I'd take 20 ounces for myself and the other 20 the guys would sell. They'd bring back cigarettes or drugs or whatever I wanted, so I just continued my lifestyle of drinking and smoking but in a different crowd. Nothing really changed in my life.

I was the first person to use the still in our group and I lasted about five or six months before it blew up. I had overheated it and my hose was not big enough so pressure built up and the top popped. The stuff went flying to the ceiling and overflowed. It went out the door when the guard was doing his count. I tried to stop the stuff from going outside but I couldn't step on it because it was extremely hot. I had a towel on my shoulder and threw it at the bottom of the door so it wouldn't go out but I missed. He saw the stuff on the floor and left. I emptied all the alcohol and brew into a bucket and a plastic bag, took the still apart and threw it underneath my bed. Then two guards came in. The first thing they did was look up because the ceiling was dripping.

So I said, "Yeah, I think there's a pipe broken up there."

They said, "Yeah."

I thought, good, they're going to leave and I can clean up. But another guard came and said, "No, no, something happened in here." They searched my cell and found the still.

I ended up going to the hole, a room with a mattress. I was asked if there was anyone else involved. I said, "No, I was alone." I spent three weeks there. When I came back, someone else had taken my job. The operation was going strong and I was still part of the team. There were five of us in the group and we all had our time with the still. I was no longer doing the production because if I would get caught again I would be in segregation for three months.

When I was in the hole I assumed responsibility to be accepted and liked, the same reason as on the outside. In jail it was interpreted that you can be counted upon in times of trouble. You're not scared of the guards roughing you up, beating you up. You respect the people around you enough that you're willing to inflict damage upon yourself instead of dragging everyone with you. You are man enough to assume responsibility. I think it was the first time that I felt fully appreciated. My taking responsibility had value. I did everything all my life to be accepted, to belong, and nothing happened. All of a sudden you're in jail with murderers, rapists and have everything you have always wanted.

Now instead of the alcohol deadening the pain, the opposite was happening. It was bringing back the memories, the anger, the frustration. I'd get extremely depressed and annoyed. I was extremely aggressive toward staff. I'd start throwing and smashing things in my cell. I'd lose control and it wasn't the ideal spot to lose control. The guards all have guns. To top it all off, when I'd drink I'd be sick for three or four days. I got off the alcohol and there was no shaking, no craving. It was sudden relief and I became a bit more aware of my emotions.

The others would sometimes offer me a drink and I'd say no. No problem. It was the first time I was not harassed or pressured into something and was still part of the group. A certain feeling of calm comes over you because you belong. You have something to identify with. The respect for taking responsibility helped to anchor me. I wanted to look at that because I think I had a little more self-respect based on what happened. I needed to explore this.

After five-and-a-half years in maximum I asked for a transfer to medium. I felt I belonged to this group but wanted to see something else, explore different avenues, meet different people. I wanted something better.

I asked three times to be moved. The first two times they said no. The third time I said I wanted to move to a specific penitentiary. They said, "No, but we'll send you over there."

I said, "I don't want to go there, I want to go here."

In prison you learn the reputation of other places. The place they had picked out for me was a heavy medium which is more like a parking lot. I said, "Forget it, and left."

Several weeks later they called me back and said, "OK, we'll send you where you want to go."

The difference between Archambault and Centre Fédéral de Formation was day and night. In Archambault I could walk up to a guard sitting behind a glass, kick it a few times and call him a few things. In medium the guard was walking beside me, going somewhere. And someone is actually going to talk to him nicely. Here I was the loud, dangerous, violent guy. Yet I appeared to be quiet all my life. It was an eye-opener to see how loud and aggressive I was. I was extremely on edge.

Some acquaintances I knew from maximum noticed my behaviour and said to me, "Take it easy, relax a bit." That helped. I wanted something safe, secure, familiar. Who's familiar in medium? The people you saw in maximum. They told me who to talk to, who to definitely stay away from. One of the fears of going to medium was that you run into all kinds of what we called low-lifes, anybody who would work directly with the police or prison authorities. Before I was always totally insecure and wanted people around me, it didn't matter who they were. Now I was staying away from certain people.

The transition period was six months. During that time I got into one fight. But it was in a sporting event, cosmo hockey, floor hockey, which was considered to be OK to a certain degree. The guy I fought was a lot bigger than I was. The fight lasted three seconds. I hit him and he hit the floor. This was in a gym where there's a lot of people watching, so it established me as a rough and mean person. He's from maximum and he beat up that big guy, stay away from him, he's dangerous. That pushed a lot of people away from me and attracted other people, like some of the leaders within the prison community. From that point on I got favourable treatment from all these people. I had opportunities to get prestige jobs in sports, the canteen. If I had no money I could always get cigarettes because I was from maximum, beat up a big guy and I knew how to handle myself. For once violence actually profited me, it allowed me to be noticed and be someone. I was extremely respected in sports after that fight. The referees were intimidated by me, so I could get away with things.

People who had come from maximum now said, "You should do this program, it'll look good on your record." So I did things based on the record, to look good. Went to the programs and just sat there. I was kind of listening, having coffee in the back, talking to someone, smoking a cigarette. I had a paper saying that I was there on a weekly basis. But I was just going through the motions.

After a while I hung around with Frank who was referred to me by the people I had made alcohol with in maximum. He was one of the drug dealers. We trained together, played sports together. He was the leader of this group, so that allowed me to be part of another group. I was with him for about a year. During that time we attended groups together. I felt more protected, so there was less need for violence and fights.

The people I met in medium were not as violent as the ones in maximum. Some of them just dealt in drugs and were extremely intelligent people. I got a little help from them. They said, "If you want to get out of jail, you have to go see a psychologist. Go to NA [Narcotics Anonymous] and AA." So I was doing all these things I was supposed to do for the wrong reasons. Not for me but for my freedom.

275

When I was on drugs and alcohol I was projecting onto other people what I was feeling. Attacking people before they attack you. I was denying responsibility. I didn't want anyone to get too close, so I had a rough edge, a rough exterior. In maximum I stopped alcohol and now I stopped the drugs because I wanted to be more aware of what was going on, not just with me but around me. In a drug haze things are not what they seem to be. I was afraid that the change I was going through would actually scare people away and leave me standing alone. It was strange because Frank was a negative influence on me, but oddly enough he was one of the people who supported the fact that I didn't want to take drugs anymore. Frank didn't consume drugs, he just sold them. Here was a drug dealer, I stopped taking drugs, and there was no one happier around me than him.

Now I was off alcohol and quit drugs. There were no other devices to hide myself from myself. So it became a time of dealing with things. I no longer saw everything as a threat. I felt more comfortable with myself, so it was nice to be alone. I didn't mind being alone. I kind of enjoyed that feeling.

Some of the people I had been with left, some had been released, others had been transferred, so the friends I had actually started to diminish. The more I found myself alone, the more I discovered. I had spent a lifetime surrounding myself with people because I was too scared to be alone. Now I desperately wanted to be alone.

Being alone was like getting rid of the static on TV. It's just such a relief. There was no more background noise, no more thoughts, feelings, perceptions being distorted. I connected with myself. And then I started taking up something I hadn't done in a long time—boxing. I used to box to become a better fighter, so I could hit harder and beat people to a pulp. Now I was taking boxing as a sport. It was you and the bag. Boxing not only gave me a chance to be alone, it also gave me a release from frustrations, anger, hate. You just beat up on a bag. Before I released the anger and frustration on someone else, making them feel the pain I had. Boxing allowed me to go back to my life and assemble pieces.

I was isolating myself and that made me see people differently. I stopped seeing people for what they looked like, what job or position or crime they committed. I began to relate to people as human beings. I mellowed out. I enjoyed being alone but I also reached out to people in a real sense instead of just wanting them there for protection. I was dealing with people as individuals and I found that so much less threatening. At first people ducked their head when I approached them because they were still threatened by me, but later on I could walk up to anybody and talk to them. It was really strange because all of a sudden I had a lot of things to say. And I found that other people also had things to say. I was exchanging with people. Wow, I'm communicating, this guy is telling me his problems. I was telling people how I should live my life. I was using people to think out aloud. It was a lot of fun.

The fears were slowly slipping away. It was strange because I was going through all these depressing things, like my childhood and the abuse, and for once in my life I actually felt happy. I had made a discovery. I realized that these things were behind me. They were not going to be my future. I was basically freeing myself. I was dealing with horrible things and I was happy. It was the first time I actually stopped and faced things instead of constantly running away.

You watch how you react to different things. The best indicator for me is to see how people react to a given situation. Then you can look at yourself and say, how do I react in the same situation? I was watching sport events to see how people deal with things. Then you reflect. When I got into a cross-check I got into a fight, I punched a guy. Other people yell and scream. Some people don't do anything. This one guy got up and started laughing.

Frank was a leader and a lot of people respected him and feared him as well. He was extremely big, muscular, strong, and he was an intelligent person. He was a real smoothy. He knew his way around people. Frank was more of a protector to me, my last line of defence. I went to groups with him and in groups we'd just sit around and do nothing. Eventually Frank left and it was a good turning point. Now I found myself in some groups where I actually had to work on myself. I felt a need.

STAR was a group that focused on changing people's patterns, making them more aware of their fears, anger, making people look at themselves, look at how they interact with others. At first when you had to name what you fear, I said, "I fear nothing."

After Frank left I actually started putting down some of my thoughts, something that was safe, superficial. You have two notebooks. You do your work in one, the next week you hand it in and you keep switching books. The people read it, write in it and hand it back to you.

You touch and smell things and try to associate it with a memory and work on the memory. When I was there I lied about everything but it was actually an awakening. I put different things down in the notebook, but in my mind I'd think that reminds me of when I was a kid.

I went back to my cell and thought about what had happened. I'd get depressed and when I get depressed I get violent and aggressive. Sometimes the group would end at 9:30 and we wouldn't have to be in our cells till 10:30. That would leave me an hour to be destructive, harass people. The only way I could feel better about myself was to crush other people.

Things began to change. It was slow, gradual, and you don't notice it. I'd be in the group and it brought up something. I'd write something else but in the group I'd verbally attack someone.

I didn't want to go too deep. I didn't want to deal with things I wasn't ready to deal with. It was self-preservation. The masks were still there. This group allowed me to take them off slowly.

One of the books came back and it said, "I notice a change in you since Frank's been gone. You seem to be more your own person." It was the first time I was called a person instead of Morris, Frank's friend. First time I was called a person in my life. So, I thought, I'll try a little harder.

I found that the more I could listen, the more I was able to reflect about my own life. By listening to others, I learned to listen to myself. It was something gradual. Someone is talking about a problem within the group. You listen and think, I had the same feeling too. Why? The reasons I felt the same as he were different but the initial emotion was the same. It allowed me to look deeper into myself. Slowly. Normally the STAR session lasts three-and-a-half months. I went to five of them over a two-and-a-half-year period.

After two-and-a-half-years I still wasn't able to express the feelings associated with my childhood. But it allowed me to deal with other things. Why I felt insecure was because of the sexual abuse, but things I did to cover it up, I took away. I was taking off one layer at a time till I came to the source, the root of everything.

I also started seeing a psychologist and was with her for roughly two years. I was transferring part of the program over but going a little deeper.

The first mention of my childhood happened with another psychologist. I chatted with her for an hour-and-a-half and at the end, as I was about to leave the office, she said, "Is there anything you would like to say off the record?"

I said, "Yeah, I was sexually abused as a child."

And I left. It was off the record, so it was fine. But when the report came back, it was on it. I felt betrayed yet I was happy; look, it's there. It was out. This happened when I was 27, 22 years after the fact.

I couldn't even say the word abused. I couldn't even think about what happened to me. Before that I dealt with my crime and the people involved. But even at that there was something missing. It wasn't till I put all the pieces of my life together that I began to realize who I am.

When I went back to my regular psychologist, we discussed it for a long time till one day, in the office, she asked me, "What about the people?"

I said, "I hate them."

She continued to ask me questions and I kept repeating the same answer, over and over. "I hate them." Then I just broke down and started crying. I hit the desk and she jumped back. All my anger came out, the pain, the hurt. I said, "I really hate these people." There was silence for a while. I was crying. That was the first time I actually unleashed the anger I had. This was the first time I actually told someone why I was so angry, why I had so much hurt and why I was always beating on people and myself. After I left the office I felt such relief. I felt 200 pounds lighter.

Beside the sexual abuse, there was the fact that I was taken away to this total unknown. I dealt with that feeling of rejection, of not being wanted. You're here because your parents don't want you. As a child that was repeated to me by the family. This is all your fault. Look what you made me do. That was repeated over and over again. So I always had a sense of responsibility, rejection, and a sense of not being wanted, not belonging. I was Indian and I felt like I didn't belong anywhere. You don't belong to your family, you don't belong to your culture, so you're always looking for a place to belong.

Here I was in jail, going to these groups and seeing a psychologist to get out, and I sat there one day and said to myself, hey, I'm not ready to be outside. I'm not ready to be freed from jail because there are so many different things I still have to deal with and understand before I can go out in society. Otherwise I'm just going to repeat the same thing over again. In one of the groups we talked about fears and that was my fear, forgetting who you are once you get outside. At this point I was roughly into my eighth year of incarceration.

There was a native group and I went. Coming in contact with my culture helped me focus. Understanding your people helps you understand yourself, your way of thinking. I was bombarded with emotions, feelings, thoughts. I'd talk with the elders when they came in. At this point I was starting to go out on one-day passes. My outings were based on going to schools on the reservation, talking to them about alcohol and drugs and what it's done to my life, going to pow-wows, seeing different aspects of native culture: the dancing, the drumming, the crafts.

The crafts reminded me of a time in my childhood where I helped my mother in the kitchen part of our tent. She used to do beadwork and I was making little flowers. It brought me in touch with the child within, with the happy years. I looked at different facets of myself. You start to understand where your attitudes, beliefs and misconceptions all came from. That allowed me to reflect on how I got here. What am I doing in jail? Yes, you killed somebody, but why?

I was being thrown aside again by my girlfriend. She was my security blanket. She was gone and it was a feeling that I could only remember having when I was young. A feeling of being tossed aside and abandoned. And there was a violent explosion.

As a teenager I used to read a lot about injustice, the Third World, poverty, exploitation of people. In prison I read the same things. Then I started to read things on natives. I got a subscriptions to radical native journals. The Native Paralegal Services gave me magazines and one had an article about the law on native children. That pointed me to a direction. One of the policies the government had was the White Paper to abolish all native rights. I researched more and found out about the forcible abduction of children, the relocation of people. In a war, what do you do when you conquer a country? You divide the children from their families so you can brainwash them and change their mode of thinking. Here I was reading this and I thought, this is what happened to me. It wasn't my fault. What could my parents have done? It was a policy.

I had a friend, Mo, who was a Micmac, and I pass the journals to him. Mo was two years older than me and played quite a role in my life.

It was the first time I actually identified an Indian with something other than violence, alcohol and broken homes. Mo came from a broken home and had a problem with alcohol but he had something else. He had a little knowledge of culture. We'd be doing things with other people, someone would make a comment and Mo would counter, "In our culture we don't believe in that. In our spiritual beliefs this is how it is."

One day Mo and I said it would be nice if we had an elder to come in and talk to us. It would be nice if we would have a little party and bring some traditional food to eat. In medium there was myself, Mo and four other guys. Mo called his place and got some food sent up. I called Wasawanipi in northern Quebec, where my mom was, and asked her for some meat. My mother moved to Wasawanipi years before, when housing became available. Other people's parents also sent up food. Elders came in. We had a feast. The elders spoke and did a prayer. An elder talked to us individually. It was nice to get a point of view of culture, spiritual beliefs, a way of life. It was like coming in contact with yourself. I've always had the sense that I was different, that I thought differently from other people. I didn't understand why.

The elder would be telling me about the two commandments, respecting and sharing, things that I have always done, even before I was five. I was always sharing things, being respectful towards other people. Respecting property. He was talking about praying and giving thanks for everything we had. Thanking the animal spirits for giving up their lives so we may eat and survive. I remember I used to go pick up my snares as a child and I looked at the rabbit and said a thank you. I was all happy and excited and I thanked the rabbit and here he was with his tongue hanging out.

I was at CFF for roughly two years before they changed the security level from medium to minimum. You were graded and depending what grade you get they might move you because of the reduction of staff and security. So I had this fear of being out of there. But much to my surprise they gave me a low-security risk rating.

I was an extremely reliable person. Always at work on time. Did my job well. I was able to take initiative, make things happen, so I got the job as sports commissioner. I organized sporting activities, recreational activities for the entire population. I had a crew of nine other guys under me who I had to co-ordinate and distribute jobs to.

I was also doing volunteer work at the prison TV channel. Then a friend said, "We need someone to do English news, why don't you come over?" I quit my job as sports commissioner and did the English news a half-hour a day. Prison news. I did it for two-and-a-half years. I did commentary. I did things like top tens, deep thoughts. Commercials.

The television allowed me to be creative, work with important issues in a different way. I learned to joke about problems, take a serious concern and break it down to something funny. I did this on a daily basis. Our show was half an hour and I had 15 minutes. I talk about what was going on in the prison that particular day but would expand it to what was going on in the world today.

I did conferences in Montreal on natives in the educational system, natives in urban settings. A lot of times I would make fun of things just to show how sad and real they are. It made people more comfortable with what I had to say and what we had to discuss.

I spent three years learning to be a machinist. I spent a year studying cabinetmaking, learning how to repair and make furniture. I was trained to be a geophysicist where you learned how to use various machines in order to get a sampling of what's underneath the earth and based on that you make a map. I had ambition. I had trades. But I finally realized that what I wanted to do was to work with people.

I passed the parole board and asked for something called projects where you go out, work all day and come back at night. You volunteer your services five days a week. I asked for it because I wanted to go out slowly.

I did my volunteer work at a rehabilitation centre for people who have had accidents, are suffering from cerebral palsy or other diseases. I worked in the shop area with handicapped people who assembled things like filters for humidifiers. I was helping them and made sure they had filters and boxes to put them in. I loved it. I was dealing with the people and seeing how fortunate I really was. Some of them had been in car accidents, the people they loved had died. Their loss was a lot greater than mine yet they survived and did it sanely.

I was always frightened to say anything about their individual handicaps. They made it easy for me, "Yeah, you can talk about the fact that I have muscular dystrophy and I'm going to die in two years. It's OK." They showed me how to live today, in the present, savouring every moment of my life now, not living in yesterday's nightmares or tomorrow's fantasies. They showed me not to be fearful. It was the first time I totally enjoyed life, with these people. Go to bed at night, be thankful. Wake up and be grateful for what was about to come. Savouring every moment. All my life I've tried to deaden, suppress the moment as opposed to accepting it, being open to it.

They knew I was in jail. They knew I had killed someone. They ask you what happened and you tell them. These people really listened and did not judge. They accepted it. It happened, now move on. That made it easier for me to feel better about life, about myself.

I was there for nearly seven months. Unfortunately I had to move on. They don't like to keep you in one place too long. I went back to the parole board and they gave me a halfway house. We were into the tenth year.

Waseskin House, a halfway house for natives, run by natives, allowed me to implement some of the theories I learned during my time in prison. I wasn't going to allow myself to be stepped on and I wasn't going to allow other people to be exploited. Because I was swaying people to fight for themselves, they got rid of me. After seven months they wrote a report which fell short of calling me God. The whole report just praised me and cut me out of the system, onto the street, living alone. I was released on full parole.

As soon as I left Waseskin House I enrolled in a CEGEP, at Dawson College, taking Third World Studies. At the time that's what I wanted to do. You question your choice, was this the right one? Maybe I feel I need to serve a purpose and be with people, solve problems and expand my mind. In school I sometimes sit at my desk, twiddle my thumb and fall asleep.

I've been out two-and-a-half years. I can complain but I won't. I'm surviving. I'm learning new things about myself and other people every day. I seem to be growing and evolving and sometimes regressing. It doesn't only go one way. I have moments where I have bouts of depression and I think, what am I doing out here? Things are much easier in jail. You question yourself every moment of every day. Surviving is a struggle.

Theoretically I should finish Dawson in May, but I'm homesick, it happens even if you're 33. Home is where your heart is, with my family and friends, my community, nature. That's where I feel I belong and that's where I feel most comfortable. People are telling me, "Morris, stay in the city for another six months and you'll be finished." There's a stronger calling. I can come back and complete the course at a later date. I want to be at home. Over the years I've had summer jobs on the reserve, I've been home for Christmas. Wasawanipi is not the greatest place to be in. There's violence, alcoholism and the suicide rate is high, but it's where I feel most comfortable. I usually work at the Youth Centre. I'd like to go back and create something, give something back to the community and give something back to society as well. I find we limit ourselves constantly.

I have a cabin that I built over the summer, basically a shack. I'd like to live there, commute to the village and back, from my family's traditional hunting grounds and what they call a trapline. I'm not the greatest hunter or trapper; I'm barely a fisherman sometimes.

I still have to find myself. It's not a complete recovery. We learn and discover new things about ourselves and each other every day. Now I'm able to speak to people in a calm and relaxed way. When I'm angry I talk about it more, I don't allow it to accumulate. When I feel depressed I look for people who know me the most, who know my past. Talking helps even if the solution that comes out from the other person is not all that great. Get it off your chest. If I can't find someone to talk to, I usually just call home.

I'm still dealing with different aspects of my childhood, my teenage years and my crime. It's so easy to fall back on past patterns. The easiest thing is to go back to where you came from. The fact that I'm dealing with my past every day, and continuing to do so, is making it a lot easier. It's making the future a lot brighter. I can be broke and penniless but still be happy. True happiness doesn't come from outside, it comes from within. As long as I'm comfortable with myself and believe in myself whatever I do, whether it turns out or doesn't, is OK. If it doesn't work out, it wasn't meant to be and I'll find something else.

Today I find I do things and meet people effortlessly. I see a bum, he says something to me and I learn from this man that everyone ignores. There's so much to learn from different people. I talk to anyone and everyone.

If you take care of today, tomorrow will take care of itself. We always thought like that. When I worked with the handicapped people, it brought me back to that philosophy and now I'm going back to my community. In the city people don't take the time to smell the flowers.

Back home we take the time to watch them grow. It's a slower pace of life. Everything has its place and everything has its time. We live by that philosophy. I love the Cree culture.

The person I killed is always in my prayers. I pray for her soul and I ask forgiveness for all the pain and trauma I created by my actions. I'm not a religious person but I do give thanks and I pray. As a child when I went to collect the rabbit from the snare I thanked the Creator. Sometimes I look at the murder that way. This was the path I was meant to take. I'm here today because this is the way things are supposed to be. All the people I met, who have helped me along the way, occurred because of that incident, because I killed somebody. I wouldn't have gotten the help I had if I hadn't been to jail. I wouldn't have gotten to know myself. I do give thanks, not for the murder, but I do give thanks every day because I'm alive. When I wake up in the morning I give thanks. When I go to bed I thank the Creator for the wonderful day he has given me, even if it was a shitty one.

Acknowledgements

Thanks are due to those who opened doors for me within the prison system: John Edwards, Commissioner, Correctional Services, who put me in touch with Loretta Mazzocchi in Communications, Correctional Services, who in turn put me in contact with Guy Petit-Clair, Regional Administrator for the Quebéc Region, who met with parole officers and passed my requirements onto them; and François Lagarde, head of Correctional Programs at the Federal Training Centre, a minimum security prison, who chose a number of prisoners for me to screen, helped them to be free for numerous, lengthy interviews and made space available in prison for the interviewing process.

I owe a debt of gratitude to all the people who accepted to be interviewed, including those in the book and the ones who did not make it into the book due to overlaps. They have all helped me to understand and appreciate the work required to face oneself. I am grateful for their openness and honesty.

Affectionate thanks to my father-in-law, Isaac Hausmann, who extended his support in numerous directions, both seen and unseen, not least of which was a belief and interest in the project. And, of course, Dani, whose love, faith in me and jokes have provided a consistent and much-needed respite from the emotional roller-coaster ride that this project has taken me on from start to finish.

A heartfelt thanks to CZ for putting me in touch with J. Gordon Shillingford, the publisher.